The Culture of Lies

Post-Communist Cultural Studies
Thomas Cushman, General Editor

The Culture of Lies

ANTIPOLITICAL ESSAYS

Dubravka Ugrešić

Translated by Celia Hawkesworth

The former Serbo-Croatian language is now officially
divided into three languages: Serbian, Croatian and
Bosnian. It seems that the Hague tribunal is the only
institution which does not care much for the finer points
of linguistic divorce; it is more interested in crimes
committed against humanity. So, within the organisation
the languages are referred to by the abbreviation CBS
(Croatian-Bosnian-Serbian). It has been used here at the
suggestion of the author. [CH]

THE PENNSYLVANIA STATE UNIVERSITY PRESS
University Park, Pennsylvania

Published in 1998 in the United States of America and Canada by
The Pennsylvania State University Press, University Park PA 16802

First published in Great Britain in 1998 by Phoenix House

Published in Dutch by Nijgh & Van Ditmar, 1995.

Published in Croatian by Arkzin, 1996

Library of Congress Cataloging in Publication Data

Ugrešić, Dubravka.
    The culture of lies : antipolitical essays/Dubravka Ugrešić ;
translated by Celia Hawkesworth.
      p.   cm. — (Post Communist cultural studies)
    Includes bibliographical references.
    ISBN 0–271–01834–8 (alk. paper)
    ISBN 0–271–01847–X (pbk.: alk. paper)
    1. Croatia—History—1990– 2. Croatia—Intellectual life—
20th century. I. Title. II. Series.
DR1601.U37   1998
949.7203—dc21

                                  98–18867
                                      CIP

Printed in Great Britain

Contents

Foreword

The present work won the Charles Veillon European Essay Prize, an honor shared by such prominent European intellectuals as Roger Caillois, Leszek Kolakowski, Timothy Garton Ash, and György Konrád, and thus it places its author, Dubravka Ugrešić, in the best East European tradition of dissident, critical writing. At first glance, this collection of literary essays appears to be much more suitable for a series other than 'Post-Communist Cultural Studies.' Yet, these essays represent cultural analysis of the first order and, as such, are highly relevant to a series that, among other things, was conceived partly as an attempt to blur the sometimes rigid boundaries that demarcate disciplines in the contemporary academy. The classification 'cultural studies' ought to include genres such as the autobiographical essay, since it is in this genre that the irony, parody, and wit of the critical and reflective intellectual find their clearest expression. Many social-scientific studies elide these central modes of expression, but the literary essay, especially one that is informed by the author's experience of living through a critical historical moment, forces us to consider those aspects of life – especially the ironic ones – that we often consciously or unconsciously hesitate to think about in our social-scientific work.

Thus it is that Dubravka Ugrešić's *The Culture of Lies* serves as a fitting introduction to a series that is meant not only to describe and interpret historical events, but also to capture the experience of post-communism in Yugoslavia and its relationship to the past. The experiences that she discusses are not characteristic of post-communism in general. For the most part, and contrary to what one might expect, the general dissolution of communism was a nonviolent process. Not so with Yugoslavia. Indeed, the latest 'Balkan wars' are a fitting epitaph to a barbaric century in which abject cruelty has been masked by the rhetoric of civility, progress, and other Enlightenment dreams. Ugrešić captures the violence and madness of the wars in Croatia and Bosnia, and thus her account denies attempts to classify post-communism as a period characterized by the emergence of a 'new truth' or a 'new civilization.' On the contrary, the visions that led to the demise of Yugoslavia and the subsequent carnage there were not true at all, but constituted a 'culture of lies.'

This culture of lies is made possible by the collective fears of people in groups who respond to situations of danger by dichoto-mizing the world into categories of 'us' versus 'them.' Ugrešić stands by and watches not only the destruction of Yugoslavia but also the destruction of a collective identity and the reconsti-tution of 'the people' under a 'new truth' that was simply a modern version of an old historical story in which, as she puts it, 'one set of "truths" has been transformed into "lies" and "lies" transformed into "truths."' Ugrešić captures with bril-liance the fallacy of Hegel's idea of the end of history; while the nationalists would have us believe that the dead Yugoslavia is a symbol of the end of history, she reminds us that, instead, what we have seen is a repetition of the past. 'The war on the territory of the former Yugoslavia,' she writes, 'is only a repetition of the old story of disappearance and appearance, the story of human civilization.' In general, while her accounts are often humorous – or, perhaps, more accurately, tragicomic – there is little in these essays that is uplifting or utopian. If there is anything positive about them, it is the story of Ugrešić's own struggle with irrationality. Hers is the narrative of a critical intellectual who, by sheer power of intellect and will, resisted the hege-mony and tyranny of the collective mind.

Unlike many intellectuals of the former communist world with whom she might be compared, Ugrešić experienced *war* and, more than that, a war that destroyed an entire way of life and thus a whole collective identity. Throughout these essays, she offers a phenomenology of dissolution, nationalism, and war. It is a phenomenology that is tragic, but it is at the same time characterized by a high degree of analytical profundity and a sardonic apprehension of contemporary history. Her formid-able analytical and literary talents bring us into the netherworld of danger, fear, and irrationality, and as we read her words we feel those things as she did. We may not agree with her interpretations of all events, but we are nonetheless unable to deny that her work deserves a central place in the pantheon of accounts that depict events in the former Yugoslavia. This collection will certainly provoke heated discussion and, one hopes, continued analysis of the variety of social and cultural phenomena that the author explores.

Ugrešić's essays are characterized by a steadfast refusal to see the breakup of Yugoslavia in the same terms as the nationalists who caused it. From the beginning, Ugrešić was destined for an unhappy fate at the hands of intellectuals, who, instead of lending their critical voice to the madness, abetted it. In an especially insightful chapter on intellectuals, one is reminded that the *trahison des clercs* described by Julian Benda in the early part of the century is alive and well in the former Yugoslavia. Ugrešić's own experience at the hands of her comrades is a saddening testimony to the fate of a critical intellectual at the hands of those who would claim that mantle, but who actually lent their talents to the new spinners of the culture of lies. She chose to write critically about Croatian politics and culture at a time when criticism was considered an act of treason, when self-reflection was seen as an act of national betrayal, and when those whose identity was bound up with the Yuguslav idea rather than ethnic particularism were seen as traitors.

Throughout the book, Ugrešić draws attention to an important problem for post-communist studies: the loss of identity that accompanied the demise of communism in the later twentieth century. Ugrešić is both a commentator and a 'victim' of this process. She is a Yugoslav, yet Yugoslavia exists no more. Furthermore, she is forced by others to renounce her more universalist position and 'become' a Croat. Ugrešić, like many Yugoslavs, was clearly at home in Yugoslavia and, as her essays show, decidedly ill at ease in the new nationalist Croatian state. Alternately branded as a traitor, whore, and witch, Ugrešić left Croatia to live in Western Europe. Her experience with the 'new Croatia,' though, is a continuing source of her critical spirit, and in many ways the book is her reckoning with her unwanted masters. The essays offer a critique of Croatian society and culture, although they are liberally interspersed with important references to and discussions of other dynamics in the successor states of the former Yugoslavia. Ugrešić has accomplished the difficult task of being critical of Croatia while not losing sight of the central responsibility of people like Radovan Karadžić, Ratko Mladić, and Slobodan Milošević for war crimes and genocide in post-communist Yugoslavia. Unlike many observers in the West, she is able to mount an effective critique of Croatian nationalism and other cultural trends without engaging in moral equivocation. That is to say, she displays a clear sense of the history of responsibility for what has ensued in the former Yugoslavia and provides a sense of scale that is so often lacking in Western accounts of the wars in that place. She is able to recount facts about General Mladić or Radovan Karadžić that illustrate the qualities that define their actions as evil, and she is able to do this while resisting the idea that, because of this evil, her 'own people' are, by default, good. This is a remarkable achievement, and one that is absolutely crucial, not only because it provides an accurate sociological picture of events in the former Yugoslavia, but also because it provides a model for the preservation of the autonomy of the intellectual in an age when criticism is so easily seen as an act of disloyalty or a betrayal of 'the group.' Ugrešić is, in this sense, a model intellectual for a troubled time, and we learn through her example about both the exhilaration and the pain brought on by critical engagement and speaking truth to power.

Thomas Cushman
Wellesley College

Antipolitics is being surprised. A person finds things unusual, grotesque, and more: meaningless. He realises that he is a victim, and he does not want to be. He does not like his life and death to depend on other people. He does not entrust his life to politicians, he demands that they give him back his language and his philosophy. A novelist does not need a minister of foreign affairs: if he is not prevented from expressing himself, he is capable of doing so. He does not need an army either, he has been occupied for as long as he can remember. The legitimation of antipolitics is no more or less than the legitimation of writing. That is not the discourse of a politician, nor a political scientist, nor a technocrat, but the opposite: of a cynical and dilettante utopian. He does not act in the name of any mass or collective. He does not need to have behind him any party, state, nation, class, corporation, academic council. Everything he does, he does of his own accord, alone, in the milieu which he himself has chosen. He does not need to account to anyone, his is a personal undertaking, self-defence.

György Konrad, The Antipolitics of a Novelist

Lately, a friend of mine keeps saying: '*I don't know.*' And she keeps on repeating the phrase. '*I don't know,*' she says, shaking her head.

Lately, out of the blue, another friend of mine has been saying, apparently concluding some inner monologue: '*Well, what can you do?*' 'Nothing,' I say. He stares at me, not understanding what I had said.

The other day an acquaintance of mine fell asleep on the bus in broad daylight and spent three hours circling the town like a basket left on the seat.

Lately, I have been meeting some acquaintance or other, sighing deeply, gazing somewhere over his or her head and letting out an unarticulated sound, a combination of the vowels *e* and *a*. Aeeee, I say, patting my companion compassionately on the back. I never used to do that.

More and more often, people in the street talk to themselves. I've noticed some of my acquaintances among them. In cafés people sit taut as strings. Their ears pricked. Sniffing the air around them.

Somewhere in *Hope Against Hope*, Nadezhda Mandelstam wrote that Russia spent the time of Stalin's purges – lying down. People drank, ate, talked, lying down . . .

I meet an acquaintance, a television producer. How are you, I ask. I feel like a tic-tac, says the producer and goes zig-zagging off.

A Montenegrin peasant was once asked how he had felt during the earthquake in Montenegro.

'I felt something trembling, I went out of the house,' he said, 'and there was the epicentre a couple of steps away from me. There it was, trembling . . . I dashed to the left, but the epicentre followed me, I turned to the right, there it was again . . .'

And what about me? Lately, I have been buying fewer and fewer newspapers, I turn off the television more and more often, I don't plug in the telephone, I close the windows, pull down the blinds, draw the bedcovers over me, bury my head in a book and, why look, the letters are trembling . . .

Dubravka Ugrešić, 'The letters are trembling', *Danas*, 18 October 1988

And so, what is left us? A box of lead type, and that is not much . . ., but it is all that man has so far devised as a weapon in defence of human dignity.

Miroslav Krleža, *Banquet in Blitva*

1
Dark Beginning

1.

I was born in the fifth decade of the twentieth century, four years after the end of the Second World War. I was born in Yugoslavia, in a small industrial town not far from Zagreb, the main city of the Republic of Croatia. Many children were born in those years. The country which had been devastated by war was rapidly building its future. According to my mother, in my second year I developed vitamin deficiency. However, in my fifth year I tasted my first orange and was given my first doll, which I myself remember quite clearly. From that first orange on, with each day life confirmed its unstoppable march into a better future.

2.

When I went to school, I learned that Yugoslavia was a country which consisted of six republics and two autonomous regions, six national communities and several national minorities. I learned that there were in Yugoslavia several linguistic communities, and that in addition to Slovene and Macedonian, and the languages of national minorities – Albanian, Hungarian, Romany, Italian and others – there was Croato-Serbian or Serbo-Croatian, or just Croatian and Serbian, the language spoken, in different variants, in Croatia, Serbia, Montenegro and Bosnia. I learned that Yugoslavia had three large religious communities – Catholic, Orthodox and Muslim – and a lot of smaller ones. I learned that Yugoslavia was a small, beautiful country in the hilly Balkans. I learned that I must preserve brotherhood and unity like the apple of my eye. This was some kind of slogan, whose true meaning I did not really understand. I was probably confused by the poetic image *apple of my eye*.

3.

When I was a little older, everything I had learned was shown to be true, especially the beauty of the country in the hilly Balkans. In my first documents, where I had to fill in 'nationality', I wrote

3

'Yugoslav'. I grew up within an ideological framework which historians and political scientists call 'Titoism'.

Titoism presupposed (false or real) *internationalism* (even when he, Tito, went travelling and we looked in wonder at the newspaper photographs of his distant travels). On the level of ordinary life, this ideological notion had such a powerful effect that my parents agreed to adopt two children from the Congo. I remember how impatiently I awaited the arrival of my 'brothers' from the Congo, who for some reason I no longer remember never arrived.

Then, Titoism meant (false or real) *brotherhood and unity* (that was the most popular Yugo-ideologeme), which resulted in a common Yugoslav cultural space. On the level of everyday life, things were far simpler: the first boy to kiss me was called Bobo, he came from Zaječar, and the kiss occurred on the bank of a river whose name I no longer remember, but it was in brotherly Serbia.

In addition, Titoism meant (real or false) *anti-Stalinism*, which on the level of culture meant a break with the in any case short-lived socialist-realism, and on the level of life and death for a time Goli Otok, the Yugoslav Gulag. On the level of daily life things were simpler: my childhood culture consisted of Greek myths, stories about brave partisans and Hollywood films. My childhood idol was Audie Murphy, the hero of American Westerns. American films were the most effective and cheapest propaganda support for Tito's famous NO to Stalin.

4.

I grew up in a culture that quickly adopted values: from Italian shoes to cult writers. Once I attended a literary evening where there was a well-known American writer. The collective complex of a small nation was immediately activated in the home-bred audience. 'Do you know Ivo Andrić, Miroslav Krleža, Danilo Kiš,' my countrymen asked with the cordial politeness of good waiters. 'No,' said the American writer calmly. 'What about Milan Kundera?' asked someone in the audience hastily. 'Of course,' said the American writer. The audience sighed contentedly. At that moment they were all prepared to swear that Kundera was *our* writer. They were all ready to swear that our country was called *Yugoslovakia*, just so long as Kundera could be that. *Our* writer.

5.

I grew up in a culture that was proud of keeping step with the Western world, although – however unlikely it may sound to a Western reader, and to our own countrymen, suffering from collective amnesia – some things at home could be artistically more interesting than what was happening abroad. That is why I listened with the deep understanding of an 'Easterner' and the benign scepticism of a 'Westerner' to a Russian colleague who told me a few years ago with sincere 'perestroika' enthusiasm: 'Come, you'll see, we've got postmodernism till it's coming out of our ears! It's only soap we're short of!'

6.

I grew up in a multinational, multicultural and monoideological community that had a future. I was not interested in politics. My parents taught me nothing about it. The words 'religion', 'people', 'nationality', or even 'communism' and 'the party' meant nothing to me. I only ever wrote one 'political' sentence (and I stole that from a child): 'I love my country because it's small and I feel sorry for it.'

7.

I lived surrounded by books and friends. I simply could not understand my mother who, about ten years ago, for some unknown reason, began sighing: 'If only there isn't a war, everything will be all right, if only there isn't a war.' I was irritated by that sighing without evident cause, I attributed her anxiety to old age. The only associations that the word 'war' could conjure up in my head were the popular children's cartoons about Mirko and Slavko, boy-partisans. 'Watch out, Mirko! There's a bullet. Thanks, Slavko!'

8.

That is presumably why, in the autumn of 1991, when I first found myself in a bomb shelter, I felt like an extra in a war film. 'What's on television tonight?' my neighbour, a senile eighty-year-old, asked her daughter. The daughter replied: 'A war has started, mother.' 'Absurd, the film has started,' said the old woman, settling herself comfortably in her chair.

9.

Time rolled up into a circle, and exactly fifty years later, in the ninth decade of the twentieth century, a new war began. This time there were no 'wicked Germans, black fascists', the local participants divided the roles between themselves. Thousands of people lost their lives, homes, identity, children, thousands of people became émigrés, refugees and homeless in their own country. The war raged on all fronts, permeated all the pores of life, spilled out of the screens of televisions which were permanently on, out of newspaper reports and photographs. In the fragmented country both real and psychological wars were waged simultaneously. Mortar shells, psychological and real, wiped out people, houses, cities, children, bridges, memory. In the name of the present, a war was waged for the past; in the name of the future, a war against the present. In the name of a new future, the war devoured the future. Warriors, the masters of oblivion, the destroyers of the old state and builders of new ones, used every possible strategic method to impose a collective amnesia. The self-proclaimed masters of life and death set up the coordinates of right and wrong, black and white, true and false.

10.

And everything existed simultaneously: some were dying for their homeland, others were killing and looting in its name; some were losing their homes, others acquiring them; some were losing their identity, others maintained that they had at last found theirs; some became ambassadors, others cripples; some died, others began at last to live. Everything fused in one moment, everything became blatantly and shamelessly simultaneous. At the same moment life and death took on the most varied forms.

11.

Some soldiers asked to be sent back to the front: they claimed that, for all the shelling, life in the trenches was more peaceful. Others, who had escaped from Sarajevo, sought ways of returning: they maintained that life was more human in Sarajevo. Peaceful cities have lived an invisible hell. Out of their brittle confidence, they have produced hatred without realising that their hatred prolongs the real war. The quantity of evil heaped on the innocent in Sarajevo has spilled over like radioactive poison.

Without realising it everyone has received a dose of radiation. Cities, towns, villages have been like laboratories. Without realising it people were participating in an invisible experiment.

12.

If they are denied food, after a while rats begin first to eat their own young, and then each other. We have all been deprived of food: our past, present and future. There was no future because it had already happened. It happened because, in its own way, the past had repeated itself.

13.

In the spring of 1993, when I was sitting with some friends in a restaurant in Antwerp, a little Gypsy girl came up to our table selling bunches of roses. 'Where are you from?' I asked. 'I'm Yugoslav, a Gypsy,' replied the little girl. 'There's no more Yugoslavia,' I said. 'You have to be from somewhere, maybe you're from Macedonia.' 'I'm a Yugoslav, I'm a Gypsy,' repeated the little girl tenaciously.

The Yugoslav Gypsies who have scattered all over Europe are the only remaining Yugoslavs today, it seems, and the left-over ex-Yugoslavs have in the meantime become homeless, exiles, refugees, countryless, excommunicated, new nomads, in a word – Gypsies.

14.

'I don't know who I am any more, or where I'm from, or where I belong,' said my mother once as we ran down to the cellar, in panic at the air-raid warning. Although I now have Croatian citizenship, when someone asks me who I am I repeat my mother's words: 'I don't know who I am any more . . .' Sometimes I say: 'I am a post-Yugoslav, a Gypsy.'

15.

In September 1993, when I myself joined the new European nomads, a journey late at night in the local Munich–Tutzing train threw up a scene, the real author of which could have been Milan Kundera. At one of the stations a man battling with a large framed picture got into the compartment and sat down opposite me. The man was a little tipsy, he was muttering something, fiddling with the picture, not knowing how to put it down. On the picture was a portrait, or touched-up colour photograph, of an important man in uniform.

'Who's that?' I asked.

'Someone . . . who played an important part in my life . . .' mumbled my companion.

'A general?'

'Someone . . . from Chile . . .'

'He looks more like a Russian general to me . . .'

'He's not Russian . . .'

'Then who is it?'

'Klement Gottwald,' said my companion resignedly. The resignation referred to his absolute conviction that I, a passenger in the late night Munich–Tutzing train, wouldn't know who Klement Gottwald was.

'Oh, Klement Gottwald!'

'How do you know about Klement Gottwald?' said my companion in amazement.

'From a novel by Kundera!' I cried, remembering the episode with the photograph of the communist leader Klement Gottwald on the balcony.

'The one with Clementis's fur hat on his head . . .' I added, sinking further into my own foolish associations. But my fellow passenger livened up. He was a Czech, of course. He had been living in Germany for twenty-five years already, he had got the picture, he said, for his children, he had to explain the history of his emigration to them.

'And then we'll spray over him . . . We'll spray him!' he called gaily as he got off the train.

As I watched the man battling with his picture on the empty platform, it occurred to me that some cruel insults do not fade even after twenty-five years. From the perspective of the one insulted, of course. From the perspective of the observer, they are simply a barely comprehensible quotation from a novel read long ago.

16.

The texts in this book have grown out of a similar, deep sense of insult, even when they do not mention its origin. My fellow passenger's twenty-five-year-long personal nightmare is over, named and framed. My nightmare is still going on, it is different in kind and it cannot be put in a frame.

From the perspective of a distant reader (a passenger in a night train on some European line), my texts do not exceed the significance of a small footnote to events in Europe at the end of the twentieth century. But even when they are read from the closest possible perspective these texts still do not exceed the significance and extent of a personal footnote to a time of war in a country which no longer exists. My texts do not speak of the war itself, they are rather concerned with life on its edge, a life in which little is left for the majority of people. For writers – insofar as they do not become presidents, warmongers, patriot-profiteers and sales agents of other people's misfortune – the only thing left, it seems, is self-defence by footnote.

2

The Palindrome Conspiracy

My First Primer

> This happened during the war, somewhere roughly around nineteen forty-three. It's all absolutely true, the portrait of a life, a life story. I have no idea how else it could be written. I have realised that there's no special biographical order of events and that everything is in indescribable chaos. It still is.
>
> Bora Ćosić, *Tales about Professions*

The other day chance quietly placed in my hand an innocent little key to the door of the not so distant past. The role of Proust's madeleine was played by my primer which slunk out of a dusty box along with some old papers.

The first four pictures filled me, just like Proust, with the joy that comes when chance brings us 'true remembrance'. Or perhaps more exactly with the mixture of feelings brought by belated sudden recognition. I remembered staring long and fervently into those fresh clear colours, mostly bright blue and bright green. I remembered adding depth to the simple, flat lines through my entranced gaze. It was not that I was thinking up stories, I was just meticulously examining every detail, every smallest detail. I examined the pictures with my gaze as a fish does the limpid river bottom.

And now I recall the pleasure with which the pencil in my hand multiplied the apples, pears, plums, the joyful little spheres (clusters of grapes); the pleasure with which it drew symmetrical little tails on tree trunks, green pines. I filled my notebooks with orderly forests of them. I remember those endless rows of orderly carrots, onions, beetroot, potatoes. I recall the touching optimism of that endless multiplication. And I can almost hear those pears and apples of mine now soundlessly rolling out of the notebook and filling another imaginary space. All those lines and streaks, thick ones and thin ones, all those little windows, circles and snails, all those little hooks and snakes, all those loops and dots – they all rustle, crinkle, mingle in that imaginary space, they have not disappeared. Perhaps one day someone will let them out to become a real window, a real pear, a real word, a sentence.

I scrutinise the pictures. I can't read yet. I notice the brightly coloured, pleasing harmony of the most various objects and concepts: here are a horse and a harp, a man and a mouse, fingers and a flower . . . Each of them happily (as I would later discover) pronouncing their own sound: a boy – ah, a girl – oh, a sheep – baa, a cow – moo. I notice the objects: an antiquated radio, archaic pens and erasers. I notice the passionate faith in progress: on one picture children are waving at an aeroplane, on another a happy family is gathered round a table. And on the table – a radio. An antique steam engine is racing into a cloudless future. Bridges span rivers, chimneys puff cheerful smoke, tractors plough the soil, and ships the sea. The ship is called *Bakar* (as I would later discover). People (men, I see now) are working cheerfully: pilots and tractor-drivers, doctors and miners. Like Colin Collier digging coal.

Women are only mothers. Or little girls.

The sky is blue, the sun is shining, there are no clouds or rain anywhere, not even at the letter C, nor at the letter R.

I learn the letters. A for apple, E for elephant, O for orange, U for umbrella. Seka, see the sea! Hooray, hooray, the sea! Bit, sit, hit, bat, sat, mat, how now cow!

I learn sentences. *Jemal and Jafer are good friends. They come from Bosnia. Jafer has no family. He lives with Jemal. Jemal's mother loves him like her own son. Jemal and Jafer go to a distant town to learn a trade. Jemal's mother puts an apple in each of their pockets. As they leave she says: 'Work hard, children, light of my life. Gladden your mother's heart with good reports!'*

The sentences make soft imprints, outline common co-ordinates in the empty fields of our future personal biographies. Some letters stand out: F for family. (*There are mummy, daddy, brother, sister . . .*) H for homeland. (*Like a mother, with its Plan, the state takes care of every man.*) The state is something quite incomprehensible. The homeland is sea and mountains, and that's entirely comprehensible. B for brother. All people are brothers, especially Africans. (*A long way away, in Africa, live peoples with dark skins. They greet our sailors joyfully. They point to the red star on our flag. They shake our sailors firmly by the hand and shout in their own language: 'Yugoslav sailors are our brothers!'*)

There are Serbs and Croats. They are brothers too. And *when brotherly hearts unite – nothing can oppose their might!* So my primer proclaims.

The coordinates of the primer's system are not built on opposites. In the world of the primer there is no evil. There is only good. It's good to learn, to be clean (*Every day / come what may / wash the dirt / and grime away*) and diligent (*All young and strong who never shirk / Come along, and join in our work!*). For the moment only the fascists are evil. They usually come with the adjective black.

The primer gives us new faithful friends. This is written in large letters in my primer. These new friends are letters. *Bad luck all those who are without them!* – the last page of my primer threatens.

I started school in 1957. That year I got my passport to the Gutenberg galaxy, and another, inner, indistinct one. The primer is a kind of passport for several generations. Several generations are a whole nation, of a kind.

We all have our own primers. I don't know the nation which hatched out of the primers of a few decades before me. They were taught about an orderly, righteous, strict world in which not only did Africans not utter strange sentences, they simply didn't exist. This strict, orderly world is suggested by the hardback price printed on the first page and the publisher: 'The Royal Regional Government of the Croats, Slavonians and Dalmatians', 1885. As for the nation which is about to emerge from the new primer (I have the one for 1990 in my hand), I shan't know them and they won't interest me at all. I don't like their primer. The title to start with. *Good Morning 1* and *Good Morning 2*!

The world of the last-century primer is dominated by absolute certainty: it has a God (*Oh gentle Jesus, meek and mild / Send blessings on your humble child, / Give to him drink and food each day / And teach him how to work and play*). This primer is a guarantee of indisputable truths (*The beech is a tree. The rope-maker is a craftsman. The wolf is a savage beast*). In the world of this primer the borders of the homeland are clear (the homeland is Croatia, Slavonia and Dalmatia), and letters are learned with the help of the villages, towns, rivers and mountains within the borders of that homeland. K for Križevci, P for Papuk, P for Petrinja.

In my primer the homeland has no borders, there is Pula. (*Let's send a postcard to our pal Pero the pioneer in Pula. We are proud of our new pen.*) There is Filip from Slavonia and Frane from Dalmatia. There are sailors (again!) and our sea. ('*There's the sea!*' *shouts Slava. 'It's big and blue. There are big waves on the sea.*') But it's not called the Adriatic anywhere.

In the primer from the last century you acquire knowledge about life (about flour and wheat, about the Gospels and ploughing). The words are broken up, you learn by syllables. Be devout, humble and industrious – these are the virtues of the orderly world of last century's primer. The rules for life are: *Fear God! Respect your parents! Obey your elders! Learn willingly! Do good! Tell the truth! Be honest! Don't touch what's not yours!* And that's all, the beginning and the end of it.

That primer teaches children about coins, measures, months, seasons, holidays and holy days, work.

There are lots of names in that primer. Ladislav, Šišman, Ljudevit, Sofija, Gavrilo, Cvjetana, Čestislava, Čutimira. Silver is white, the sun is bright, reeds are green, melons are succulent, conch shells are long. Čestislava is a name.

In my primer the names, Croatian and Serbian, are equally distributed. As many Petars as Mitars, Djordjes as Ivans.

The names in the new primer are Bobo and Beba, Bibo and Biba, Nino and Nena. And Jafer. Somehow he got a ticket into all the primers. He's here too. Without Jemal this time. And in a quite different text.

In the pages of the 1885 primer there is no doubt in the truth of the world. In the 1990 primer the world does not exist. There are no towns, rivers or mountains, the homeland is not measured. There are no Jovans or Ivans. The alphabet is the same: an apple for A, a boat for B, the inevitable umbrella for U. The pages have begun to fall out of the new primer; mine was firmly bound.

The drawings in my primer are realistic, with innumerable

tiny details. The colours are clear, like freshly painted village houses. The drawings in the new primer are stylised, like caricatures or cartoon films. In pastel shades, pinkish, yellowish . . . The children's faces have dots for eyes, dashes instead of smiles. The faces of the adults are indistinguishable from those of the children. Boring dots and dashes.

In the new primer there are pictures of a world which no longer exists, like old flags people have forgotten to take down. Tito and pioneers. The top children in their class, who are right now learning from this primer, are no longer enrolled in the pioneers ('to enrol in the pioneers' is a sentence from a bygone age), Tito is only a monument (a photograph of a monument), and in the children's minds partisan might easily be confused with marzipan. No single reality matches the drawings, no single drawing matches reality. The world of the new primer resembles the world of cartoon films (*Skipping in the sun / Oh what jolly fun! / Laugh the clouds away / What a lovely day! / Smile at all you meet: / Every day's a treat!*). The world of the new primer doesn't exist, it's a world of paper happiness.

The world of my primer matches reality. The picture of a mother in a clean apron seeing her little boy off to school is overlaid for me now with a picture of my own mother. I remember clearly the snow-white aprons, the clean bedlinen, curtains and cushions, the aesthetics of poverty. In the general post-war deprivation we all shared, a vase of wild flowers, a little curtain and a cushion, and that faultless cleanliness successfully concealed the lack of material things.

C for car – and the drawing of a car opens up domains of unwritten and unarticulated (were we ashamed?) Yugo-mythology. A car, a *fićo*, the first Yugoslav car. I remember that passionate faith that each new day would bring a better future (this year we're buying a car, and next year we'll go to the sea).

The 'Red Star' shoe factory (that's what's written in the primer) with a picture of children's shoes with little straps (I had shoes like that, some with the toes cut out, I was growing and shoes were expensive) draws with it a whole history of Yugo-actuality: memories of real 'winkle-pickers', plastic macs, the first nylon underwear, white nylon shirts, the first orange, the first sweets, the first chocolate, the first trip to Trieste . . .

Seka, Sanda, see the sea! Hurray, hurray the sea was not an alliterative sentence to practise writing the letter S, but what we

17

said every time we caught sight of the sea. The picture of the family at the train window (you can clearly see the initials of the Yugoslav State Railways, in Latin and Cyrillic scripts) matches the exciting reality of travelling by train (school trips to Zagreb, the capital of Croatia, to Belgrade, the capital of Yugoslavia).

In the drawing of the radio I clearly recognise the first 'Nikola Tesla' Yugoslav radio (I remember staring intently in the dark at the magic flickering green eye), and the family gathered round the table is listening trustingly to the 'Sailors' Requests' programme broadcast every Monday at eight. It was heard by people on ships, people who had relatives on ships and people who had never seen either a ship or the sea. The attentiveness with which the family was listening to the radio concealed the reality of Yugo-daily-life at the time. It too was a substitute for poverty: huddled round the radio people listened to the magical names of distant ports and oceans, and also to Mato Matić requesting the song 'Yugoslav Sailors' for his family, his wife Kata, daughter Vlasta and son Joško. It had the same importance as the first landing on the moon.

The Tito of my primer was a real Tito, the one to whom we sent letters on his birthday rolled up into tubes and pushed into hand-made wooden batons. I remember rolling the letters into tubes and pushing them into that important object, and then it wasn't merely 'a letter in a bottle' but a letter with a clear addressee which would be read. There was no doubt about that.

I started school in 1957. That year I got my passport to the Gutenberg galaxy, and another, inner, indistinct one. The primer is a kind of passport for several generations. Several generations are a whole nation, of a kind. I recognise that nation of mine. It hatched out of the primer like those armies of pears and apples. It's hard to recognise, it's neither East nor West, neither Russian nor English. But I always do recognise my people. I recognise them at international airports, where they are more easily hidden mixed up with others. I recognise them by a kind of twitch, by their eyes, by the way they glance shyly around them, and the way they try not to, by the way they check in their luggage, I recognise them even when they're travelling in the opposite direction, when they're well disguised in foreign clothes, and pretending, therefore, to be something else.

The people who will be writing the next primer for their pupils belong to a nation which has wrapped itself in national flags as its only identity. That identity makes it secure and gives it a sense of reality, like a coat with the trusty 'Burberry' label. They will pass through international airports as firmly convinced Croats, Serbs, Slovenes, with no twitch on their face and without glancing shyly around them. The language, alphabet, symbols, concepts of those primers will be different. But the new generation will get its passport too: one for the Gutenberg galaxy, and another, inner, indistinct one . . .

April 1991

Postscript

The primer, a little Utopia, which was initially synchronised with life, very quickly became a dusty document from the past. Life set off to conquer lovelier, richer images. However, in 1991, when the last, bloodiest phase of dismantling the Yugoslav Utopia began, time rolled up into a circle and everything went back . . . to the beginning! Tired of the breathless strategies of the media war with all its 'sound and fury', the dismantling returned to the bare, clear little sketches from my primer! Jovans are attacking Ivans, the Cyrillic alphabet is quarrelling with the Latin script, Serbs with Croats, Djordje and Jafer are fighting, the green aeroplanes with a red star from my primer took off and began bombing first Croatian villages and towns, then Bosnian ones. From their ships our Yugoslav sailors shelled our ports, towns and our lovely blue sea. The homeland without borders began to carve its new borders. Books, our best friends, burned, splinters of centuries-old churches flew through the air together with splinters of Tito's plaster heads. Letters, figures, symbols from my innocent primer rushed to annihilate themselves. Like Eristochtones, the Utopia was devouring itself before our eyes, and in the wastelands, like harmless little eggs, there began to appear the outlines of new . . . primers!

The Palindrome Story

1.

A palindrome (Greek: 'running back again'), according to the *Dictionary of Literary Terms*, is a word or sentence that reads the same whether it is read forwards or backwards. For instance, *civic, level, minim, radar*. In enigmatics a palindrome can be a riddle on this basis, and it can be used in verse and in prose. A palindrome can consist of letters or syllables. It was introduced into enigmatics by the German poet and dramatist Theodor Körner. There have been examples of whole palindromic sentences since the earliest times.

2.

a) Among the oldest palindromes are those of the Roman poet Virgil. A famous example is the so-called Latin *sator* formula, in the form of a magic square, found in 1936 during the excavation of the ancient Mesopotamian city of Dura (now Salahyeh):

SATOR
AREPO
TENET
OPERA
ROTAS

This square inscription can be found on several buildings in Italy, the most famous of which is the one on a nineteenth-century mosaic in the floor of a church in Piave-Terzigani. The sentence means roughly: *Arepo the sower holds his cart with difficulty.*

   b) According to some sources, the palindrome was invented by the Greet poet Sotades (third century BC). Legend has it that because of his sharp tongue, Ptolomy II had him tied up in a sack and thrown into the sea. Palindrome verses are sometimes called *sotadics* in his honour. Apparently the best-known Greek palindrome is *Nipson anomemata me monan ospin* (Wash not only my face but also my sins), which is inscribed on many fonts and churches.

c) The most popular English example of a palindrome is the sentence *Able I was ere I saw Elba*, attributed to Napoleon. Other favourite examples are: *Sums are not set as a test on Erasmus; A man, a plan, a canal – Panama!* A recent example by W. H. Auden is: *T. Eliot, top bard, notes putrid tang emanating, is sad. I'd assign it a name: 'Gnat dirt upset on drab pot toilet.'* The poet Sir Thomas Urquhart is said to have invented a universal language based on palindromes. Apparently the longest palindrome in English (consisting of 11,125 words!) was written in 1979 by the New Zealand poet Jeff Grant. It begins with the line: *No elate man I meet sees a bed . . .* Another well-known example is the half-meaningful creation of an anonymous nineteenth-century poet, beginning: *Dog as a devil deified/ Deified lived as a dog.*

d) In Russian literature there is the famous line of G. R. Derzhavin: *Ja idu s mechem sudija* (I go with a judge's sword). V. Bryusov wrote palindromes, as did Velimir Hlebnikov, who wrote the palindromic poem 'Styenka Razin'.

e) In Croatian literature the poet Petar Preradović wrote palindromes, and Brabalić's sentence in the form of a magic square is often cited as an example: *Šešir Elidi širiš idile rišeš* (You stretch Elida's hat. You sketch idylls).

3.

The palindrome is a poetic word game, in the category of technopaignia, or *carmina figurata*. In the theory of puzzle-writing a false palindrome is called a palindromoid. That is a word or sentence that has one meaning when read forwards and a different one when read backwards.

4.

According to *A Dictionary of Symbols* by J. Chevalier and A. Gheerbrant, in cabbalistic tradition Lillith is the name of the woman made before Eve. Lillith was made like Adam, not that is from a man's rib, but from clay.

We are both equal, she said to Adam, because we are made from clay. After that they quarrelled and, having uttered the name of God, Lillith ran away.

According to a different version Lillith was the first Eve, and Cain and Abel fought over which of them she belonged to. Some see in her traces of androgeny, the first man and the incest of the first couple. As a woman who was rejected or abandoned in favour of another woman, Lillith symbolises hatred of family, married couples and children: she reminds one of the tragic image of Lamia in Greek mythology. Since she could not fit into the framework of human life or social norms, she was thrown into a chasm, into the depth of the ocean, where she is tormented by depraved desires. Lillith is the little nocturnal nymph who tries to seduce Adam and give birth to mirages. She is the vampire nymph of curiosity who removes and replaces her eyes at will and gives human children the poisonous milk of dreams.

5.
'*Madam I'm Adam*', said Adam to Eve, and she introduced herself equally palindromically: '*Eve.*'

6.
According to the encyclopaedia Croats speak the čakavian, kajkavian and štokavian dialects. All three dialects make up one linguistic diasystem, but since the štokavian dialect is also spoken by Serbs, Croats and those former Yugoslavs who are categorised by nationality as Muslims, this diasystem is known in scholarship as Serbo-Croatian or Croato-Serbian, and belongs to the South Slavonic group of languages.

The Croatian literary language dates back to the twelfth century. The oldest Croatian monument, the Baška Stone, from 1100, is written in čakavian, with Old Church Slavonic elements. The first alphabet was Glagolitic, then Cyrillic, with Latin script dominating from the fourteenth century. The contemporary Croatian literary language has an unbroken tradition from the sixteenth century, when the Republic of Dubrovnik (Ragusa) developed a rich literature in the ijekavian variant of the štokavian dialect. A major contribution to the unification of the Croatian literary language in the štokavian dialect was made by the Franciscans who were active in Dalmatia, Bosnia and Slavonia, so that by the middle of the eighteenth century it was sufficiently sophisticated to have a standard form. It was only with the endeavours of the Illyrian movement in the first half of the nineteenth century that all Croats were united by one štokavian language. The main influence on the formation of the Croatian literary language in the nineteenth century was that of the Zagreb linguistic school. The orthography was etymological. Towards the end of the nineteenth century Croatian followers of the reformer of the Serbian literary language, Vuk Karadžić, predominated and endeavoured to take the Croatian literary language in a similar direction. On the basis of the work of V. Karadžić and Đura Daničić, in 1892 Ivan Broz published his *Croatian Orthography* following phonological principles, and in 1899 Tomo Maretić published his *Grammar and Stylistics of the Croatian or Serbian Literary Language* with new forms and Karadžić–Daničić accents. In 1901 Franjo Iveković brought out his *Dictionary of the Croatian Language* based on the same principles and compiled in cooperation with Ivan Broz. These three works laid down the orthographical and grammatical norms of the contemporary Croatian literary language. This activity brought the Croatian language significantly closer to Serbian.

7.

'When I get up in the morning,' said Kšvebt, a Croat, 'I say the whole alphabet, it includes all the prayers of the world, so let the Lord God Himself gather up the letters and make of them whatever prayers He likes. I can't do it as well as He can, He's better at it.' (Moscherosch, *The Amazing True Characters of Philander of Sittewald*, 1665; quoted by Gustave Rene Hocke in his book, *Mannerism in Literature*.)

8.

In his book *The Sky and Hell*, Emmanuel Swedenborg – who according to his servants often conversed with invisible beings in an unknown language – discovers something about the language of angels. The speech of the angels of heaven is like 'a tranquil river, gentle and almost uninterrupted', while the speech of the angels of the spirit 'seems to flutter and hesitate'. Further, Swedenborg affirms that the vowels U and O predominate in the speech of heavenly angels, E and I in that of angels of the spirit. The speech of heavenly angels has no hard consonants.

Swedenborg distinguishes between the groups of angels of the sky and spirit, as those which are concerned with good and those concerned with truth. Speech which expresses truth contains the vowels E and I, while that which expresses good contains U and I, and sometimes A.

In the speech of angels altogether there is a kind of 'harmony which cannot be described'. The speech of hell is heard like 'a gnashing of teeth which instils horror'.

9.

D. O.[1] is a Croatian poet. She writes in the Croatian language and belongs to a little literature in which for a long time women wrote only children's books, then poems, then autobiography, then romances . . . D. O. did not write a single a) children's book; b) autobiography; c) romance. She wrote two books of poetry and numerous articles, including one about Khlebnikov's *language of the stars*.

The language of the stars is a universal language system, far more elaborate than the one which Swedenborg attributes to the angels. Angels speak the language of heaven, the language of the stars is a language of the universe, of 'heavenhell'. It seems that this *language of the stars* marks the beginning of the end of this story.

10.

In 1981 D. O. wrote a palindromic poem entitled '*Rim i mir ili ono*' (lit. 'Rome and Peace or That'), which she called a palindromic apocalypse. She was familiar with the ideas of Raymond Lully and his tables of combinations, his endeavour to construct the theological-ontological composition of the world with letters and words, she was enthusiastic about Khlebnikov, she wrote about his unusual forms, she translated him, delving into his paraphilological system, was carried away by the 'transmental' language of *zaum* and Dada, she read Kruchenych carefully, and like Mallarmé she thought that *everything in the world exists in order to end up in a book*, she knew his idea of a superbook, the poetic book of the world – and then she herself began to play,

[1] The 'Palindrome Poem' by the Croatian poet, Dubravka Oraić Tolić, served only as a starting point for this essay. Its meaning and the figure of the poet known as D. O. are products of the author's imagination.

rejecting Eve's, rejecting Adam's language. Completely alone in the Croatian language, this Lillith took the Croatian language into her mouth like the sacred host, winding herself in it like a divine larva in her own cocoon.

In total darkness, lit from within, from the little nest of the Croatian language, she listened to the pulse of the globe, the stars, space, the universe.

11.

As she wrote her poem, she sorted her words as a bird does seeds in its gizzard. She wanted every word to be as perfect as a seed, as an atom, she sorted letters from right to left, from left to right, forming the words in her own saliva, and finally, drugged, she spat from her mouth a perfect palindrome – a rich rosary which can be counted equally from the left and from the right.

The most frequent vowels in the poem were E and I. And sometimes also A.

12.

According to *A Dictionary of Symbols* a rosary is a series of pearls on a string, mentioned in the *Bhagavadgita*, and the string is Atma, on which all things are strung, that is all the worlds, all the states of the phenomenal. Atma, the universal spirit, links those worlds; it is the breath that gives them life. Guenon mentions that the formulae accompanying each seed are spoken in the rhythm of breathing.

In Indian iconography rosaries are attributed to a small number of deities, but above all to Brahma and Sarasvata, who is the alphabet, the creative power of the word. Her rosary (aksa-mala) has fifty seeds (aksa) which corresponds to the Sanskrit alphabet of fifty letters. Like every wreath of letters, the Indian rosary is connected with creative sound and the sense of hearing.

In India, particularly in the Bhuddist world, the rosary has 108 beads, which is a cyclical number and therefore expresses the growth of the phenomenal. The Muslim rosary has ninety-nine which is also a cyclical number. The beads are connected with the names of God, while the hundredth, the unread bead, expresses the return of the multiple to the One.

13.

According to *A Dictionary of Symbols* the apocalypse is above all the declaration of mysterious realities, then a prophecy because those realities are yet to take place, and finally it is a vision. That vision has no value in itself, but only through the symbolism it contains: in the apocalypse everything has symbolic value; numbers, objects, characters. Symbols, like tarot cards, may have different meanings and be read in different ways.

14.

The apocalypse in D. O.'s poem occurs in 1991, a year which can be read equally forwards and backwards. Then, in 1981, it would have been possible to chose 2002 as a palindromic year, but she needed the figure *one* as a symbol of beginning, being and discovery, and the figure *nine*, the last in the series of numbers, as an indication of the end and the beginning, death and rebirth, as the last number of the phenomenal world. A fragment of the poem was published in 1981 in a literary journal. The same number included texts by Gustave Rene Hocke about *ars combinatoria*, Italo Calvino about cybernetics and fantasy, Jacques Roubaud about mathematics in the method of Raymond Queneau. This fragment is the only public proof of the fact that the poem existed as early as 1981.

15.

Seeing what she had done, she trembled with foreboding and withdrew her rosary.

Like a golden ring, coiled like a snake, the poem lay under her tongue gleaming with an ominous dark glow. Holding her tongue, she restrained the phantoms she had blindly given birth to, removing her own eyes from her face, so as to be closer to the stars.

For some reason, in her poem E and I rang . . . like knives.

And when the outlines of the phantom world from her palindrome apocalypse began, in the same order, in the same rhythm of a breathless step, to appear on the horizon, accompanied by the clink of metal, she was not surprised. All the palindromic phantoms, one after another, were there, before our eyes . . . A mere ten years later reality was unfolding just as her palindromic scroll dictated. Reality just corrupted the beauty of the metaphors of reality discovered before.

Real events, as they took place, extinguished the visionary gleam of the lines. The work of art became . . . truth.

16.

And it all happened: the Third Rome shook, the worm-eaten East European empire creaked, the sad grey empire disintegrated. The palindromes produced 'rings of Hell', the embittered masses burned symbols: lengthy, black 'beards of care'. The Third Rome – Moscow – burned.

And then everything rolled in, marched in, heaved in here, towards us. The scroll of the poetic palindrome unwound to the end and stopped here, just here, 'at the loud edge'. A gong sounded announcing the beginning: an introduction to destruction. The riders are coming, bringing monosyllabic words: death, war, grief. *Idu ludi, na rub buran.*[2]

17.

At this moment, when her own poem reads like a horoscope – in which everything foreseen in it did in fact take place, apart from the end for which there is still time – D. O. wants only one thing: that reality should vanish, that the poem should remain what it was to start with, a game, a work of art. But the palindromic genie has been let out of the bottle, it's too late. At this moment, when she reads bloody reality like her own poem, D. O. wants only one thing: that the poem should become what it was not to start with – one, unambiguous language, the language of one truth, for there cannot be more than one truth.

Because the fact is that her palindromic rosary written in the little Croatian language, an unknown, unrecognised jewel of Croatian literature, may be read from left to right, but also from right to left, in Croatian, but also in Serbian, in the Latin script, but also in Cyrillic; the palindromic truth is here, on the left-hand side, but, so they say, also over there, on the right; it may be read equally in a Western and in an Eastern way!

In reality both sides of the tormented land in their fight to the death speak Croatian, but also Serbian, they are dying on one side, and on the other. Truth is on our side – they shout from left to right. Truth is on our side – they shout from right to left. But they are killing us! – comes the cry from left to right. But they are killing us! – comes the cry from right to left. O Jugo! O gujo![3]

---

[2] Crazed men are marching to the wild edge.

[3] **Juga** was a widespread colloquial abbreviation for 'Yugoslavia'. It seems that the word entered into general use via the slang of Yugoslavia *Gastarbeiters*. **Guja** is a synonym for **zmija** (serpent) common in folklore, in fairy tales and songs (e.g. **Ijuta guja**). The palindrome **O Jugo! O gujo!** means: Oh, Yugo(slavia)! Oh, serpent! (Translator's note)

Even the Jesuses in the tragic game of mirrors hang strung like the beads of a rosary, from left to right, from right to left. *I vise sivi Isusi. Isti, sivi* (Grey Jesuses hang. The same, grey). The palindromic language has been let out of the bottle like a genie. Like a mirage truth becomes two, the same! Two truths are two truths, are two lies, two truths are one lie. One of the two is a lie . . .

No one foresaw this bitter, terrible farce. The farce was foreseen by the palindrome.

Let out of its bottle the palindrome genie creeps back, towards its end, towards its beginning, it wraps round our necks, throttles us like a 'serpent', takes our breath away.

18.

Apart from the little fragment in the literary journal of exactly ten years ago, D. O.'s poem has never been published. She is not thinking of publishing it.

Grandiose creations are as fragile as houses of cards. As in a dream, as in a flashback, she, *avet Eva* (the phantom Eve), the first *Eve*, the tragic Lillith – who does not wish to repeat the history for which she is, they see, responsible – destroys her creation, puts away the cards. There is no point whatever in destroying the poem, the terrible reality is already here.

One of the most meaningless, one of the most meaningful creations of Croatian literature will destroy itself, the pages will burn, they have written the apocalypse, they will vanish in it. That is one possibility. The publication of the poem later, when it is all over, on the ruins, will reveal a palindromic summary of events. And how to prove then, and to whom and why, after all, that she described everything that was yet to come long before it happened, how to justify the choice of genre. On the ruins of the former world, on the ruins of the future world, that will be unnecessary, inappropriate. That is another possibility. On the ruins of the former world, on the ruins of the future world, the palindromic snake under her tongue will slide out, clang like a golden ring, glow with the gleam of a work of art. The truth contained in it will no longer be important. The palindrome will become its true nature, a serpent, Lillith, the production of phantoms through art, through the phantom of art. That is a third possibility.

At this moment D. O. is not thinking about that, she is

trembling with fear, and wondering whether in her starry inspiration, trying to wrap the Croatian language around the globe, to set the stars alight, it could be that, without knowing what would happen, knowing what would happen, could it be that she actually produced everything that occurred?!

19.

And how is it that I, who am jotting down these fragments, laying them out like cards in a game of patience, came to know all this? D. O. gave me her text then, in that distant 1981, to devour – as the angel to John . . .

The other day I took it out of my drawer to read (I believe that she did so as well). From the television come the sounds of shooting, gunfire, tanks, people are dying, images of funerals, destruction, blood . . . *O Jugo! O gujo!*

The circle is narrowing, the noose is tightening like the figure 9. Time has been rounded off into a loop, like a snake swallowing its own tail. *O Jugo! O gujo!*

A century of solitude begins and ends. I unroll the scroll of the palindrome, I reach the 'bright end' *(jarki kraj)*.

Shall we destroy each other, will the 'atom furl' us all in the end, will we be left with one single, final palindromic wail – *kisik*![4] Will at last the final *teleks* really be a *skelet(on)* . . .

20.

I am completing these fragments on 1.9.91. There are another 122 days until the end of this palindromic year. I'm waiting. As I wait, I tremble, gun shots from the television screen merge with those around my house, they knock at my door, and as I wait I devour the pages of the palindromic apocalypse, I feel *a sweet taste in the mouth* and *bitterness in the stomach* . . .

21.

According to the *Dictionary of Literary Terms* palindrome means 'running back again'. An ancient term for a word, sentence or line of verse which sounds the same whether it is read from right to left or left to right. Such a line is also called *versus diabolicus*, the devil's line.

September 1991

---

4 Oxygen.

Postscript

In his *Book of Laughter and Forgetting*, in the chapter about the two laughters, Milan Kundera touches on the essence of the palindrome. When he first heard the Devil's laughter, the Angel felt weak and helpless. As he understood it, the Devil's laughter was aimed against God and the wonder of His works. Since he could not think of anything else, he decided to imitate his opponent. And so, writes Kundera, *there they stood, Devil and Angel face to face, mouths open, both making more or less the same sound, but each expressing himself in a unique timbre – absolute opposites.*

Accepting the division into Good and Evil, the Devil and the Angel, means to accept the demagogy of the angels, maintains Kundera. As far as laughter is concerned there exist authentic laughter (that of the Devil) and its imitation (that of the Angel). There are, therefore, two kinds of laughter, but we have no words to distinguish them.

I gave D. O. the text about the palindrome poem to read I think on the very day I finished it, 1.9.1991. Soon afterwards I went abroad; in any case, important events consigned the text to oblivion.

In the meantime D. O. wrote an essay, a kind of hidden reply, and published it. When I returned after being away for several months and came across her essay in a magazine, I was startled, just like Kundera's Angel, just as D. O. herself was, I assume, when she read mine. I thought I recognised the rhythm (my prose rhythm!), the intonation (mine!) . . . Her text, however, contained quite the opposite meaning.

Finally, two years later, D. O. published her palindromic poem, and that is, I think, why I am writing this *postscript* now. Writers rarely burn their works, writers are, after all, only people, fallible beings. The poet had invested too much effort in her demanding linguistic puzzle simply to forget it. And my poetic assumptions about how to solve her as yet unpublished poem turned out to be mere romantic raving. D. O. published her poem. I understand that decision perfectly. I believe she could not in fact resist the call of the Devil, her right to *authenticity*.

She published her essay, 'The Palindrome Story' again, alongside the poem. The essay is a commentary in which she rejects her own poem (*I was ashamed of every word, every line . . .*). Because, the poet writes in her commentary, *the language of the*

*palindrome is a Utopian linguistic game. No one speaks it and
no one ever will. It works on the Utopian principle that both
sides are the same, that the words can be read equally from the
left and from the right, from the east and from the west. In our
normal discourse, in our normal orientation in space, in our
normal understanding of European civilisation it is normal for
there to be two sides, right and left, an East and a West, and it
doesn't cross anyone's mind to suggest that they are identical.*

What has in fact happened in the meantime is that palindromes
have become too subversive, too dangerous not only for the poet
herself, but, and this is far more important, for the newly
established *Truth*. In publishing her poem and her commentary,
the poet has at the same time, consciously or unconsciously,
bound *the official truth* between covers. She did this with the
same urgency and passion with which the *New Truth*
endeavoured to enter anthologies, textbooks, encyclopaedias,
monographs, an urgency which seems to spring from the fear that
she could lose her right to *one, single* reading.

At this moment, two years later, therefore, I cannot say with
any certainty why I wrote the text about the palindrome poem. I
believe what drove me to write it was fear of the palindrome
madness which was beating at our doors as I wrote and which is
still raging; the same fear, in fact, that drove the poet herself, the
author of the palindrome poem, to deny it. As though by that act
she had put an end to the madness, the palindrome reality, and
returned to a *normal* orientation in space, to a *normal* understanding of the world.

Our palindrome story, hers and mine, begins of course with the
authentic, with the Devil. D. O., a true poet, unconsciously
opted for the *authentic*, for the *Devil*'s language. Unexpectedly
seeing her reflection in my text, my *interpretation* (which is
nothing other than *a search for the authentic*, that is, *an
imitation*) she was suddenly afraid. She discovered a different
reading, a different possible meaning which she had not herself
foreseen. In this sudden reversal I helped her to recognise the
Angel in herself, and thanks to that reversal I myself recognised
the Devil in me. Continuing to follow the *demagogy of the angels*
nothing remained for the poet but to *imitate* the meaning of her
own poem, the meaning which I had read in her text about the
authentic, her *Devil's verse*.

Ever since I gave D. O. my text to read, I have felt that I have a shadow, a reflection. At the same time as I write my text, my reflection, my shadow is writing the same but different text by way of reply. The palindrome game continues, without either she or I wanting it. Whatever I utter, she will utter as well; when I laugh, I shall see before me my opponent *letting out a wobbly, breathy sound*, but the meaning of that sound will be the absolute opposite.

In order to destroy her palindromes for ever, that *dead utopian language* (as she herself described it), the poet D. O. used the strategy of the palindrome. Has the Angel outwitted the Devil?

I am not, however, writing this *postscript* in order to relate our palindromic happening, D. O.'s and mine. I am writing these lines because of a new anxiety, because of my fear of the ever more suffocating song of the angels, a song which *defends God and the wonder of his works*, fear of the *demagogy of the angels*, of reflections, of imitation. I am writing it because of a foreboding that tells me that before long in this unhappy wasteland the Angel will come face to face, as in a mirror, with the Angel, the imitation of an imitation, and in his blind, righteous passion he will believe that he is still waging war against the Devil. That is why I am opting for the language of the Devil. Even at the price of being the only one who knows it. For however paradoxical it sounds, here, at this time, the Devil is alone.

And finally, let us add, the palindromes, which wiped a whole country from the map and drove its inhabitants insane, have woven ironic lassoos of destiny around the two of us as well, the author of the palindromic poem and myself.

The poet, in opting to *protect God and the dignity of His work* or, more briefly, in opting for the language of one *truth* (for truth cannot be but one), became the chief editor of a substantial volume of photo-reportage about the war in Croatia. She expended a vast amount of energy and more than a year working on the volume. As truth about the war, the lavishly produced documentary volume has become a kind of state souvenir. The poet personally handed the book to the President of the new Croatian state, Franjo Tudjman, as was reported in the Croatian media with fitting attention. Further, the poet was received, promoting the truth (and erasing her 'palindromic past'), by Hans-Dietrich Genscher, as was confirmed by photographs displayed for days in the window of a Zagreb bookshop. These photographs show the poet cordially handing her book to the German politician. Driven by the same deep and sincere sense of mission, she sought an audience also with Margaret Thatcher and Pope John Paul II. Whether she reached them, I don't know.

So, the poet rejected her poetic language (the language of lies) and chose the photograph (the language of truth). The tragedy of her choice lies in the fact that her sincere mission ended up bound into a topical state souvenir, and still more in the fact that the photograph too is a palindrome. In a media-propaganda war, what is most frequently manipulated is the language of truth, poetic language is in this sense barely usable. It is well known that photographs of dead bodies and burned houses have been adopted as *their victims* by both sides; both the side of the *victim* and that of the *executioner*, in other words.

As far as I, the author of these lines, am concerned, the palindromes of destiny have shown themselves to be unimaginative. In our shared story, they allotted me the expected and therefore banal path which I experience as a quotation: for a while now I have been living in exile. Voluntary, of course.

As for the country, Yugoslavia, which was known colloquially as Juga to its inhabitants, pronouncing the vowel *u* as a hollow, long-drawn-out sound, has found its place in the prophetic palindrome of a Croatian poet and really become Juga-guja.

July 1993

Priests and Parrots

A writer is a mixed breed of parrot and priest. He is a parrot in the loftiest sense of the word. He speaks French if his master is French, but sold in Persia he will speak Persian: 'Polly is a fool' or 'Polly wants a cracker'. A parrot knows no age, nor can he tell day from night. If he begins to bore his master, he is covered over with a black cloth, and that, for literature, is the surrogate of night.

Osip Mandelshtam, *Fourth Prose*

1.

'If only I were Czech or Hungarian . . . Given that I can't be English or French,' mused my countryman, my colleague, a writer.

'How do you mean?'

'My surname bothers me.'

'I don't understand . . .'

'If only it began with a *K* . . . that would be a help.'

'What do you mean?'

'It could go with Kundera, Konrad, Klima . . .'

'If only you were called Krleža or Kiš . . . that would be a help,' I said.

'That would make a fundamental difference . . .' sighed my colleague.

'How about changing your name?'

'What to?'

'I don't know . . . Kefka? That begins with a *K* . . .' I suggested cautiously.

'Um . . . Kafka . . . Kefka . . .' mumbled my colleague and countryman Petar Petrović.

34

And as I nodded sympathetically, it occurred to me that as a rule a person can choose a lot of things: friendships, way of life, often even death itself, even the country he or she is going to live in (if it has come to that), even a surname (if it has even come to that) . . . There are just two things one can't choose: one's place of birth and – one's colleagues!

2.

This jokey dialogue could have taken place up until a short time ago. Step by step, the identity of the Yugoslav writer has been completely destroyed. That is, he, the Yugo-writer, did not take refuge in time under the umbrella of *Central Europe*, his cultural milieu, myth, cultural longing or 'dream' (as Gyorgy Konrad would say), his cultural label. How could he have done when he had been brought up in the conviction ever since 1948 that we (we, Yugoslavs) were something quite different from them (Czechs, Hungarians and Poles . . .), which was after all confirmed by everyday reality (we could go to Trieste for a coffee, and they couldn't!). And so that *Central European* identity had slipped out of his grasp, and he, Petar Petrović, was enviously wishing he could see himself among them. He gaped, he had missed out, and everything had been there: he had had Krleža, he had had Kiš, and, after all, Europe had been and still was his cultural home.

And then those 'Westerners', always ready to invent marketable political labels, had suddenly discovered *Eastern Europe* and shoved him there with the Romanians and Bulgarians . . . The Romanians! Appalled, Petar Petrović leafed through the foreign anthology in which he was himself included. On the title page there was a photograph of tired, grey people queuing for sour cabbage or something, somewhere in Bucharest. But I didn't have to queue! Petar Petrović protested angrily.

And off we went. Everything had happened too fast. The Berlin wall came down, and that *East European* identity escaped him . . . It was all because of that Italian coffee, grumbled Petar Petrović. It wasn't that it made him feel Italian, but it did distinguish him clearly from them . . . from Bucharest. Never mind, I'm Yugoslav, that's what I've always been, after all, thought Petar Petrović calming down.

And off we went again. Everything had happened too fast again. The Berlin wall had begun to sprout like magic beanshoots in his country. And that Yugo-identity – which he had never in fact invested with meaning, articulated, never attached any value to – that too had disintegrated.

At this moment bullets are whistling over Petar Petrović's head, towns are being destroyed before his eyes, people are being killed. No, that couldn't possibly be me, that's not my country, that can't be my life, I've translated Rilke and Proust, I write hermetic poetry . . . Petar Petrović mutters in consternation. And he tests his own reality in the foreign press. In *Newsweek* he sees a photograph of a woman. In one hand the woman is holding a plastic bag with an innocent leek poking out of it, and in the other – a rifle. The caption reads: *Yugoslav national costume*. No, it's not possible, is that really the face of my country, can that be my identity!? Petar Petrović wonders in horror. And suddenly he feels that he is disappearing, that he and his country are dissolving like an ice cube in water, that he is being reduced to a number, to a name and surname . . . And what kind of an identity is that, a name and a surname?

'Yes!' say the Great Manipulators, already standing behind him. 'That is your identity. Because there are various kinds of Petar Petrović. Petar Petrović the Serb is radically different from Petar Petrović the Croat. Make up your mind which you are!'

And Petar Petrović stands on the border between before and after, between one age and another, between one reality and another, between one Utopia and another, between the past and the future – and he trembles. And he sees clearly: those who stand confused on the border seem to disappear; those who make up their minds hold in their hands a ticket for the future, a ticket for the Balkan Express . . .

3.

Contemporary manufacturers of happiness function according to the magic formula 'before and after'. 'Before' is of course always worse, 'after' obviously always better. The world is always moving towards its optimum variant. The tested formulae rarely let one down.

Let us leave our colleague Petar Petrović for a while and consider what it was actually like, 'before'.

The literatures of Yugoslavia were written in relative freedom. The word 'freedom' sounds old-fashioned and somehow insincere to those who bandy about concepts from the dictionary of

East European stereotypes ('communism', 'the iron curtain', 'censorship', 'repression', 'totalitarianism').

Contemporary Yugoslav literatures were free of imposed aesthetic and ideological norms. After diplomatic relations with the Soviet Union were broken off in 1948 (I apologise for the fact that I, a post-Yugoslav, mention again that already threadbare mythic moment in the history of a country that no longer exists), the door to normative socialist-realism and the import of Soviet culture was closed, without ever really having opened. There were, of course, forbidden topics, but they were never part of a system of aesthetic and ideological norms. And then, those restrictions were soon lifted, the taboos revoked, and in 1971 in Croatia we saw that there was only one serious veto: nationalism (although this concept had the colour of those times, it has a different meaning and value today).

As there had never been an official culture established in Yugoslavia (which did not prevent the existence of official figures in cultural life), there could never be its natural opposite, an underground, alternative or parallel culture, such as was richly cherished by other socialist countries. All in all, the Yugoslav writer rarely had the opportunity of being a dissident, or at least not for the same reasons and not as often as in other socialist countries. If he did happen to become one in his own environment, others would set to healing his wounds. A Zagreb dissident would have his books published in Belgrade or Ljubljana, and vice versa, of course.

The contemporary Yugo-writer had never had the same importance in Yugoslav cultural life as, traditionally, a writer in Russian cultural life, for instance. The socialist slogan – 'workers, peasants and honest intellectuals' – had forever placed the intellectual on the periphery and that's where he stayed. The contemporary Yugoslav writer was rarely called upon to be the 'spokesman of the people'. The writers of the small nations on the soil of Yugoslavia lost that role in the nineteenth century and never regained it. After the war the Yugoslav republics selected living writers who would, like it or not, fulfil the function of 'Yugoslav classics'. Miroslav Krleža and Ivo Andrić, the greatest of them, were fortunate enough to die in time.

The contemporary Yugoslav writer was free also from the tradition of so-called 'great literature'. He could not point to a Tolstoy (or toss that same Tolstoy out of the 'steamship of contemporaneity'), because he simply did not have a Tolstoy. Conscious of belonging to small literatures, Yugoslav writers were freed of the obligation to create 'a great novel'. Yugoslav writers just wrote their novels, many of which are – you'll have to take my word for it – great.

The contemporary Yugoslav writer wrote free from the laws of the literary market, of the phenomenon known as the 'publishing industry'. He could not rely on his own wild, disorganised market, he didn't even dream of relying on foreign markets.

The contemporary Yugoslav writer wrote free from the attention of the world, in a cul-de-sac somewhere, on the periphery. From time to time the attention of the outside world was beamed like a spotlight on the commercially, politically or aesthetically more interesting literatures: Russian, Czech . . . The Yugoslav literatures regularly remained outside its focus.

The contemporary Yugoslav writer created in the freedom afforded him by his position as an outsider. He wrote conscious of his insignificance within his own culture, without pretention of any significance abroad. He wrote in Europe, but on its edge; he wrote in the European *East* but on its *Western* edge. The Yugoslav writer lived an underprivileged social life but a privileged literary one. Because it was only in a wild, non-commercial, disorganised and unarticulated culture that astonishing un-provincial gestures could occur, such as the abundant translation of books which could not have been translated in other, commercially oriented cultures. It was only in that confused, half-literate and at the same time highly literate culture, that our own books could be printed in lavish bindings. Only in an extravagant, crazy country between *communism* and *capitalism* (to use words from the dictionary of East-European stereotypes) could books be printed whose costs could not be covered by sales, the expense of whose production exceeded their price. From an entirely literary point of view, the Yugoslav writer lived like a rich pauper.

The contemporary Yugoslav writer lived in a literary centre oriented and open to the *West*, but at the same time open to all the different centres within Yugoslavia. The Yugoslav cultural space was shared, it was made up of different cultural and linguistic traditions which blended and communicated with one another. In practice, for the Yugoslav writer who knew the literatures of the Yugoslav peoples, both the Latin and the

Cyrillic ones, that meant living in Zagreb and having publishers in Belgrade, readers in Ljubljana, Sarajevo, Skopje and Priština. It meant freely living different cultures and experiencing them all as one's own.

4.

Was it really like that *before*? And who is speaking? I. Who am I? No one. I come from Atlantis. Atlantis does not exist. Therefore, I do not exist. If I do not exist, then how can what I am saying be taken as true?

The truth has shattered into pieces like a mirror. Every piece reflects its own truth. At this moment the peoples of the former Yugoslavia are zealously assuring themselves and others that everything *before* was a lie. Nothing like that ever existed, they say. Because if it had really existed, how could what happened *afterwards* have happened?

That is why our Petar Petrović, standing on the imagined frontier, wonders in confusion whether he exists at all and what is the state of his identity?

5.

And what did, after all, happen . . . *afterwards*?

Having established that Yugoslavia was a big lie, the Great Manipulators and their well-equipped teams (composed of writers, journalists, sociologists, psychiatrists, philosophers, political scientists, and . . . generals!) began the process of dismantling the *big lie*. At first it was easy, they accused the communist regime of every evil (of manipulating the people!), they threw ideological formulae out of the dictionary of ideas (*brotherhood and unity*, *socialism*, *Titoism*, etc.), they dismantled the old symbols (the hammer and sickle, the red star, the Yugoslav flag, the Yugoslav anthem, busts of Tito). The Great Manipulators and their teams composed a new dictionary of ideological formulae (*democracy*, *national sovereignty*, *Europeanisation*, etc.); they established new symbols (parliament, national flags, national anthems, etc.); they changed the names of streets, squares and cities; then they moved into the same buildings (usually Tito's); they surrounded themselves with the same people: communists transformed into nationalists, nationalists transformed into liberals, liberals transformed into conservatives . . . The Great Manipulators, *transformers*, dismantled the old system and built a new one out of the *same* pieces! And then they stopped to rest from their work and suddenly noticed that the country was still whole.

And they set about dismantling the country. Well-equipped teams (composed of writers, sociologists, political scientists, psychiatrists, philosophers and . . . generals!) began to produce hatred, lies and madness. In order more easily to dismantle the country, multinational as it was, multicultural as it was, the Great Manipulators and their teams offered the most effective formula, a new Utopia: the nation. But in order to awaken the dormant national consciousness, it was necessary quickly to establish differences: in what way were we different, that is, better, than them. Colleagues: university teachers, linguists, journalists, writers, historians, psychiatrists worked fervently in the teams to secure the dormant, lost, 'repressed' national identity.

To start with there was mild, secret counting, then somewhat more obvious dividing, and then very clear branding. How else can one mark one's stock, distinguish one's own herd from someone else's?

To start with, the shifting about of the people was carried out in the name of the fine and vague phrase *national homogenisation*. Then the popular shifting about acquired an organised administrative shape in the *population census*. Then the statistically indifferent censuses took on the warmer, more emotional form of voluntary public declarations (I am a Croat, Serb, Muslim, Slovene . . .). New words began to enter the language of the media: *ethnically clean* (territory, team, side, workforce), as opposed, therefore, to ethnically unclean ones. *Clean* and *unclean* quickly spread to the *dirty* war, with accompanying formulations (*cleansing terrain, ethnic cleansing*). Every day new maps of Yugoslavia surfaced in the media with differently coloured patches; everyone experienced some colour and patch as threatening. And of their own accord people began to proffer their behinds, asking their Great Manipulators (the *fathers of their nation*, their defenders, their *leaders*) to brand them. They maintained tearfully that this brand was what they had always wanted, but they dared not say so during the *red, commie* period, it was what they had wanted for centuries, indeed. Then, within the clearly designated national groups a new agitation began: people began to look for a new, additional nuance in the brand, one that would place them in a special position, which would distinguish the *great* Croat from the good Croat and the good Croat from the bad Croat, the *great* Serb from the mere Serb.

That minority of undetermined, those who had identified themselves in the census under the heading 'nationality' as Mercedes, Toshiba or Red Indian, that minority which had observed the process of dismantling the country as a fancy-dress ball that would pass, were sadly mistaken. Branding was not a sweet which could be accepted or politely refused. If you can't yourself think who you are, I'll help you, grinned the people from the Great Manipulators' teams, holding glowing national branding irons in their hands.

Even the dead did not succeed in escaping the national realignment. Danilo Kiš, the last Yugoslav writer, a writer who emphasised his Central-European, his Yugoslav identity, who escaped to Paris to avoid the local manipulators, not even he succeeded in escaping. It is true that they did not catch him alive, but they fixed him when he was dead, burying him to the accompaniment of a great Orthodox spectacle. Now his name is waved like a national banner by the same people who once drove him away.

Not even the long-since and thoroughly dead can manage it. The only Yugoslav Nobel prize-winner, the writer Ivo Andrić, has been torn apart by passionate necrophiliacs. They beat their tribal drums with Andrić's bones, until it occurred to someone, following the old communist formula of 'culture to the people', to destroy his monument in Višegrad. The town of Višegrad exists thanks to Andrić's writing. As for Andrić's bones, they have been definitively dragged away by the Serbian tribe.

Not even the very well-known can manage it. Milorad Pavić, the Serbian and international writer, travelled through the world (*before*), explaining to the Jews that his Khazars were in fact Jews, he paid a brief visit to the Croats, giving them to understand that maybe his Khazars were actually Croats, he suggested to the Basques that maybe they were Basques. Today (*after*), slipping joyfully into the Serbian war camp, Pavić travels through the world explaining that the Khazars are none other than the Serbs.

Not even foreigners can manage it. Milan Kundera once said something in some newspaper and ever since then he has been inscribed in Slovene hearts as . . . a Slovene. The half-Slovene

Peter Handke said something in some newspaper and since then he has been erased from Slovene hearts and from publishing programmes. György Konrad said something in some newspaper and upset absolutely everyone. No one will ever forgive him his lack of clarity and his refusal to join any side.

Not even those who have left the country in order to avoid all of this have managed it.

'So, what are you then?' an English colleague asked me recently.

'What do you mean?'

'What are you *technically*?'

I wriggled, stuttered. 'How can you ask me for my blood group, I'm a writer, that's what I am . . .'

'You're fudging the issue. It's all quite obvious in any case. You are technically . . . Balkan,' said the Englishman coldly and his tone brought the conversation to an abrupt end.

'Yes, I'm Balkan,' I sighed, resigned. The Englishman had stuck an identification label on me which for a moment I experienced as balm. For a moment. Because my English colleague could not have known about the joke current in Yugoslavia at that time. The joke about buying tickets for the Balkan Express. One-way. Return tickets were not available. There were no return tickets for that train.

6.

Whoevever is not with us is against us, shout the Serbs. Whoever is against us is not with us, shout the Croats. Petar Petrović is still standing on the border, trembling. He watches the terrifying speed with which his colleagues change colour, flags, symbols; the passion with which they practise the genres of oral and written confession on which they cleanse themselves of communism and Yugoslavism, in which they denounce each other. Petar Petrović watches the terrifying passion with which his colleagues scuttle after power and the powerful, the joy with which they accept functions, become loudspeakers, the *voice of the people*. Petar Petrović watches his colleague, a novelist, rapidly turning into a writer of notes for a thick illustrated monograph about *the father of the nation (The President shaving. Good morning. Mr President! The President playing tennis. Try a backhand, Mr President!)*. Petar Petrović watches his colleagues suddenly introducing themselves as Havels (How come there are

so many Havels all of a sudden? Had they all been in prison?),
he watches these Havel look-alikes becoming ministers of culture: he reads publishing plans in which works by the ministers
of culture suddenly predominate. Petar Petrović watches his
colleagues, writers until the day before, now becoming ministers
for the press and ambassadors; he watches people who were
editors the previous day now becoming deputy chiefs of police.
Petar Petrović listens to his colleagues harmoniously practis-
ing genres: the genre of war poetry, patriotic poetry, war diaries
and polemics, open letters and patriotic slogans. He watches
his female colleague, a poet until the day before, handing the
father of the nation and founder of the state, with a deep
curtsy, his (the father's of course) works bound in fine leather.
Petar Petrović watches critics, writers, journalists, university
teachers, academics, all harmoniously uniting, having previously tested one another's national pulse. Petar Petrović watches
a former upholder of fascism, now a patriotic poet, becoming a
respected citizen, the bearer of numerous functions, and being
wished a happy birthday personally by the President, on television. Petar Petrović watches his colleagues proposing in
parliament that the people (Serbian) drop napalm bombs on the
people (Croatian). Petar Petrović looks at newspaper photographs
of his colleagues dressed in military uniforms, colleagues holding
literary evenings at the front, he reads newspaper reports of
colleagues publicly boasting that they had thrown grenades at
Dubrovnik. Petar Petrović reads a statement in the newspaper by
his Serbian colleague saying: 'The Serbs are not killing out of
hatred, but out of despair. And to kill out of despair is the work of
the killer and God, while to kill out of hatred is the work of the
killer and the Devil. God is responsible for Serbian crimes, while
the crimes of those others are the work of the Devil.'[1] Petar
Petrović watches images of the reality of war unfolding before his
eyes interwoven with images of totalitarian reality, he watches
the Yugoslav hullabaloo, sees his colleagues initiating crimes
and then justifying them, he sees destroyed, impoverished
peoples, he watches the Great Manipulators and their teams, war
criminals who will never answer for their crimes, because the
people elected them, because the people wanted them, because
that was just what the people wanted. Petar Petrović stands on

[1] The thought of the Serbian poet and parliamentarian Brana Crnčević.

the border as on a rickety bridge, with the same abyss on either side.

And Petar Petrović does not know who is right: those who are in the majority or he who is alone. He does not know whether to kill himself, to burn himself in public or to accept togetherness as the sacred sacrament, to incline to the majority; whether to go abroad (where the brand which is his destiny will follow him), to go to a lunatic asylum or to the front, whether to die for his homeland or to die of shame, to bury himself in the earth, to turn into a beetle, to disappear . . .

7.

And is that the truth about the great Yugoslav 'after'? I have told the story from the point of view of Petar Petrović. If I had told it from the point of view of a *Croatian Petrović* or a *Serbian Petrović* we would have had new, different stories. So why Petrović then? Out of pity. He is the one whose country, Yugo-Atlantis, has vanished. He is the Yugoslav writer who is vanishing, they, the others, are just appearing and they will get the chance to tell their own stories.

The truth about Yugoslavia and its intellectuals is like that broken mirror: each fragment reflects its profound truth and its profound lie. It is only the practice of daily living which produces results as the truth.

Multinational Yugoslavia paid a heavy price for its post-communist democracy, if it can be called that at all. The tragic Yugoslav spectacle is not yet over. Croatia and Slovenia have achieved independence and international recognition, Bosnia and Macedonia are waiting in line, the Federal Army and the Serbian leadership continue to display pretensions of conquest, disguising their crimes with the worn-out idea of Yugoslav unity.

The great majority of intellectuals stood at the side of their leaders and governments, supporting their official policies. Under the slogan of democratisation of the government in their republics they have created indisputably poorer countries and unhappier people. Instead of real democracy, they have created small, totalitarian communities. Instead of citizens they have created an obedient numerical figure; instead of free media, rigid control; instead of dismantling the old state apparatus they have strengthened little state replicas; instead of demilitarisation, a new militarisation – necessary, they say.

The new national states and their rulers demand a new national culture, one that will represent their national being, they demand a new art which will, they say, have 'the function of spiritual renewal'. And that is what they will get, it is already what they are getting. That is just what our colleagues are already fervently working on.

8.

And is that really how things are?

The identity of the writer, the intellectual, is called into question in the turbulent times of the destruction of old values and the establishment of new ones. Some have found an identity, others have lost one. To speak about identity at a time when many people are losing their lives, the roof over their heads and those closest to them seems inappropriate. Or else the only thing possible: everything began with that question, with that question like an unfortunate noose everything ends.

During the bombardment of Dubrovnik, the Dubrovnik poet Milan Milišić died, sitting at his desk in his Dubrovnik flat. Dubrovnik, a Croatian and once Yugoslav city, was bombed by the Serbian army claiming that it was defending the threatened Serbs. The dead Dubrovnik poet was a Serb by nationality. His death was one of a series of 'jokes' produced every day by the Yugoslav tragedy of disintegrating identity.

Yugoslavia never had a large emigration of humanistically inclined intellectuals, as other socialist countries did. She was better known for her export of unofficial *Gastarbeiter* labour. At this moment there are many intellectuals in Paris, London, New York. Those who could manage it, of course, those who had the opportunity, those who made that choice, those who had no choice, the terrified, the confused, those who were sickened by the events around them, by the events around others, or both . . .

That is why it is not impossible in this story about our colleagues that a dialogue such as the following should take place between me and my imagined Petar Petrović:

'Hello, Petrović? I'm phoning . . . It doesn't matter where I'm phoning from . . . I just wanted to say, I just wanted you to know . . .'

'What is it you want to say?' says Petrović.

'I'm changing my surname. To Kefka, if you don't mind . . .'

'I've changed mine too,' says Petrović calmly.

'What?'

'Don't worry. To Petrović . . .' says the former Petrović.

9.

That was a short and incomplete story about our colleagues. As I told it, I left myself out. By leaving myself out, I emerge as better. But is it really like that? I still think there are only two things a person cannot choose: his own birth and his colleagues. And therefore my story is an invitation to all of us to face our other aspect, the history of our profession which has been compromised so often, our race which often emits an *unbearable stench*, as Madelshtam put it, an invitation to face ourselves, *priests and parrots*, to face the fact that some of us forge words like knives, the fact that many of us find ourselves once again in the trap of master and servant, executioner and victim. And is there anything that we can do in this weary, indifferent age which hardly distinguishes between real and celluloid death. Is there anything we can do so that there are return tickets for this train, this sad *Balkan Express . . .*[2]

April 1992

[2] a) This text, in this form, was read at an international literary meeting held at the beginning of April 1992 at an American university. The concluding question was posed there as well. Then and now, the question directed to my colleagues seemed pathetic, naive, senseless, indeed second-hand, a quotation. But nevertheless, I asked it. Just as I do not omit it now either, when it seems even more pathetic and more senseless. Despite the fact that we know that the 'letter in a bottle' is only a genre, its content, a call for help, was and remains . . . authentic.

b) *After ten months of war, you can hear 'intellectuals' in Sarajevo asking: why has this happened to us, and why is it so brutal? They are not clever enough to see the answer: Because!*

Just because.

And because all questions come too late. (Šemezdin Mehmedinović, 'Sarajevo Blues')

3

Sweet Strategies

Gingerbread Heart Culture

Nationalism is the ideology of the banal.

Danilo Kiš

In his book about Gogol, Vladimir Nabokov uses the term *poshlost'*. *Poshlost'* is a Russian word which, because of its wealth of meanings, Nabokov prefers to English equivalents such as *cheap, inferior, sorry, trashy, scurvy, tawdry* and the like. By way of illustration of poshlost' Nabokov takes Gogol's description of a young German. This German is paying court in vain to a young girl who spends each evening sitting on her balcony, knitting stockings and enjoying the beautiful view over a lake. Finally the German devises a strategy to capture the girl's heart. Every evening he undresses, dives into the lake and swims before the eyes of his beloved, while at the same time embracing two swans he has acquired especially for this purpose. In the end the young man wins the girl thanks to the witty notion of the swans. While this pure form of poshlost' merely provokes a benign smile, the other – the one which, as Nabokov says, is 'particularly strong and pernicious when the falsity is not obvious and when it is believed, rightly or not, that the values it imitates belong to the highest reaches of art, thought or sensibility' – is disturbing.

In the schizophrenic head of the citizen of former Yugoslavia not only are two realities refracted, past and present, but two types of kitsch: the old type, already long since dead, and the new which reflects the old, on the assumption that the recipient has long since consigned the first model to oblivion.

In the new political age state socialist kitsch has been replaced by a new brand: nationalistic kitsch for which Danilo Kiš found a precise metaphor in the gingerbread heart, a traditional cake sold at village fairs. Both types of kitsch are populistic (because the essence of kitsch is populistic), and as their seductive strategy is aimed at the people, they are both above all connected with folklore.

As Yugoslavia falls apart (the process is still going on even if the governments of the new states have declared and signed its clinical death) to the accompaniment of whistling grenades, screams, groans, howls of grief and explosions, in my split consciousness there echo fragments of folklore melodies: Montenegrin, Macedonian, Croatian, Serbian, Albanian . . . The key symbol is the ring dance, the 'kolo', which was performed for years at all ceremonial state occasions. The 'kolo' was danced by representatives of the nations and nationalities of Yugoslavia dressed in their national costumes. They all danced all the different dances from all the different regions, in harmony: they hopped, skipped, pranced, capered, stamped, as required. That ring dance – the symbolic image of Yugoslavia, comprehensible to all literate and illiterate Yugoslavs alike – has now been transformed into its opposite, a lethal noose. Today, the participants in the Yugoslav 'kolo' are maiming and slaughtering one another, with the same verve, accompanied by the sounds of the same folk tunes.

The citizen of the former Yugoslavia has not yet forgotten his former, state kitsch: socialist spectacles, Tito's relay race. Ex-Yugoslavs remember that wooden baton which was carried by runners once a year (in May!) from village to village, from town to town. It was passed breathlessly from Slovene to Croat, from Croat to Muslim, from Muslim to Serb, who would finally lay it at the feet of the mythic father, Tito. The citizen of the former Yugoslavia remembers the monumental productions in which the main and only part was played by the pliant, collective body which was ready for its President to transform itself into a word, a slogan, a flower, a sumptuous picture on the stadium grass. The citizen of former Yugoslavia still remembers these spectacles, including the last one, dedicated to Tito, although Tito himself was already dead at the time. An anonymous socialist designer had dreamed up a swansong: an enormous polystyrene sculpture of Tito. Then there was a sudden gust of wind which nearly swept the polystyrene Tito away, and with him the live workers who were trying with all their might to stop Tito flying heavenwards.

Just as every tragedy recurs as farce, so all the former Yugo-symbols have been transformed into their ironic opposite: Tito's baton (the symbol of brotherhood and unity) has become a fratricidal stick (a gun, a knife) with which the male represen-tatives of the former Yugo-peoples are annihilating each other. The towns and villages through which the relay passed are today being demolished like towers of cards: in almost the same order, from north to south. The collective human body has become human flesh, all ex-Yugoslavs are today merely meat. The fact that some perish as Croats, others as Serbs, others again as Muslims – or even because they are Croats, Serbs and Muslims – does not mean much in matters of death.

In an utterly shattered world there is a cacophonic mixture of fragments of the former and present regimes, tunes which we have already heard, but in a new arrangement, symbols which we have already seen, but in a new design. In the new reality, which has become a phantasmagoric nightmare, the quickest thing to adapt and come to life again in all its irrepressible splendour was kitsch.

In a country which has fallen apart, kitsch, as an important element of that country's ideological strategy, has also disinteg-rated: each side has now dragged relevant parts out of the ruins, and stuck them together in new strategic monsters.

The Croatian Catholic-folklore variant of kitsch has rede-signed itself using a blend of ancient inscriptions and folklore motifs, Catholic candles and crosses, gingerbread hearts and national costumes. Out of the ruins of what was once a shared home, it has taken Tito as a souvenir. Tito has suddenly come back to life in the shape of the new Croatian President.[1] The

---

[1] It is a banal fact that totalitarian societies merely feign a complex organisational order. The most appropriate metaphor for that order is the *family* with the *father* at its head (Stalin, Tito and Tudjman are all referred to by homely local words for 'dad' – 'batya', 'stari', 'ćaća', 'tata'). National heroes are *sons* (who are *loyal* and *lay down their lives on the altar of the homeland*), while women, of course, serve for the production of *sons*. The old hierarchical order is preserved by handing down the roles from father to son (Stalin following Lenin). In the Yugoslav case, however, there is an evident confusion in relation to the successor. The newly composed political folklore, both Serbian and Croatian, is fighting for its leader-successors. At the beginning of the disintegration of Yugoslavia the new Serbian folklore connected its 'leader' Slobodan Milošević to Tito more frequently than did Croatian folklore (*The*

Croatian President wears white jackets like Tito's; he gives children apricots from his garden (Tito used to send them baskets of mandarins from his gardens on Brioni); he kisses any child who happens to find itself in front of the television cameras with him (Tito used to like being photographed with children in identical poses). In the redesigned state spectacles the Croatian President is more active than Tito: where Tito used to sit calmly permitting the people to demonstrate their skills in front of him, the Croatian President himself takes an active part in the performance. On the day of Croatian independence the President took part in a pathetic pantomime: on a public stage, surrounded by young girls in Croatian national costume, he solemnly placed a ducat, traditionally given for the good fortune of a newborn child, into an empty cradle (symbol of the newly born Croatia).

The other, Serbian, side has created its own monster out of elements of hysterical Orthodoxy, mixing Orthodox icons and candles with traditional peasant shoes, folklore clamour with Chetnik caps and bearded cut-throats; mixing historical ages, epic songs with the ghosts of unacknowledged kings, the traditional lyre with war bugles, bugles with the barrels of field guns. Out of the ruins of what was once a shared home, the Serbian side has dragged the grey suit of communism and put it on its President. In the chaos of elements, in which crimes are committed in the name of (the Serbian) God and more extensive territory, and the torture of others is carried out in the name of the struggle against fascism (!), the Serbian President is becoming a monstrous icon.

Although the kitsch of today fits the old one like a photograph torn in half, the two pictures are different. Socialist kitsch declared its ideology: brotherhood and unity, internationalism, social equality, progress and the like. The fundamental ideas of nationalist kitsch are: national sovereignty and privilege for the individual on the basis of acceptable blood group. Socialist kitsch

---

Serbs now a question face/When will Slobo take Tito's place). In the war over the succession, at least as far as the image is concerned, it seems nevertheless that Franjo Tudjman has won. The inherited image has been reinforced by abundant documentary material: a thick volume of photographs 'Franjo Tudjman' (which is stylistically connected to similar volumes about Tito), documentary films (such as *We have Croatia*), newspaper articles about Tudjman (which resurrect the already forgotten genre of socialist hagiography), new textbooks for primary schools (in which Tudjman replaces Tito), and political rituals (speeches, celebrations, etc.).

has a futuristic projection, and therefore a strong Utopian dimension. Nationalist kitsch draws its content from passionate submersion in 'the essence of the national being' and is therefore turned towards the past, deprived of any Utopian dimension. The key symbols of socialist kitsch are connected with work, progress, equality (railways, roads, factories, sculptures of peasants and workers with their arms round each other and such like). The key symbols of nationalist kitsch are connected with national identity (knights, coats of arms, Catholic and Orthodox crosses, sculptures of historical heroes, and so on). Both kinds of kitsch employ an identical strategy of seduction.

There is, of course, another fundamental difference. The socialist state kitsch was created in peacetime, in a country with a future before it. This other kitsch, this 'gingerbread heart culture', is poured like icing over the appalling reality of war. In the reality of war 'gingerbread heart culture' intensifies its strategy of seduction and penetrates all the pores of daily life like a virus, transforming real horror into the horror of *poshlost'*. The sad voices of reporters, long TV shots, pictures of dead bodies, funerals, corpses wrapped in national flags, the ritual receipt of military honours which resemble taking communion, the general theatricalisation of death, horrors accompanied by newly composed Yugoslav drumming, cassettes threatening to annihilate the enemy with folkloric gusto, posters, a newly composed patriotic squeal, the kitsch propaganda industry of war – all of this is bubbling in a Yugoslav hotpot between tragedy and farce, suffering and indifference, compassion and cynicism, terror and parody.[2]

To go back to the beginning: the Yugoslav power-wielders (both elected and self-proclaimed) and their successors are extraordinarily reminiscent of Gogol's swimmer in the lake, embracing two swans and seducing the girl on the balcony. We

---

[2] The following detail will complete our tale from the most grotesque angle. During the Christmas holidays of 1992, a meat factory produced a new salami with the Croatian coat of arms. The coat of arms was printed into the meat of the sausage itself. If we give in to mischievous associations and believe those who tell stories of domestic pigs in the war areas feeding on human corpses (Croatian, Serbian, Muslim) and that now those pigs are being turned into sausages with the state coat of arms, then we really must praise the natural organisational wisdom of the new states.

I was in Slovenia recently, in Maribor. On the wall of a Maribor butcher's shop I read the grafitto *We're all pigs!*

can add to Gogol's picture just a few more details – there are corpses floating in the lake, drowning people, mortar shells, burned houses, red stars and crosses like swastikas, dead children and the bodies of animals, but the essence of the dance with the swans remains the same: seduction. The large, dejected, sweating heads of our Yugoslav swimmers peer out of the water and seduce Europe, as it knits stockings on the balcony. And, of course, what is left of their people as they sit, impoverished and starving on the shore. Our swimmers embrace their swans and swim without paying any attention to the unseemly stage design. And as always the seduction achieves its aim. The peoples on the shore clap enthusiastially, seeing the performance as 'the essence of the national being', as something beautiful, grand and true. For, in 'the empire of poshlost', says Nabokov thinking of literature, 'it is not the book itself but the reading public that ensures triumph.'

A complex picture, isn't it? How is it for me, then, sitting on the shore among my fellow countrymen, obliged to experience defeat as triumph? My only consolation is the thought that perhaps I am nevertheless not alone. And what Europe is doing on the balcony knitting stockings and enjoying the view of the lake, I really couldn't say.

August 1992

The Realisation of a Metaphor

Do not be obsessed by the urgency of history or believe in the metaphor of the trains of history. Do not therefore jump aboard the 'train of history': it is merely a stupid metaphor.

Danilo Kiš, *Homo poeticus*

1. About a stylistic device

If we were to read the terrible reality of war as a literary text, we would be able to put together a whole repertoire of narrative strategies, a whole lexicon of stylistic devices, tropes and figures. And such a literary method of analysis of the reality of war would be just as accurate (and inaccurate) as any other: political, economic, military-strategic or psychoanalytic. That is to say, it all began with words and it will all end with words. And the intervening reality – thousands of real deaths, refugees, wounded and dispersed citizens, ruined houses, villages and towns – will one day be ground down by a steamroller of words, and the real tragedy will be concreted over with interpretations: historical, politological, military-strategic, culturological, literary . . .

The quotation by Danilo Kiš is taken from his advice to young writers. As he warns writers not to believe that metaphor is reality, at the same time Kiš expresses the fear that such a thing may be possible. Cultural practice today shows that in just three years of war literature has been destroyed (as have all other forms of 'the artistic transposition of reality', to use an old-fashioned term) simply because the first assumption has been suspended: the borderline between words and life, between the unreal and the real. By turning *words into deeds* the ex-Yugoslav peoples have moved into a new dimension, into 'mythic time' in which the borders between existing and non-existent worlds have been erased.

In Russian folklore there is a form of sorcery known as chertyhan'e, which freely translated would be 'summoning the devil'. The most imaginative repertoire of chertyhan'e can be found in Bulgakov's novel *The Master and Margarita*. It is enough for the characters simply to say the word devil and – there is the devil in front of them, life-size, with his whole cheerful entourage. Superstitious people are often cautious when using certain words: they are afraid that what they have uttered may occur in real life. Writers often have the same kind of superstitious fears. Besides, they know better than anyone that dealing with words is . . . devilish work!

The mere word war echoed for a long time in the media, many people struck it doggedly like a flint until the first spark flew. By then it was no longer difficult to create a great conflagration. Tormented by the media war, by mutual accusations and hatred, the citizens of a country that no longer exists could be heard to say in desperation: 'Let it burst once and for all, just let all this stop!' And it really did 'burst'. But nothing 'stopped'.

A few years ago, at a public meeting, a Serbian poet announced euphorically: 'A nation has occurred!' And the nation that had begun to exist was told poetically by Slobodan Milošević: 'If we're not much good at working, at least we know how to fight.' In defensive elation, the Croatian 'father of the nation' announced: 'Every state is born in blood.' And a Serbian political folk song confirms this idea: 'From time immemorial, we have nursed you with blood.'

Originating in writer-politicians' workshops, the Serbian national-socialist programme (words, that is!) was elaborated in the 'lighter' literary genres of 'newly composed' folk literature. 'Wherever the bones of our ancestors lie, there are the frontiers of the Serbs' is the briefest treatment of the Serbian programme of conquest. The linguist and ethnologist Ivan Čolović subdivides this new folk literature into the *language of love* (through which the Serbian ethnic identity is established) and the *language of hate* (through which the national ethnic identity is strengthened, thanks to those who 'threaten' it).[1] *The language of love* in folk songs shows 'those same features of ethnic communality which

[1] Ivan Čolović, *Bordel ratnika*, Belgrade, 1993.

have become the almost obligatory commonplaces of today's public discourse about the ethnos and identity: collective memory, faith, language, tradition, territory'. This repertoire of stereotypes (identical ones may be found on the Croatian side) served to adapt the 'image of the Serbian ethnic identity to the needs of the new nationalistic and populistic ideology and war propaganda'. *The language of hate*, to judge by the examples given, is far more creative. Thus Čolović finds in the new folk literature several mutually interrelated 'registers of *the language of hate*'. These are accusations and charges (against all the 'traitors' and 'degenerates' from Sultan Murat, the Turks, Hitler, Genscher, America, Titoists, communists, to the 'Ustashas', foreigners and Serb-haters); threats (informing all enemies of what is in store for them: 'Hey, Ustashas, never fear / a deep pit awaits you here./ In its width it measures a metre / and in depth a kilometre'); curses (cursing all enemies from America to Tudjman); swearing ('Tonight's our night, we freely boast / tonight's the night Tudjman will roast. / Let him roast, turn on the spit / who messes with him ends in shit.'); and finally mockery (of Croats, Slovenes, Albanians and others). With such a prepared package of texts (and we have not mentioned also many texts of so-called creative literature/) it was possible, but not essential, for war to begin. The devilish mystique consists in the fact that much of what had been uttered or written began later to occur in reality.[2]

But if we return to the original thesis – that it is, therefore, possible to read the war as a literary text – then one of the predominant stylistic devices is metamorphosis. Roman Jakobson defines the essence of metamorphosis as the realisation of a trope, as the 'projection of a literary device into artistic reality, the transformation of a poetic trope into a poetic fact, a

[2] Radovan Karadžić is the perpetrator of the 'visionary' project of Greater Serbia, conceived in the heads of writers such as Dobrica Ćosić and supported by power-lovers such as Slobodan Milošević. Karadžić is the perpetrator also of his own visionary project as witnessed by the frequently quoted lines from his poem 'Sarajevo', written in 1971: 'The city burns like a lump of incense/ and our consciousness wafts in that smoke too./ Empty suits slip through the city. The dying stone/ glows red, built into the house. Plague!/ Calm. A company of poplars in armour/ marches upwards. The aggressor/ runs through our bloodstream/ one minute you're a man, the next in space./ I know that all this is the beginning of a howl/what is the black metal in the garage for?/ See – like fear transformed into a spider/ it seeks the answer in its computer.'

construct, content'. Such a metaphor, comparison, symbol may become in the text the generator of content. Unlike a literary text, in which the original metaphor (the 'heart's flame', for example) develops in the text according to the logic of its component parts as a story (so that we might well expect . . . firemen), in the *war text* the original metaphor (spoken or written) continues to develop, according to the same logic, in reality.

The war topography of terror unfolds on a deeply symbolised foundation. Thus, many buildings are destroyed because of their symbolic value; thus many dates of the fiercest war terror are connected with dates of symbolic value from the Serbian collective memory. Thus, according to one eyewitness Serbian soldiers forced captive Croatian soldiers to swallow crosses (Catholic crosses, which the Croatian soldiers wear round their necks because of this same symbolic value!).

A television broadcast showed pictures of wounded Croatian soldiers. A young man in plaster was lying on a hospital bed. Over the empty bed next to his was spread the Croatian flag. Thus the soldier was lying in a double bed with his symbolic bride, the Croatian flag. 'This is all I have,' said the young man to the camera, tenderly stroking the flag. 'As soon as I have recovered, I'm going back to fight,' he added. Incidentally, in the funeral ritual, soldiers' coffins are draped with flags. The symbolic brides thus accompany their bridegrooms even into the grave.

The authors of a newly composed Chetnik song experience Croatia as a girl (in the song the girl is called Tudjmanka) who has abandoned her boyfriend (a Serb), preferring another (the West, Germany above all). The song goes on to say that there, in the West, no one will marry her but she will become a 'Western whore'. The Serbian war rapes, may, therefore, be read as the realisation of the metaphor contained in the Chetnik song, as the (real) revenge of the (metaphorical) 'young man'.

I am a passionate reader of newspaper advertisements. In the summer of 1991 my attention was drawn to some mysterious advertisements announcing the sale of 'hens' and 'chicks'. A 'hen' cost about 500 German marks, I don't remember the price of the 'chicks'. I made enquiries and learned that 'hen' was the name for a revolver, and 'chicks', logically enough, for bullets. A year later all the international newspapers published one of the most appalling war photographs. It showed the shattered skull of an anonymous soldier with a hen calmly pecking at his brain.

There is a similar zoological metaphor connected with another, far more destructive weapon – the grenades, which are called 'sows' in war slang. There's a story going round that in the devastated villages of Slavonia pigs (sows, real ones!) devoured human bodies (also real ones).

All in all, the leaders, political manipulators, generals, murderers, criminals, and then the people themselves who elected them, had in fact, played the divine card ('In the beginning was the Word, and the Word was with God, and the Word was God'), and have experienced a just, diabolical punishment! The Word has become a diabolical reality. And this terrible reality is being restored by the global media industry (devil's work!), to its beginning, turning it into word and image, into non-reality, into a market-product, into 'literature'! There is a story going around that authentic war rapes in Bosnia, recorded on videocassettes are now being sold in European and American porn-shops. So the circle is closed. If we continue to follow this devil's logic, then the peoples of former Yugoslavia have entered a circle from which, it seems, there is no way out; they have moved into a different reality, virtual reality, virtuality . . .

Such a (potential) perspective confirms a recent statement by a Serbian writer. Accusing Europe of 'throwing this world of ours into the despair of the beggar's staff' (the author is thinking of the sanctions against Serbia, or rather rump Yugoslavia), the Serbian writer finds consolation in the fact that 'in torment and mere physical survival, what remains are words, tales told from generation to generation, in which dust, blood and bondage forge an exalted epic which bridges All, what remains are the tales heard with a sense we have carried with us from our ancient, pagan gods'.

2. Analysis of a little text

Two years ago, when the Croatian nation was euphorically declaring its independence, there were unusual tin cans on sale in kiosks in Zagreb. They were like Coca Cola cans, with the red and white Croatian coat of arms and the message: Clean Croatian Air. This message coincided with the (then) most popular TV advertising slogan for cough-sweets: Breathe more easily. Thus one message, already quite clear, doubly reinforced the other: Breathe more easily with Clean Croatian air!

Today you can't find these politico-ecological tins any more, there's a different souvenir on sale now: a chocolate-box designed like a Croatian passport, with the same 'Coca Cola-look' coat of arms. The budding kitsch industry has followed the development of political events closely and from 'clean Croatian air' (or the proclamation of independence) it has moved on to the 'sweet Croatian passport' (or to a sovereign, internationally recognised state).

But what happened to the air? That innocuous (!) linguistic message written on the empty tin can has come to life like a spirit released from a bottle, and begun to occur in reality in various different ways. That little phrase – clean Croatian air – has attached itself to the Croatian language like a burr, come to life in newspapers, on television, in politics, in thought, in everyday speech, in everyday life. Today there is hardly a newspaper article or television broadcast without the word clean, which, of course implies its opposite – dirty. And with the newly established system of values, based on the opposition clean–dirty, life suddenly seems very simple.

In addition to external enemies (i.e. the Serbs, who are waging, and because of whom we are waging, this dirty war), the spirit from the bottle – like the diligent Mr Clean or Meister Proper – has in recent months been cleansing all sorts of things in Croatia.

So the numerous (paid and voluntary) blood-group police are diligently verifying the blood of Croatian citizens. Croatian citizens themselves have begun frantically digging through their own and other people's biographies in search of an undesirable blot. Public declaration of national allegiance has become a new rule of Croatian etiquette. Hence the recent pronouncement by a well-known public figure: 'Everyone knows there hasn't been any Byzantine blood in my family for three hundred years' – which would have sounded at the very least odd in any other place, has become a part of normal behaviour here. This new kind of behaviour was introduced into public life by politicians. It was begun by the Croatian President himself when he announced that he was glad that his wife was neither a Serb nor a Jew (but a Croat). Immediately afterwards, following the President's example, a humble member of the Assembly announced that he too was glad his wife was a Croat, and not, therefore, either a Serb, a

Jew or, heaven forbid, black! What would have seemed two years ago like a bad joke not worth repeating, or a passing nationalist virus unworthy of attention, has become established in the unwritten rules of generally accepted behaviour.

In the new system of values (clean–dirty), 'Byzantine blood' is the most dangerous polluter. 'Byzantine' is simply another (more refined) word for Serb, Orthodox, which, in the same linguistic and ideological system, means: sly, dirty, deceitful, in other words whoever is different from us. Or as the author of a newspaper article recently defined it: 'Ordinary Croatian people are not the same as ordinary Serbian people who are aggressive and collectively frustrated by the Serbo-Byzantine philosophy of life – kill, seize, steal, dominate.'

The magic spray-formula 'clean Croatian air' cleans Croatian territory not only of 'Byzantines' who are of a different blood type, but of all internal enemies who are different from the ruling majority. Such dirty enemies are insufficiently good Croats, 'saboteurs', 'traitors', 'anti-Tudjman commandos', 'commies', 'Yugo-nostalgics', 'unlike-thinkers'. In this spirit all the candidates of the parties in the recent pre-election campaign, including the President himself, promised 'a great clean-out' of the above-mentioned polluters.

The spirit from the tin can, Mr Clean Croatian Air, cleanses Croatian territory not only of animate, but also of inanimate enemies, of 'symbols of the power of the non-national regime', as was explained by the writer of a newspaper report justifying the mass destruction of monuments to the victims of fascism, symbols in other words. The spirit from the can has inspired self-appointed cleaners as well, the 'bombers', who have taken on themselves the difficult patriotic task of cleansing, with dynamite, Croatian towns of houses whose owners are Serbs, and also insufficiently good Croats. In their zeal for cleanliness the cleaners sometimes use dirty methods. One of these is the collective smearing of the house with collective shit, to ensure that the undesirable owner abandons the house for ever. This original method of cleaning was adopted by the inhabitants of a small island town on the Adriatic. The house in question belonged to a former Yugoslav minister, a Croat. The local police did nothing to suggest that such methods of cleaning were unacceptable. It is itself, after all, deeply imbued with the spirit of the new hygienic slogan.

The spirit from the can has crept into institutions as well, especially the Ministry of Culture, where the officials, with the new minister at their head, have proved themselves diligent cleaners. They have cleaned the school curriculum of everything 'undesirable', and for the sake of 'clean Croatian air' the minister has publicly recommended that teachers of the Croatian language in schools should be pure Croats. At the same time, the Croatian public has silently approved the minister's instructions. Not one institution – not even the Croatian Arts Faculty, which trains teachers of the Croatian language and literature – made a single public protest.

Mr Clean Croatian Air has entered the libraries. Following the indistinct instructions of the Croatian Minister of Culture, patriotic librarians are quietly putting books by Serbian writers into the cellars, cleansing the shelves of enemy Cyrillic, and also of Latin-script books imbued with the 'Yugoslav spirit'. A nicely designed strip, with a folk motif, has appeared on books by Croatian writers. In future this little sign will distinguish Croatian from non-Croatian books, including Shakespeare.

Mr Clean Coatian Air has cleaned up all the old names of streets, schools, institutions, squares, because the old ones sullied our Croatian surroundings. That little zealot's spirit has entered businesses, all kinds of working places, and for two years now has been cleaning away all political unlike-thinkers. All these quiet, invisible, and of course, in the context of the great disgrace of the war, insignificant cleansings simply confirm that this small spray-formula has experienced a great affirmation.

The zeal of cleanliness which has gripped the Croatian lands does not shrink from the most grotesque forms (after all, at last we're 'our own people in our own land', so why should we be ashamed of strong feelings?). So in an interview, a once popular Yugoslav comedienne (who owes her fame to the character of a crude chatterbox, a cleaner!), announced in a recent interview that after her death she wanted to be wrapped in the Croatian flag and buried in Croatian soil, then she would be happy for her corpse would be devoured by . . . Croatian worms!

The words *clean* and *air* have entered the lexicon of the best-known Croatian minds: in a television appearance, in response to the presenter's stupid question – what kind of women he liked – a famous Croatian intellectual replied briefly and just as stupidly: *clean!* A few months later that intellectual was to invite those *clean* Croatian women to give the lives of their sons for *the defence of liberty*, and a little later still in a funeral oration for dead Croatian soldiers, he was to say that we must not in any way *soil* our liberty, i.e. that *even our death must be clean.*

A second Croatian intellectual, euphorically greeting the idea of the 'spiritual renewal' of the Croatian people concluded poetically: 'That is the path of spiritual renewal, of a beautiful and *clean* [my emphasis] generation, the path to the people, to us, with a clear and *clean* [my emphasis] conscience.'

A third Croatian intellectual was more concerned with the 'airiness' of the metaphor and, explaining the concept of 'spiritual renewal', he wrote: 'That is why when we speak of spiritual renewal, we must start from the meaning of the concept "spirit" [. . .]. The Croatian word "duh" retains its original reference to the air we breathe, "dah" (breath), or "duša" (soul).'

The spray-formula has evidently adapted to the Croatian everyday reality and does not care much for the rules of good taste, but continues energetically cleaning everything in front of it. The Croatian newspapers are full of threatening texts, and one of the most frequent threats is again connected with the air! 'If so and so wants to go on breathing Croatian air, and behaving the way he does . . .' the angry regime journalists usually write. And they are profoundly right. Because breathing Croatian air is the only thing left to the Croatian citizen. Soon, that is, he will not have enough money to buy Croatian bread.

And so, let us just add that it is August 1992, the sky over Zagreb is clean and blue, the air with each day ever cleaner and thinner. One breathes as in the Andes, almost with gills. On the other hand, the doctors assure us that just such air favours the creation of red blood cells. And red, as we know, is the colour of patriotism.

August 1992

Postscript, five years later

'Analysis of a short text' was first published under the title 'Pure Croatian Air' in the German weekly *Die Zeit* ('Der Saubere Kroatische Luft', 23 October 1992) and a little later in English in the *Independent on Sunday* ('Dirty Tyranny of Mr Clean', 6 December 1992). Although the text was not published in the local press, everyone immediately knew what was in it and the author was suddenly cast into the role of isolated target of frenzied attacks by her compatriots: the new political élite, newspapers, television, radio, fellow writers, colleagues at the Arts Faculty in Zagreb, friends, anonymous writers of threatening letters, unnamed righteous telephone callers . . . Her furious compatriots – proclaiming the author a liar, traitor, public enemy and a witch – fuelled a pyre and the author, consumed by fire in her own homeland, left to continue her life in exile.

During a brief Christmas visit to Zagreb in 1996, the author was greeted by an anonymous message on her answerphone: *Rats, you've been hiding! So you're still here! You're still breathing under the wonderful Croatian sky? Get out of Croatia!* The message might be interpreted as a very belated joke by some anonymous Croatian patriot were it not so much in tune with the Croatian government's firm, stubborn policy of pest-control, which is still, tacitly or actively, supported by the majority of Croatian citizens. After all, the Serbs are cleansing even more furiously, so why should we be ashamed . . .

The 'cleansing' policy file has become terrifyingly thick over the last few years. It contains numerous instances of citizens of Serbian nationality being dismissed from their jobs, threatened, expelled, bombed in *Serbian* houses, abused and intimidated, the legal appropriation of houses belonging to Serbs, the refusal of the right of Croatian citizenship to many people who had lived in Croatia all their lives, Serbs, Albanians, Muslims, anationals . . .

The fiercest 'pest-controlling' action occurred in August 1995 when tens of thousands of Croatian citizens of Serbian nationality were driven out of Croatia. This final act of ethnic cleansing was declared an act of liberation, and the 'pest controllers' were awarded medals for patriotism and heroism. Through the liberated territories ran a triumphant 'Liberty Train' filled with the euphoric, half-drunk Croatian élite around the Croatian president who made triumphalist speeches at every little provincial station in front of audiences who were not the least ashamed.

The well-known Croatian writer Slobodan Novak explained the Croatian hygienic euphoria in the following words: 'Croatia is cleansing itself of Yugo-unitarist and Great-Serb rubbish which had been spread all over it for a whole century. Croatia is simply being restored to its original form and returning to its true self. If today it has to make painful incisions in its language, history, scholarship, and even the names of its towns and streets, that only shows the extent to which it was contaminated and how polluted were all facets of its life and all segments of its corpus.'

From today's perspective, the author's tale of Mr Clean looks like a children's story. Especially if it is compared with the confession of Miro Bajramović published on 1 September 1997 in the Croatian opposition weekly *Feral Tribune*. Miro Bajramović, a member of the notorious Croatian military unit poetically named 'Autumn Rain', describes the bloody sequence of torture and murder which he (who killed eighty-six people with his own hands) and others carried out against Serbian civilians in Croatia. After his public confession, Bajramović became the target of the enraged Croatian public. But not because of what, by his own confession, he had done, but because what he said was a lie.

'He's lying when he says he killed people. Criminal imagination, details . . . the man must have seen too many films or something and his imagination's working overtime . . .' was the comment of the former Minister of Police, Bajramović's superior, on this public confession.

'This is a single case whose authenticity has yet to be established. Such cases six years on create an image of Croatia as aggressor and not as victim,' proclaimed the leader of one of the opposition parties and member of the Croatian parliament.

The Culture of Lies

People are always shouting that they want to create a better future. It's not true. The future is an apathetic void of no interest to anyone. The past is full of life, eager to irritate us, provoke and insult us, tempt us to destroy or repaint it. The only reason people want to be masters of the future is to change the past. They are fighting for access to the laboratories where photographs are retouched and biographies and histories rewritten.

Milan Kundera, *The Book of Laughter and Forgetting*

I.

I was in a Zagreb hospital recently and happened to come across an acquaintance from Sarajevo. He looked pretty wretched: right leg in plaster, left arm bandaged, a mass of dark bruises . . .

'My God . . .' I exclaimed, because I didn't know what else to say.

'I've just come from Sarajevo . . .' he said.

'My God . . .' I shook my head. 'So, how did this happen?' I asked. I couldn't have asked a stupider question.

'I'll tell you, but promise you won't tell anyone . . .'

I nodded, filled with a sense of guilt and deep compassion for my acquaintance from Sarajevo.

'I was sitting in my room, when suddenly – wham – a grenade flew in through the open window . . .'

'And then?!' I gasped.

'Nothing. It didn't explode . . . I picked it up . . . and threw it out of the window, what else could I have done . . .'

'And then?!'

'Nothing. It exploded and took off the front wall . . .'

'And then?!'

'Nothing. I peered out through the broken wall of the room and fell, from the second floor . . . into the street.'

'And then?!'

'Nothing. I smashed myself up . . .'

2.

My Sarajevo acquaintance had told the truth. But his truth was self-discrediting, for a moment it destroyed the terrible, general truth of the sufferings of the inhabitants of Sarajevo, it sounded like a parody of their real collective suffering. All in all, at that moment I felt betrayed, as though my acquaintance had told me a tasteless joke (looking for sympathy too!). The fact that the unfortunate fellow had barely survived, that he had lived through the terrible fate of his city for a whole year, that, when he did get out, he had told me only the last, personal episode – somehow none of that was able to prevent my slight sense of disappointment. With all those bandages he could have invented a heroic tale. Which, *really*, would have been true!

3.

His situation was like that of all those who tell their *own* truth in these terrible war times. Terrible times are usually collective times. The truth is only what may be smoothly built into the picture which the collective accepts as the truth. If we add to that a time of general postmodern confusion – then the truth will sound like a lie, a lie like the truth.

4.

In the times of war, apart from the culture of death, the things that come irrepressibly to the surface, like hologram grimaces, are the shapes of parallel lives. In the chaos, an infernal balance is established: suffering masks its parody under a black mourning cloth, tragedy drags farce in its wake, as unhappiness does cynicism, brutality and compassion go everywhere together. Times of great truths are usually deeply permeated with the all-pervading culture of lies.

It seems that this culture of lies is something that the small nations of Yugoslavia created long ago, learning to live with it and reinforcing it to this day. Lying – just like dying, – has become a natural state, a norm of behaviour, liars are normal citizens. And if one really should give any credit to Dobrica Ćosić, Serbian writer and failed President of the *false Yugoslavia*, then it must be for his remark: 'Lying is an aspect of our patriotism and confirmation of our innate intelligence.'

5.

'What is most astounding, as everyone who has taken part in the negotiations in today's Yugoslavia will tell you, is the unbelievable capacity of people at all levels – to tell lies. An incredible phenomenon. Just look at how many ceasefires have been broken. And they carried on signing papers with the obvious intention of disregarding them. In ex-Yugoslavia our norms of honour don't exist, it's part of the culture. It's so widespread that you won't be at all surprised when you realise that X or Y is a liar, here people live with a culture of lies,' said Lord Owen on one occasion. Owen himself discredited Western 'norms of honour', if such a thing exists and if that was what was at stake, by signing agreements with liars.

6.

Is this matter of the culture of lies really so simple?

The peoples of Yugoslavia lived for several decades in their own country, building not only cities, bridges, roads, railways but also a certain complex of values. Built into the foundations of that complex of values were, among other things: 'the ideology and practice of socialism' (today those same ex-Yugoslavs call that 'communism', 'Tito's regime', 'communist dictatorship'). It was a practice which to a considerable extent confirmed the earlier break with Stalin (even if the break was carried out on the principle of 'the same medicine': numerous individuals, usually out of a sheer inability to cope with the rapid ideological U-turn, ended up on the Yugoslav Gulag, Goli Otok). Then there was that famous 'Yugoslavism'. This implied a multinational and multicultural community and was reinforced over the years not only by Tito's popular slogans – *'Preserve brotherhood and unity like the apple of your eye'* – but also by the practice of daily life. Today those same peoples claim that they lived in *a prison of nations*, and that it was that idea, the idea of Yugoslavism – not *they themselves* – which is responsible for the present brutal war.

7.

Some ten years ago the nations of now former Yugoslavia wept sincerely at the funeral of their long-lived mummy, Tito. Now those same nations claim unanimously that they lived under the 'repressive boot of a communist dictator'. The more extreme settle their scores with plaster heads of Tito as though they were clay pigeons. And so, belatedly (ten years on!) they are exorcising the ghost of *their* communism. The necrophiliac Yugoslav passion for digging up old bones (and burying new ones!) spares no one: the Serbs threaten the Croats by saying they will dig up Tito's bones, buried in Belgrade, and send them to the Croats.

Today the same *national, collective* language is used to proclaim their truth by all those who kept silent for fifty years, that is by all those who, in that same *collective* language, lived out their *multinational* togetherness for a full fifty years as their own truth.

8.

Other totalitarian states articulated their dissatisfaction with their regimes in strong intellectual undergrounds, both in the country and abroad. Yugoslavia had virtually no intellectual *underground* (apart from an insignificant number of *dissidents* in the early communist years). After the Second World War 'Ustashas', 'Chetniks', 'collaborators' and 'anti-communists' were driven out of the country (dead or alive); some twenty years later there was an economic migration out of the country, of *Gastarbeiter*. The intellectual emigration was numerically insignificant. If a strong intellectual underground did exist, as everyone swears it did today, then how is it that no one knew about it; and if it didn't exist, how can we believe that *the truth* which people craved behind the walls of the so-called *prison of nations* is the one that has now come to the surface? Perhaps the regime, that soft Yugoslav totalitarianism, was not so soft after all, perhaps it was worse than the Albanian or Romanian versions? If that was the case, how come there was so little protest?

At this moment it is an indisputable and statistically verifiable truth that many intellectuals from the former Yugoslavia are *voluntarily* joining the ocean of *involuntary* refugees and knocking on the doors of other countries. What, then, is the truth and what is a lie? Could it be that a new lie is springing up in the place of the old truth? Or is it the other way round?

9.

Terrible times are marked by the rhythm of destruction and construction, chaos and order, rapid demolition and simultaneous building. What was there is destroyed (cities, ideological notions, bridges, criteria, libraries, norms, churches, marriages, monuments, lives, graves, friendships, homes, myths) the old truth is destroyed. What will become the new truth is rapidly built in its place.

In Duga Resa, a small town in Croatia, a little wood was planted: eighty-eight trees, for Tito's birthday. Today the inhabitants of Duga Resa have cut down the wood: they say they were removing 'the last remnants of the communist regime'. The people who cut the wood down were the same people who planted it.

There is a story going round about the murderer, the Serbian General Mladić, who for more than a year has been turning the innocent city of Sarajevo into a graveyard. It is said that he aimed his guns from the surrounding Sarajevo hills straight at the house of a friend. The story goes on to say that the murderer then telephoned his friend to tell him he was about to blow up his house.

'You've got five minutes to take your albums and get out.'

The General meant family photograph albums. Before destroying everything he owned, the General had 'generously' bequeathed his chosen victim life together with the right to memory, life with a few family snapshots.

What is being annihilated with guns, grenades, murders, rape, the displacement of peoples, 'ethnic cleansing', the new ideology supported by the media, is memory. What is being built on the ruins is the new truth, the one that will one day be the only memory. In that sense, the war on the territory of former Yugoslavia is only a repetition of the old story of disappearance and appearance, the story of human civilisation.

10.

Unaccustomed to the culture of scepticism, at this moment the Yugoslav peoples are firmly convinced that they are fighting for the truth. Even if this were not the case, they know that every newly established lie eventually becomes the truth. And that is why, when the terrible times finally pass, those who survive will not be ashamed. The peoples of the new countries will not be ashamed because of the hundreds of thousands of dead, displaced, unhappy, because of the millions of destroyed lives, because of the destroyed country which they once built together.

II.

Is it possible for the media to provoke war? I permit myself the theory that the war on the territory of Yugoslavia began several years ago with the posterior of a completely innocent Serbian peasant. I still remember his surname: Martinović. For months the poor man, who was allegedly found in a field with a bottle in his backside, became a topic in many Yugoslav newspapers and TV stations, particularly in Serbia. Some maintained that Martinović had been raped with a beer bottle by Albanians, others that he was a pervert who had been masturbating with the bottle. Others again affirmed that he had been raped by Serbs so that they could blame the Albanians. Yet others calculated, on the basis of the nature of the injury, that Martinović had himself jumped on to the bottle from a nearby tree. His numerous sorrowing offspring gave statements in their father's favour, teams of doctors disagreed in public about the various possibilities of injury and self-injury. Martinović spent the whole time in his hospital bed smiling feebly at the anxious TV viewers. The media made a political spectacle of Martinović's backside, quite in keeping with the Yugoslav spirit.

So the case of Martinović simply confirmed the belief of the Serbian people that the Serbian leader Milošević's decision – to change the constitution violently and revoke the autonomy of Kosovo and Vojvodina – was more than justified! So the masses became accustomed to participating passionately and collectively in that miserable and tasteless media story. And so they confirmed once again their receptivity to any kind of media manipulation.

After Martinović there was an abundance of 'evidence', which the Serbian media 'milked' to the full, of 'genocide' carried out against the Serbian minority by Albanians, and numerous Serbian women sprang up from somewhere, having been raped by (who else but) Albanians. Justifying themselves by their injured national pride and the national myths served up by the media, Serbian nationalists collectively supported the Serbian repression of the Albanians in Kosovo, or took an active part in it themselves.

12.

And since in these lands every lie becomes a truth in the end, every spoken word becomes reality, so just a few years later a male and, from a psychoanalytical point of view, deeply homosexual war came about, and the war strategy of rape became cruel everyday reality. The women who were to be raped were, of course, completely innocent, their bodies simply serving as a medium for the transmission of male messages.

13.

The media only discovered anew what they knew already: that promiscuity with leaders and power, with their political pretensions and aims, functions perfectly; they also discovered what they may not have known before – the scale of their power! They quivered with satisfaction at the confirmation that a lie very easily becomes legitimate truth; they were astonished at the realisation that in the absence of other information people believe what is available to them, that even despite other information, people believe what they want to believe, their media, in short, their custom-built myths.

And the infernal media campaign was able to continue. In Serbian newspapers there began to appear articles about the Ustasha camps during the Second World War (and no one could deny their truthfulness, because they existed and in them perished Serbs, Gypsies, Jews but also Croats). There began to be more and more pictures of the camps on Serbian television. Croats began increasingly to be called criminals, 'Ustashas'. Serbian newspapers were full of horrifying stories of 'necklaces of Serbian children's fingers', worn by the Croat 'Ustashas', of the 'genocide' which the Croats were again preparing to carry out against the innocent Serbs.

The Serbian media propaganda (orchestrated by the Serbian authorities and the Serbian *leader*) finally achieved what it had sought: a reaction in the Croatian media. And when the Croatian media also filled with tales of 'necklaces of Croatian children's fingers' worn round their necks by Serbian 'cut-throats' – the preparations were laid for war.

Today, in what is still wartime, no Serbian newspapers can be found in Croatia (and if they could no one would buy them), nor are there Croatian papers in Serbia (and if there were no one would believe them), and television programmes waging a war to the death can only be received with satellite aerials. Which is hardly necessary in any case as the programmes are identical. The Serbs put together information in their interest, the Croats in theirs. Telephone links between Croatia and Serbia have not been functioning for a long time.

14.

Growing out of the worn-out Yugoslav system, following the same old habits, the media have succeeded in legalising lies. From being a political and journalistic way of behaving, lies have developed into a war strategy, and as such have rapidly become established as morally acceptable.

When the homeland is at stake, I am prepared to lie, said one Croatian journalist and she attained a high rating on the Croatian journalistic scene. In a completely upside-down system of values, therefore, lies have become not only acceptable but a positively marked way of behaving (we lie in order to defend the homeland, we lie in the name of that homeland, we lie, of course, only temporarily because the homeland is in danger).

15.

The culture of lies is most easily established if we have an opponent who lies more than we do, or who speaks the ancient palindromic language, 'the devil's verse', the one that is read the same backwards and forwards, from left to right. And the weary postmodern outside world, to which the nations doggedly direct 'their truths', tries reluctantly and with difficulty to set up coordinates: both sides lie equally; or one side lies more, the other less; or one side lies, the other tells the truth . . . It is only the dead who do not lie, but they have no credibility.

16.

Croatia (which I take here as an example simply because it is closest to me) establishes its public, political and moral coordinates on the basis of the formula: executioner and victim. In this tandem (from the Croatian point of view) Croatia is the *victim*, which is hard to deny: part of its territory is occupied by Serbs, they have partly (or completely) destroyed some Croatian villages and towns (which have posthumously become symbols of national remembrance, like Vukovar or Dubrovnik), railway lines and bridges (which have posthumously become symbols of past and the possible future connectedness). At the same time, of course, the Croats too have destroyed, particularly in Bosnia. This fact has not diminished the collective emotion, fostered passionately by Croatian citizens, government and the media, of being the victim.

This collective experience is in ironic contrast with what has become today one of the commonest words in Croatian public and political life: the word *image*. It is not necessary to emphasise that the word *image* means impression, representation. However, in local usage, this word implies *the truth about Croatia*. The Croatian media are full of phrases about the fact that *we must all build a positive image of Croatia in the world* (in this case the word *'world'* usually means European, then American media, politicians and public opinion).

Recently on television the Vice-President of the Croatian government invited all the citizens of Croatia *to build together a positive image of Croatia in the world*, which means, in effect, the image of a righteous victim! The Vice-President added that even ordinary citizens could help by writing letters (surely each of us has some friends abroad!) in which they would spread *the truth about Croatia*. The patriotic duty of every citizen – *to spread the truth about Croatia* – has legitimised a method which they always employed in any case with great zeal whenever invited to: denunciation of people who think differently – sceptics, 'Yugosnostalgics', intellectuals who once said something critical about the present regime; denunciation of people who travel too much ('while we sit it out here bravely because our homeland is in danger'); denunciation of neighbours (he said, 'Fuck an independent state in which you've nothing to live on'); of an acquaintance (he said, 'What kind of a state is it that has taken my two sons from me?'); of colleagues at work (he said, 'Why are we fighting when the *commies* are still in power?'). The citizens, meanwhile, as always in such cases, sincerely believe that they are carrying out a little, honourable, patriotic task.

Bit by bit, the strategy of 'spreading the truth about Croatia' has entailed several disastrous consequences: such as the virtually complete control of the media on the part of the ruling party, i.e. the state. In spite of democratic elections, all power in Croatia is in the hands of the ruling party and the President of the state (who is at the same time the leader of the ruling party), who has extensive powers. These powers were approved by parliament when they voted for the new constitution, which was not difficult because the majority of seats are held by members of that same, ruling party. Television, as the most powerful propaganda machine, followed by radio, serves the state. The main newspapers today are controlled by an editorial board, in which the majority consists once again of representatives of the ruling party!

Dozens and dozens of journalists have been dismissed from their jobs; their places have been taken by those who unanimously *spread the truth about Croatia. There are journalists who think Croatia and those who feel her. Croatia should not be thought, she should be felt*, said a journalist, the one we have already quoted. Her slogan typifies the state of Croatian journalism today. Sometimes Croatian journalists succeed in fighting for a more critical article in local newspapers. Of course, this can only be when the editors of the newspapers decide temporarily to improve their *image* and so suppress *Western rumours* that all is not well with the media in Croatia.

17.

The *image*, which is more important than the truth, is being worked on by government organisations, the Ministry of Information, offices for the promotion of Croatia in the world, but also by newly formed non-governmental organisations such as, for instance, 'The Croatian Anti-defamation League'. Maintaining that 'lies about Croatia have been spread for decades', the president of the League recently announced: 'We shall endeavour to alter world public opinion in favour of Croatia, using the truth as our strongest and sole argument. It is the duty of each one of us to defend our country, and that is our most important task. Slander is a more powerful weapon than a gun, a tank or an aeroplane.'

Looking at the local newspapers the uninformed reader might think that we were not involved in a real war but in a battle for our *image in the world*. Newspapers are full of such titles as: 'Why the Muslims have a better image in the world than the Croats', 'How the Serbs succeeded in manipulating world public opinion and improving their image in the world', 'What Croatia has to do to improve its image in the world'.[1]

[1] In answer to a journalist's question, 'What is then the best way to tell the world the truth, so people will accept that truth as the truth, and not a lie?', M. F., currently the Head of the Section for Culture and the Promotion of the Republic of Croatia at

18.

But still, in order for the system to function, it is not enough for there to be one-party power, control of the media, censorship (justified by the war), ideological propaganda (justified by the exceptional situation), and constant patriotic media 'briefings' It is not enough, in other words, to send out messages, there must also be someone to receive them.

In the autumn of 1991, the inhabitants of Zagreb (including myself, the author of these lines) went down almost daily into cellars and shelters at the sound of the air-raid warning. Fortunately this *drilling of the people* proved to be unnecessary, although in other towns (Zadar, Vukovar, Dubrovnik, Karlovac, Šibenik.) it was all too necessary. In the autumn of 1991, the people of Zagreb were reluctant to go out into the streets for fear of Serbian snipers (apparently disguised as chimney-sweeps, postmen and firemen!), who shot at people from the roofs. The snipers and their victims were curiously anonymous, despite the fact that they could have contributed to the process of *spreading the truth about Croatia*, but also rapidly forgotten, because of new dramatic events. That is how the citizens became *one*, collective, threatened body, just as the enemy became one, collective, threatening body. The collective paranoia induced in this way, based on perfectly real assumptions, brought with it also a collective readiness to interpret rumours as the truth (after all many interpreted the truth as rumour). Anguished by fear, the loss of relatives and friends, poverty, uncertainty, an information blockade, the terror of war, encroaching chaos, the citizens of Croatia are today ready to grab hold of the one and only truth they are offered, like a straw. The totalitarian mentality, collectivism and conformism – which have sprung out of the perception of the nation as victim – have now become so entrenched that every objection to quite obvious, crude offences, illogicality, political amateurism, crimes, corruption, infringements of human rights is interpreted as an attack *against the young Croatian state, as*

---

the Ministry of Foreign Affairs, gave the following reply: 'The first thing we have to do when we go abroad is to spread the truth about the enemy, and then to create an image of Croatia as a strong, courageous, unwavering, resilient and vital country with a future. That is what spreading the truth about Croatia means, that is propaganda.' (*Večernji list*, 9.5.1993) *anti-Croatian,* and, therefore *pro-Serbian, as undermining the young Croatian state, as treason, as . . . a lie.*

In order, therefore, to set up a system which manifests the clear symptoms of pathological collectivism, what was required was perfect cooperation between the authorities, the state ideology, and the citizens who identify with it. The citizens will then justify their conformism with regard to obvious infringements of human rights, disregard of fundamental democratic principles, the creation of an autocratic state, etc. – by priorities: our survival is at stake, this is still wartime, we're not going to worry about trifles such as the freedom of the media . . . And similar arguments are used by the authorities themselves.

19.

In the newly created collective climate all who do not speak the language of the collective are exposed to the danger of being proclaimed traitors and enemies of the people. It is a fact that the number of *public enemies* (compared to the number of friends of the people) is insignificant, so the same names keep turning up in the Croatian press.

The objects of public campaigns are often women (journalists, writers, artists).[2] In a milieu that has hidden its deeply rooted patriarchalism behind socialist formulae about the equality of women and men, 'democratisation' has brought a new freedom for patriarchalism. In this sense women intellectuals are almost a 'natural' choice as objects of a media assassination. Along with the female *public enemies* – who are guilty because they have publicly declared their anti-nationalist, anti-war and individual standpoint – some men have also undergone a media lynching. It is interesting that few people came to their defence: a few journalists, alternative and anti-war women's groups, the occasional friend. It is a fact that the public campaigns against *public enemies* often included colleagues (members of the Croatian

---

[2] I myself have experienced the method of media assassination. A few days ago an acquaintance came up to me in the street. 'So, you're going abroad?' she asked, meaning was I at last intending to leave the country for good.

'Why should I go "abroad"?'

'Because you keep writing all those lies about us,' she said with conviction.

'So you've read what I've written,' I said.

'Why should I! Are you going to say that everyone else is lying?' she said, emphasising the word *everyone* in astonishment.

PEN, writers, journalists, intellectuals), politicians, but also ordinary citizens. These last in the 'Readers' letters' columns of newspapers, or, if the 'victim' agrees to a dialogue, in organised interviews on television (a kind of trial-by-television), where anonymous citizens put questions to the 'accused' and comment on her / his answers.

The collective paranoia that has been induced does not stop at individuals. In an atmosphere of quite real insecurity, and fear, with the constant sense that life is on the edge of an abyss, in an atmosphere of uncertainty and quite real helplessness, the citizens of Croatia occasionally direct their enmity at all those who *do not understand them*, or, conversely, euphorically proclaim their friendship towards all those who *do understand* them. Thus it is not uncommon to find in Croatian newspapers headlines such as the recent one: 'The French and English do not like us!' And since rumour has in any case replaced information, it is not rare for various theories of an internationl conspiracy against Croatia to appear in the Croatian media.

20.

It seems that it is not only fear, aroused national (and nationalist) emotions, hatred of the enemy, vulnerability, the establishment of an autocratic system, media propaganda and war that have reinforced the culture of lies. One of the strategies with which the culture of lies is established is terror by forgetting (they force you to forget what you remember!) and terror by remembering (they force you to remember what you do not remember!). After the dismantling of Yugoslavia, after the election of the new Croatian government and the proclamation of independence, terror by forgetting was carried out in Croatia by administrative means, by means of the media and finally . . . by collective compulsion. 'Yugoslavia' (a country in which Croatian citizens had lived for some fifty years!) became a prohibited word, and the terms *Yugoslav, Yugonostalgic* or *Yugo-zombie* are synonymous with national traitor. The old symbols – flags, coats of arms, the names of streets, schools, squares – have been removed and replaced by new ones; the language and its name have been changed (Cyrillic and Serbian have become undesirable). Almost overnight a whole system of values has been changed. So 'anti-fascists', former 'partisans', 'communists', the 'left wing', 'anti-nationalists' (previously positively marked terms) have suddenly become negatively marked (despite the fact that the Croatian government, including above all the Croatian President, consists largely of political converts, former communists). The formerly negatively valued nationalists, terrorist-émigrés, 'Ustashas' and the Independent State of Croatia (NDH) itself have acquired a neutral or even a positive connotation. In that sense many historical concepts and 'historical facts' have undergone an abrupt reassessment. For example, according to the new value judgements, the 'Ustashas' did admittedly commit crimes, but on a far smaller scale than was suggested for years by the 'Yugo-Bolshevik-Greater Serb propaganda'.) So, among other things, the Independent State of Croatia has been re-evaluated. The NDH is today often seen as a state that was admittedly 'Nazi', but at the same time realised the age-old longing for Croatian statehood.

21.

Such an abrupt transformation of values, occurring in many spheres of everyday, cultural, political and ideological life has generated confusion in the head of many citizens: bad has suddenly become good, left has suddenly become right. In this re-evaluation the blotting out of one's personal life, one's identity, a kind of amnesia, an unconscious or conscious lie have become a protective reaction which enables one quickly to adopt the new identity.

22.

I know of a writer colleague who claimed to a foreign journalist that he was 'the victim of repression' under *Yugo-communism*, that his books were banned, and that he had been in prison. That colleague was never in prison nor was he 'the victim of repression' and all his books were regularly published. I do not believe that he was lying. Exposed to media brainwashing, terror by forgetting and collective compulsion, my colleague had simply forgotten his personal history, he carried out an unconscious mental touching-up, and in the general context the spoken lie became an acceptable truth. And after all, the foreign journalist had come to hear just such a story, in his Westerner's head he already carried the stereotype: the story of a repressed writer in the former communist regime and a happy end in the new, democratic one.

I know of a Zagreb Japanologist who terrorised the whole Yugoslav cultural scene for years with – Japan! Throughout the whole of former Yugoslavia there sprang up haiku circles, haiku poets, ikebana courses, anthologies of Japanese poetry, twinnings between Osaka and Varaždin, festivals of Yugoslav haiku poets. Thanks to the activity of the aforementioned Japanologist, the inflation of haiku poetry during 'totalitarianism' had given us all 'a pain in the neck'. Today the famous Japanologist claims that under the 'Tito regime' he was exposed to repression because of . . . haiku poetry!

23.

Many citizens of Croatia, among them Albanians, Croats, Serbs, Muslims and others, are today experiencing difficulty in acquiring the residence document, *domovnica*, on the basis of which they can obtain essential papers, a passport, an identity card. If their father was born outside Croatia, if they were themselves born in Skopje or Sarajevo, if they moved to Zagreb from Belgrade, if they are refugees, they will come up against an unpleasant bureaucratic procedure and the possibility that they will not be granted citizenship in the country in which they were born or lived their whole life. The country in which they have lived for years is suddenly no longer theirs. And the citizens will have to forget their former life in order to liberate the space for a new one. They will adapt, conform, sign some things and write off others in order to survive, in order that their children should survive, in order that on some 'higher' state level the space should be liberated for the building of some new (this time truly new!), bright (this time truly bright) future (this time truly a future!).

24.

Terror by remembering is a parallel process to terror by forgetting. Both processes have the function of building a new state, a new truth. Terror by remembering is a strategy by which the continuity (apparently interrupted) of national identity is established, terror by forgetting is the strategy whereby a 'Yugoslav' identity and any remote prospect of its being re-established is wiped out. Terror by remembering has its administrative-symbolic, cultural forms as well. The names of streets, squares, institutions are replaced by the names of Croats 'of renown'; monuments are erected to Croatian historical figures, writers, politicians; the language of schools and the media is changed; textbooks are changed, figures from Croatian cultural history are honoured, and so on. Terror by remembering as a method of establishing a national identity does not shrink from national megalomania, heroisation, mythicisation, the absurd accepted lies, in other words. Signs of national megalomania are visible everywhere: proclaiming the city of Zagreb a 'metropolis', and the Croatian state a 'miracle' and 'the most democratic state in the world'. National mythomania is confirmed by 'serious' claims about the Iranian origin of the Croats and popular phrases about the Croatian state as the 'thousand-year dream of all Croats'. National mythomania tends to distort, touch up or counterfeit historical authenticity. So the latest history textbooks for primary schools are exchanging the recent heroisation and fetishisation of Tito and the partisan movement for the same fetishisation of the Croatian President, Franjo Tudjman, that 'architect of Croatian defence', that 'great Croat' and 'man for all Croatian times'.

The terror of remembering is, of course, also a war strategy of setting up frontiers, establishing differences: we are different from them (Serbs), our history, faith, customs and language are different from theirs. In the war variant this complex (which profoundly penetrates the Croatian collective consciousness) is used like this: we are different from them (Serbs) because we are better, which is proved by our history; we always built, they always only destroyed; we are a European, Catholic, culture, they are only Orthodox, illiterate barbarians. And so on and so forth.

Ordinary Croatian citizens with strong national feelings express their satisfaction that the 'dream' they have dreamed 'for a thousand years' has been realised, those with weak national feelings accept the idea that, like it or not, that dream is also their reality. Croatian Serbs in Krajina are dreaming some 'thousand-year dreams' of their own. After one set of 'truths' has been transformed into 'lies' and 'lies' transformed into 'truths', in the majority of cases the citizens will always bow to the majority.

25.

I heard a story about a foreign TV-reporter who happened to find himself in some Bosnian village and paid the surviving locals 200

German marks to drag the scattered corpses into a tidy heap, so that he could photograph them. At the same time he did not quite grasp either where he was, or who was who, and he made a moving TV commentary about a Muslim massacre of Serbs. The corpses were Muslim.

I know of tales about foreign journalists who paid local photographers and cameramen to film dangerous scenes for a pittance. (Those 'natives' need money, they're dying like flies in any case!) I know of foreign journalists who, thinking they were writing 'the truth and nothing but the truth' sold the world someone else's misery for their own well-being.

I know also about those truly courageous people who risked their lives to touch the indifferent heart of the world. No one asked them to do it, but they did.

I know also of kind foreigners, whose hearts were stirred and who sent one refugee camp a large quantity of flat irons. It had not even occurred to the kind-hearted foreigners that the 'native tribes' had had electricity for ages. Or else the irons were intended for those who really did not have any, the inhabitants of Sarajevo, so that they could go to their deaths neatly ironed.

26.

War is like a cake, everyone wants to grab his piece: politicians (local and foreign), criminals and speculators (local and foreign), war profiteers and murderers (local and foreign), sadists and masochists, believers and benefactors (local and foreign), historians and philosophers (local and foreign), journalists (local and foreign).

The war carries with it the destruction of identity but also a rapid and cheap possibility of acquiring one. For foreign philosophers the war is a new toy, a test of the elasticity of old and new concepts. Europe without frontiers or Europe with frontiers? Nationalism with positive connotations, nationalism with negative connotations? Post-totalitarianism and the New World Order? For foreign politicians and strategists the war is a living polygon for examining a potential future; for the media an exciting adventure; for foreign readers and audiences a fix for quickening the sluggish moral and emotional metabolism; for criminals the possibility of becoming heroes, for intellectuals of becoming . . . criminals!

27.

Radovan Karadžić, the leader of the Bosnian Serbs and an un-doubted war criminal, is a favourite theme of much of the Western media. When Karadžić is being shown, the Western media for some unknown reason usually put him in the fore-ground. So Karadžić (a psychiatrist by training!) is able more easily to communicate with his Western 'clients'. I imagine the Western reader / viewer comfortably settled in an armchair. My imagined reader / viewer first feels secretly pleased that, thank God, he does not live in such a terrible country (after all, *they* are the Balkans, not Europe). Then he gazes at the huge, sweating head of the murderer from the wild Bosnian forests and for a moment abandons himself to romantic musings about a criminal leading the whole world by the nose. Then he mentally erases such inadmissible musings and is genuinely horrified at the 'highwayman's' barbarity. Then he turns off the television, folds up the newspaper. My imagined Western media consumer then feels an undefined sense of relief. My imagined Western reader cannot conceive that at that very moment Karadžić's dark shadow is sitting in his armchair, manipulating him, the owner of the armchair and the newspaper!

28.

As a writer, I can allow myself such a notion. Indeed, I am convinced that that outside world, that so coveted arbiter of civilisation, that Europe – so called upon and so desperately depended upon by the Croats *(Danke Deutschland, danke Gen-scher)* and the Bosnians and the people of Sarajevo (who for months have been expecting the mythical Sixth Fleet to sail into Sarajevo) – that Europe has also played its part, bears its heavy portion of blame, has its problem of a 'Western' culture of truth and lies. And the root of that problem, whether Europe wants it or not, lies in Bosnia. And that is why Karadžić's dark and terrible shadow is already sitting, comfortably settled, in the armchairs of European homes.

29.

In all the former Yugoslav territories people are now living a postmodern chaos. Past, present and future are all lived simultaneously. In the circular temporal mish-mash suddenly everything we ever knew and everything we shall know has sprung to life and gained its right to existence.

After exactly fifty years (1941 to 1991), by almost infernal symmetry, the Second World War has sprung up again, many of the same villages have been burned down again, many families have experienced a symmetrical fate, many children and grand-children have lived through the fate of their fathers. Even the weapons are sometimes the same: stolen out of necessity from local 'museums of the revolution', belonging to the partisans in other words, or else taken down from attics and out of trunks, left there for fifty years by 'Ustashas' or 'Chetniks'.

The newly created states are also 'museum pieces', quotations, and the responses of the newly elected leaders are only references to those already uttered. Like the flash of a hologram, segments of former times appear, fragments of history; from the faces of today's leaders there often gleams the hellish reflection of some other leaders, in such a gleam the swastika is linked to the red star. The hotheads of the Yugoslav people dream thousand-year dreams, some fragments flash like reality and then sink into the darkness to yield the right to a brief life to some other fragments. In the territories of the disintegrated country, which was once shared, victims and their executioners, attackers and attacked, occupiers and occupied sometimes exchange dreams, sometimes they dream the same dream, thinking they are dreaming different ones.

In the disintegrated Yugoslav territories we are also living simultaneously the future, that post-apocalyptic one, the one that for others has yet to come. Sarajevo is a city from the future and a city of the future, existing and non-existent, a city from science fiction films and cartoons, the screenplay for a new version of *Blade Runner*, for a future version of *Mad Max*. 'I am a terminator,' said my friend soon after she had left Sarajevo, 'I have seen so much death that I cannot be anything but a terminator.' My friend set off into the world. 'I must tell the world that I come from the future, from Sarajevo,' she said.

The present in which people are dying is like the permanent running of films from the past and from the future. 'I'm sitting in life like a cinema,' wrote my Belgrade friend a long time ago. On a doomed ship that is sailing nowhere, in the former Yugoslav territories, reality no longer exists. The media perpetuation of accusations and lies has cancelled their harsh reality. People watch their own death on the screen, they only do not know whether the bullet that will kill them is coming from the street or from the screen. Which comes to the same thing in any case, as we are perhaps all dead already. 'Or else we are dead already, only our nails are still growing just a little, as the nails of corpses do, they are turning into claws,' wrote the Sarajevo writer Abdulah Sidran. Perpetuating the horror destroys the horror, perpetuating the evil destroys its weight. Ultimately, nothing has happened, if what is happening is only a reference to what has already happened, and if what is happening is only what is yet to come.

30.

In this sense my story about the culture of lies also collapses like a tower of cards, destroying itself. The truth is only that I too, the writer of these lines, am covered with invisible bruises, just as my Sarajevo acquaintance from the beginning of this story is covered with visible ones. Soon I shall be *voluntarily* joining that ocean of (willing and unwilling) refugees who are knocking at the doors of other countries of the world. I have no illusions. In those other countries at least one thing is undoubtedly waiting: the TV screen and newspapers. I imagine myself opening a newspaper (and oddly I still want to) and coming across an article written by a colleague from over there, *on the other side*. The article will be about the Serbian culture of lies. As it is, my text is only half the story, half the truth. Or half a lie, as, I imagine, my Croatian countrymen would say.

August 1993

85

Good Night, Croatian Writers, Wherever You May Be[1]

But it seems to me that there is now just one single principle in our intellectual (and literary-cultural) patriotism: to think nothing, to distort the facts, to misinterpret the most basic truths, to spread lies, to foster a cult of empty phrases, in short to do everything that is contrary to the most primitive taste of common sense.

Miroslav Krleža, *Literary Survey*

1.

In these difficult times it is not easy to be a Croatian writer. Or, more precisely, to be the one we shall be using here as an example. In times when the fundamental coordinates of everyday reality have become staying alive and surviving, the Croatian writer's situation is somewhat more complex. Because he would like also to write. And writing, to put it at its simplest, means thinking. Why then is this so hard for some Croatian writers, particularly for the one in question?

2.

Our Croatian writer, the one we are using here as an example, is sitting today over a blank sheet of white paper as though it were a

[1] The sentence 'Good night, Croatian fighters, wherever you may be' is spoken at the end of all the evening news broadcasts on Croatian television. This message to the defenders of Croatia came into use in peak viewing time a year ago and is still in use today.

minefield. Many of his colleagues are on the other side of the field, they are waving to him, calling to him in friendly voices, come over, they say, it isn't difficult. Our writer shakes his head doubtfully, some of his colleagues didn't make it, some barely did. Some are standing on the edge, not daring to cross. Others do cross and have the decency to leave markers after them: beware of the mines! The unwritten sheets of white paper lie before our writer and it seems as though everything were teeming with warnings: there are little red 'stop' signs everywhere, narrow green crossings, amber lights urging caution, black death's-heads . . .

3.

The Croatian writer, the one we have chosen for this occasion, finds himself in a completely new communicative situation brought about by the new reality of war. Sometimes it seems to him that the task of sending artistic messages has been reduced to the mere process of distinguishing noises, removing barriers, to a painful endeavour to explain what he has in any case already said. It seems that a little text of a few pages demands twice as many explanatory footnotes. His text is no longer understood as before, something gets in the way, the words no longer mean what they used to, each one rebounds in his face. It seems to our writer that this is because things can no longer be implied, and they can't be implied because there is no longer a common code. Or else a code has been established and has become common to others, but not to him. It seems to him further that this is because the world *he* knew, for better or worse, has fallen apart, and therefore everything is in pieces. That is why his, the writer's, perspective, his point of view, his starting point has been called into question; it too is a consequence of the chaos of war. That is why it seems to the writer that he no longer recognises the orientation of those he is addressing. They have changed, but he hasn't, or he has and they haven't. In any case, in the very nature of things, his message is certainly read differently by those in the trenches, those on one side and those on the other, those without a roof and those with a roof over their heads, those who are hungry and those who have enough to eat, those who have experienced the new-style concentration camps and those who have only seen pictures of war on television.

4.

In such a communicative situation, and this is confirmed every day in practice, our writer is called upon to build into his text clear signals, which his readers expect: they too want to find their way through the text, to read it from the 'right' angle.

The primary signal, which determines the nature of the text in a situation such as the present one, is the writer's origin. If he is a Croat he will be condemned but forgiven for his critical stance towards the new-style reality. He's 'one of us' after all, thinks the reading public contentedly. If he is a Serb (a Croatian Serb, of course) he will never be forgiven for his critical stance towards the new-style reality (because it will be a long time before he is forgiven simply for being a Serb), but at least *it will be perfectly clear* 'which way the wind is blowing'. If no one knows who he is, he will be publicly labelled, someone will know, or think they know (and no distinction is made between 'thinking I know' and really 'knowing'). In the map of the World According to Blood Group the fundamental marker for every public act, for an ordinary 'Good morning' to a neighbour, is just that – The Holy Blood Group. In a system of generally induced paranoia one's national origin is the essential fact: it is the measure of all things, it determines perspective, it is the most fundamental assumption in the relation between Sender and Recipient. In such a situation, then, the first demand made of the writer (and his text) is the *clear and public* expression of that primary assumption. The writer makes this first signal for fear of not being understood, in his desire to be understood, no matter what. The message now slips differently along the channel of communication. We understand one another, we *belong*, even if we don't understand one another, or we don't *belong*, even if we do understand one another.

5.

Another exceptionally important signal in understanding the text (or even that ordinary 'Good morning' to a neighbour) is the social origin of the writer, or at least his implicit or explicit adherence to various political options. For instance, if the writer comes from an officer's family, if he was himself ever a communist, his readers will see his texts as coloured by a 'Yugo-nostalgic' tone, even if there is no evidence of such a belief in either the text or its intonation. *Yugo-nostalgia* is one of the most loaded of political qualifications in a paranoid communicative situation, more loaded than many other labels in use today; such as *Chetnik, nationally colourblind, commie, Serb chauvinist*, and the like. This little term, with its attractive components ('Yugo' – south – + nostalgia) evidently conceals many other, yet more dangerous things. It conceals a perfidious doubt in the new system (the old one, i.e. the *commie one*, was better!). Doubt in the new system is a hostile act against the new state, it means questioning its values, it implies a condemnation of the war, accepting the option that our enemies are also people; furthermore it implies subscribing to communism and the whole ideological package it carried with it. But most of all, nostalgia is dangerous because it encourages . . . remembering. And in the newly established reality everything starts again from scratch. And in order to start from scratch, everything that came before must be forgotten. That is why the writer more or less joyfully builds additional signals into his text. They are clear or hidden, according to the way he has been brought up and to his taste, but they must be there in order for the text to reach its audience without hindrance. I am not a 'Yugo-nostalgic', I am not in favour of 'the prison of nations', I was not a 'communist' . . . Or I was, but only for a short time. Or I was, but I always had a low opinion of them.

6.

Just as ordinary people gladly wear badges which will smooth communication with others and 'put things in their proper place' (hence all those crosses round people's necks or stickers with the Croatian coat of arms on the windows of flats, on cars) a similar system of signals, simple and comprehensible to all, is expected also of the writer. He is the sender of messages, the message must reach the recipient without hindrance. And the recipient in the new-style communicative situation seems no longer to be the reading public but the people. And our writer, like it or not, suddenly finds himself in the completely new situation of sending messages to the people! He becomes, by chance or intention, like it or not, a writer of the people. And what that is exactly our chosen instance doesn't know, just as he doesn't know exactly what *the people* is. His literary memories search and strain, connecting that whole vague complex with 'popular' novels (?), with the nineteenth century (?), with the theory of 'commissioning' works (?), with patriotism (?), with 'the role of the intellectual' in difficult times . . . And why is *the people* suddenly doing the commissioning, grumbles the writer, when there are so few books in any case, and when the *people* are not unduly concerned that there are so few, when culture in these unhappy times is in any case reduced to the level of communication of hearsay!

7.

Naturally our writer knows that the war has changed everything and that no one is the same any more. The reality he knew, the one that was the norm of his life, the norm of his normality, has vanished. In the same place, before the writer's eyes, a new reality is coming into being, new values are being established, a new world is being built into which life will be breathed once it is named. The business of building begins with naming. This is a house, this is the homeland, this is black, this is white . . . Our writer is a little confused. He humbly recalls that naming is the work of God (Authority, State, Utopia). Our writer is surprised by this general passion for naming, it appears to be intended to convince oneself and others of the real existence of the new reality. This is black, this is white, this is right, this is wrong . . . It is only in firm coordinates, in a clear and named world that we shall not be lost, not threatened by the chaos of madness, ambiguity, multiple truths. Because we are at the beginning, we need one truth. An alarm bell suddenly rings in our writer's head: his work, that of a writer, is not and cannot be adherence to one truth. And in the newly established communicative situation, between him and his audience there is room for only one truth (or what has been proclaimed the truth). Everything else is a lie.

8.

Our writer finds himself in a new communicative situation in which, like a double exposure, things overlap even within himself: he no longer knows where the private person ends, and where the writer begins, where his heart and mind are. In this fragmented state, he is being asked to provide something he does not understand, something that surpasses his strength: that he be the *spokesman of his people*, the loudspeaker and conveyor of *correct* political truths, a soothsayer and a leader, a popular singer and healer, examiner of the 'national being' and its spiritual renovator.

9.

Our writer is disconcerted, inner alarm bells ring wildly in him, the memory of his 'genetic' password, the password of *his* 'people', the writer's people. He remembers decades, centuries, times filled with the sweet appeal of national community and bitter rejection. He suddenly recalls the consequences of agreeing to roles, he suddenly remembers the history of careers, he remembers the words, those before and those afterwards, spoken by the same lips, written by the same pens, he suddenly recalls both shameful and glorious moments from the general history of the writer's craft.

10.

Our writer is a Croatian citizen: he most certainly has a heart, connected to the mega-bloodstream of general suffering. His world is split in two, reality unfolds before his eyes like a grotesque nightmare. One half of him, the writer in our writer, resists the proposed strategies: the naming of things, oblivion by order, the new Utopian project on the ruins of the old one, unambiguous language, mental florets which spring back to life in the consciousness like new blades of grass. All of this has been done already, not so long ago, he has learned about it from the history of the involvement of culture with politics. The other half, the citizen in our writer, is torn apart by the numerous miseries of his countrymen, of his present and that former country. How can he separate them and how connect them? And how should he go on?

11.

And in his search for answers, our writer turns to his colleagues: writers, journalists, intellectuals. His colleagues (or, at least, those who make themselves heard at this time) have adapted. The majority have adapted. They have accepted quite naturally the codes of behaviour of a changed communicative situation and newly established reality, they have preserved quite naturally the old mechanisms of their guild life. With little artistic or moral difficulty they reproduce the same language, the same mental and linguistic formulae, the same articulation of the unhappy reality which has affected everyone equally. From the outside they appear to be innocently and contentedly submerged in the warm, sweet, smoke-filled collectivity. It is as though they have no inkling that what is in store for them is the destiny they have already lived through, as though a benevolent amnesia had wiped out their whole memory. Our writer sees his colleagues arguing with a zeal that sometimes surprises themselves over *what needs to be done*; arguing over whether the greatest classic of Croatian literature should be published in full, or whether his political essays should be omitted, particularly the ones dealing with Yugoslavism (is it *the right political moment?*), or should such a writer be published at all. Our writer watches his colleagues discussing with a zeal that sometimes surprises themselves whether a colleague (who has in any case been getting up their collective nose for some time) should be destroyed, forgetting that they used to be guided by one set of principles and now they subscribe to another, and that, in fact, this is what used to be done to them. His colleagues discuss things in corridors, hatch little plots in barely existent editorial boards, accusing one another, the true believers accusing the heretical. In the newly established paranoid communicative system, in the system of everyday life, his colleagues are suddenly waging invisible wars *for the right way, the right idea*, they are suddenly surrounded by a self-styled army of little patriot-informers who slip them reports about the antipatriotic behaviour of this or that colleague . . . What is at stake is *what is right*, all methods are permissible, what is at stake are *sincere patriotic feelings*; and then again, let's forget methods, this is all being done in the name of the *homeland* which is in danger. Without noticing it, his colleagues are slowly becoming policemen, courtiers who take the collective patriotic pulse. With the serious, grey mask of true believers on their faces, unconsciously copied from the former executives, his colleagues are turning themselves into executives. In collective systems which confirm their vitality by the simple skills of hunting down individuals, by the practice of collective lynching, it is a logical assumption that one day the executioners will become the victims. And the other way round. Because they, the vital ones, leap up more swiftly than maize flakes from popcorn machines. And while his colleagues raise their spear-pens with holy, dedicated concentration and aim them at their enemies, while they click their carefully sharpened (temporary, it isn't the right moment) censor's scissors, convinced that they are doing it for the first time (it's our lives, our freedom, our future that are at stake!) behind their backs rises the supple shadow of a younger and more skilful hunter.

12.

And finally, to make things perfectly clear: I too, the author of this text, am a Croatian writer. I have no alternative, it was not my decision. But still, as I write on these white sheets of paper before me, I have at least decided not to take note of designating labels. I am prepared for the explosive consequences, I'm not complaining. Everyone chooses his path. Of course I allow that, in these unhappy times, everyone – from the ordinary citizen to the state President, from the arms smuggler to the fighter – believes that he has the right to expect the writer *to fulfil his duty* to the homeland, to be *the spokesman of the people,* to be *a loyal son* (where are the daughters?) of his Croatian homeland, that he declare his love for it, out loud, clearly and above all *publicly*. But I shall allow myself to refuse such demands. From the history *of my people,* this writer's people, I have learned what misfortunes the practice of confusing categories brings for the writers themselves, for their people, for freedom of speech, for literature itself. Therefore, as a writer, I shall not defend *the barricades of my homeland*. I prefer to stroll along the barricade of Literature or sit a while on the barricade of Freedom of Speech.

13.

I am still not sure whether I should quite believe Osip Mandelshtam who considered that the writer was *a parrot in the deepest sense of the word. A parrot does not know time,* says Mandelshtam, *it does not distinguish day from night. If it bores its owner, the latter will cover it up with a black cloth, and that becomes a surrogate of night for literature.* I am equally not sure whether it has become completely dark here yet. But, just in case, goodnight, Croatian writers, wherever you may be!

November 1992

Postscript, five years later

If what we have been doing up to now is translating hard facts into soft metaphor, let us now, five years on, try testing the metaphor against the facts.

What has happened in the meantime is that little Croatia has become one of the world's major producers of *public enemies, turncoats, back-stabbers, conspirators* and *witches. Public enemies* are on the whole recruited from the ranks of intellectuals. This is why some intellectuals have left the country and are now living in exile. Their places are immediately filled by other intellectuals. Many journalists have been dismissed from their posts, but they too have been replaced by others. One unacceptable writer had explosives planted under his house, another's post-box was peppered with gunshot from the revolver of an anonymous Croatian patriot. Several have been beaten up; one writer nearly paid Croatia literally with his head when one of the President's guards struck him on the head with a military metal belt. It is a fact, however, that no one has as yet died a violent death, which gives some cause for optimism. But it is also true that many *enemies* have been terrified into denying their *enmity*.

One former editor in a publishing company has become the Deputy Chief of Police, which is proof that democracy has enabled many people to realise their secret ambitions. Two or three writers have become soldiers and policemen, and, in the meantime, some soldiers and policemen have become writers. Some writers have been erased from anthologies, school text-books, school and university curricula, but an equivalent number of former (some dead, some still living) fascists, nationalist émigrés and self-proclaimed patriots have been restored to the literature of their homeland. The language of literature has also been changed: many *Serbisms* have been expelled from the language, but almost the same number of *Croaticisms* has settled into the language. The basic paucity of the language is unchanged.

Many people have taken it on themselves to pronounce judgement on the little Croatian culture. A half-literate village school-teacher has become the Minister of Culture. Her contribution to the idiotisation of the system of education and culture is enormous. Others too have done their bit towards the impoverishment and primitivisation of culture: these include university deans, professors, academicians, journalists, writers. A prominent position in cultural life has been assumed by a former pizza-seller from a pizzeria in Toronto, the current Croatian Minister of Defence. He has founded an academy of art in his native village. At frequent auctions, paintings of no artistic value are sold for several tens of thousand German marks. The purchasers are local people. And the artists are local people. At the Christmas auction in 1996 a dwarf plaster figurine of the Croatian President fetched a sum of 80,000 marks.

Over the last few years, the President of the Croatian State, Franjo Tudjman, has produced more enemies than all the fundamentalist groups in the world put together. The paranoid President publishes lists of the names of the undesirable, but at the same time mentions the names of the loyal. He also often distributes medals, and gave several to acknowledged war criminals and one to an acknowledged French writer. In addition to the official lists with the names of intellectuals for the firing-squad, there is an unofficial list going round Croatia. It was distributed by a Croatian neo-fascist group. It is of interest to note that the names of the undesirable are on both lists. The name of the author of this postscript is included in both lists.

In the meantime, the Society of Croatian writers has accepted some fifty new members into its ranks. Croatia now has 536 officially registered writers. Statistically speaking, in proportion to its population, Croatia is a real paradise for writers. In the meantime, only four *enemy* writers have left the society, an event accompanied by rapturous applause at the society's annual meeting. And while the works of the one truly great Croatian writer, Miroslav Krleža, can hardly be found in the bookshops (understandably, it's too large an opus and the bookshops are small!), the Society of Croatian Writers has elected a president to scale. The present president is the smallest living Croatian writer (just over 4½ ft). The tiny president, professor of theory of literature at Zagreb University, member of the ruling party and active admirer of President Tudjman, does not miss any opportunity to stress his great literary-theoretical idea that *writers must be the moral conscience of their people.* And thus, this little literature has at last found a president to scale, just as this little nation has found its *moral conscience.* All to scale.

4

Conversations, or Repairing the Tap in Three Episodes

Opening. A time of war

That the people learn fast is demonstrated by a true anecdote from the Zagreb Dolac market. Immediately after coming to power, the new city political élite took on the task of proclaiming the town of Zagreb a 'metropolis', of changing the names of streets, squares, schools; of redesigning symbols, taking down one set of pictures, flags and coats of arms, and replacing them with others; and of moving the tramlines on one side of the square a few centimetres to the right. And so, as one of the democratic innovations in the redesigning of the metropolis, for a short time a detachment of paid policemen appeared in the Dolac city market. These strong young men in uniform understood 'democracy' in the same way as the new government understood it. Strong and arrogant, they seriously disrupted the established life of the market: the life of shoppers, small retailers, black-marketeers, peasant women from neighbouring villages who sell cheese and cream. (Incidentally, in the opinion of the author of this note, cheese and cream are a serious reason for the patriotic pride of the nation, experienced by some of its other members exclusively as a nation of 'heroes, thinkers, giants of spirit and genius'.)

All in all, when the peasant women saw the strong young men in uniform approaching them, they would signal to one another: 'Run, women, here comes "democracy"!'

Episode one. Public enemy

A few days ago a friend called me from abroad.

'I heard you were in prison,' he said cautiously.

'Me? Prison? Whatever do you mean?'

'Oh . . .' he said, embarrassed. 'So you aren't?'

'No . . .'

'Thank goodness you're not in prison!' said my acquaintance, sounding so disappointed that for a moment I almost felt guilty that I wasn't in prison.

*

What is happening in Croatia, in one of *the most democratic countries in the world*, as the Croatian President likes to put it? And why those anxious questions and why such reassuring answers?

'We're an internationally recognised victim,' my plumber Jura instructed me recently, waving a spanner in front of my nose. 'And there's no way any victim ever can be . . . normal.'

Driven mad by the lengthy, painful dismantling of Yugoslavia, by ferocious Serbian nationalism which has in turn engendered its own, equivalent, Croatian nationalism; driven mad by elections, the change of government, the realisation of the *thousand-year dream of independence* (as those in power in Croatia put it, and the citizens of Croatia obediently dream); exhausted by war against an enemy (only yesterday a friend and brother!); crazed by ruins, corpses, massacres, lost territories; paralysed by fear in face of the fact that it is at last a recognised, independent, European state which ought to take responsibility for its actions; crazed by this sudden freedom, ready to overlook the lack of judgement of its democratically elected government; tormented by paranoia which may perhaps have been induced by others, but which it continues zealously generating itself; exhausted by uncertainty, ever deeper poverty and general chaos; crazed by both the media war and the real war, by isolation, by its own lies and those of others, by the continuing uncertainty between war and peace; crazed finally by the lack of a clear programme for the future, Croatia is most certainly not a normal country. Nor are its citizens normal people.

Just one year old, the new state shows all the signs of un-acknowledged, postmodern madness in which various references are mixed up: references from the museum of totalitarian regimes, references taken from the shattered Yugo-project, references to the Austro-Hungarian historico-cultural myth, from Croatian history (which is becoming ever more distant and ever more glorious with each day), references from the European dream, from the Croatian ethno-museum, from industrial museums displaying rare objects from early capitalism, and so on and so forth. Sometimes it seems that Croatia has knocked its official policy together out of references, twisting their meanings and altering their symbols. And in order to hold it all together, it has glued the components with the strong mucus of national homogenisation, national myth and military-defensive pride.

This *postmodern dictatorship* – which its citizens are not and cannot be aware of at the moment – is the political strategy of a country which is fighting for its future, which is attacked both from outside (by the Serbs) and from within (oh, those Serbs again!). Dictatorship under the guise of democracy or democracy under the guise of dictatorship is the only strategy of official Croatian policy aimed at restoring the ruined self-confidence of the hysterical and tormented country. All its citizens join together in the task of restoring its ruined self-confidence and all methods are permissible!

In a hysterical, paranoid situation like this, it is quite natural that citizens who express doubt – even if it is only an insignificant number of journalists, writers, university professors, artists – should be proclaimed *public enemies.* In view of the fact that Croatia has declared democracy *a public enemy* – a newly revived reference from the totalitarian age – such an enemy will have somewhat different treatment from a simple prison sentence. Other, subtler tactics will be used to deal with the *disinclined.* Today the most widely adopted and most popular tactic is that of the *media lynch.* In harmonious unison, the media (almost all under the control of the ruling party), journalists (mostly in the service of the government), and even ordinary citizens (who believe what their media tell them) round on their chosen victim, passionately and fiercely. Current tactics include the victim's quiet removal from public life, administratively justified removal from their post, public molestation and marginalisation not only of the private individual but of his or her professional or artistic work. One common procedure is, of course, accessible to all: ostracism. There is nothing more exhilarating than hatred of an enemy for which we need not have the least sense of personal guilt!

'So, what was it you had to go sounding off about?' asked Jura, my plumber and political adviser.

'The truth,' I said.

'We don't need the truth, we need peace,' said Jura. And he's right. About needing peace.

For the West European liberal who deals with such stereotypes as *repression, censorship, freedom of speech and the press, human rights,* the situation in Croatia will look bleak. For Americans who remember McCarthyism these tactics of public lynching, black lists and ostracism will be more recognisable and seen as transient. Is the situation in Croatia really so bleak? There are two good reasons for optimism, of which one is 'philosophical' and the other statistical. We live in a postmodern age, everything is simulation, everything is reference, even dictatorships. And then, in Croatia, which has four and a half million inhabitants, a mere ten *public enemies* have been publicly identified: feminists, women journalists, women writers, sociologists, actors, university professors. What's happened to the anonymous enemies, I don't know.

'The production of public enemies is an excellent therapeutic exercise for the frayed nerves of the wretched people,' said Jura, my plumber, cheerfully, waving his spanner.

Lastly, I am one of those ten. I chose the wrong time to speak the truth, that's all. Now I find someone rubbing up against my name in the papers every day. I don't get upset, why should I, I am *a public enemy*.

'At least your life isn't boring,' says Jura. And he's quite right. Every day I'm shaken by some anonymous telephone voice, I often find anonymous notes in my letter-box. *Get out of Croatia!* anonymous Croatian citizens advise me. I don't react. Why should I? I'm not in prison! . . . Although I sometimes feel I'd be better off there. I wouldn't keep bumping my head against the ambiguities of postmodernism. It would be more peaceful. And I wouldn't be able to get out.

Episode two. Mr President

There was a postcard waiting for me in my letter-box. *Bridge between Croatian dreams and reality, between longing and fulfilment, between all the social groups and regions of our lovely homeland. HDZ – zna se!!!*[1] The three cheerful exclamation marks gave my flagging spirits a lift; the bright, confident 'of course' restored my self-esteem to an acceptable equilibrium.

When I go out I am followed everywhere by the gaze of my President from enormous posters. His eyes are screened by spectacles, but his gaze penetrates the glass and darts straight into mine. Wherever I go, to the left or the right, whichever way I turn, his eyes look straight into mine. And I feel that he knows

[1] The HDZ (Croatian Democratic Union) is the ruling party whose leader is Franjo Tudjman. Its initials are pronounced HaDeZe. The slogan 'zna se' which rhymes with these initials means literally 'it is known', 'of course', 'it goes without saying'.

everything, there is no way of his not knowing, so all-present is my President T.

I like the first letter of his surname. The first letter reminds one of a bird spreading its wings. The powerful letter T! T-t-t – the tip of the tongue taps the palate, flaps like a fish on dry land, T-t-t – the tongue taps the palate driving out air in little, muffled bursts of gunfire. Te-te-te – HDZ – zna se!

I like my newly elected President. I like it when he is made honorary citizen of our cities, Zagreb, Zadar . . . Although, I think, it isn't much, where are the other cities, Rijeka, Pula, Osijek, Split, where is Dubrovnik, I think, heaven knows we have plenty of cities, big ones and small ones.

I am impressed that my President is a doctor of philosophy, an academician, a scholar, a *historian*, as he says himself. I am impressed by the way he speaks, the way he dresses, how benevolently he watches over his people from posters, from stages and television screens – mildly but firmly. Ever since we elected him, I have been regularly cutting out all the news about him, my study is filling up with press cuttings, more and more with every day.

'As we have learned from the general secretary of the IV World Triennale of Ceramics, Hannibal Salvar, and from the Association of Applied Artists of Croatia, it has been confirmed that the President of the Republic, Dr Franjo Tudjman, will be the patron of the world-famous exhibition of contemporary ceramics. The World Triennale of Ceramics is the most important international gathering (on a small scale) and the best-known among ceramicists throughout the world.'

I read little news items like that ten times a day, there are plenty of them, there's something every day. As I read I run my tongue over my favourite words: *most important, best-known, world-famous* . . . The only thing that bothers me is that *small scale* . . .

I like the way he expresses himself, so clear, so concise, and yet so rich. I like the sincerity of his statements.

The nation is just a big family, says my President and leader, for instance. *If a person in a family wants to get more, then he must contribute more to that family, both by his behaviour and his work. That is how it is also with the nation . . . All of a sudden you have democratic rights, so you think you can do what you like! Ah, but you can't! In our openness to all freedoms and to democracy, there have been some phenomena which have no place here and to which we shall not be reconciled.*

That's right, I think, we shall not be reconciled! But then I feel a sudden misgiving, what have I contributed to make things better for my family, my nation, I wonder? I have written a few books. So what, so has the President. He's an academician, and I'm not, his books are thick, and mine are thin. He had already published a book when I was just starting school, a thick volume, about the partisan war. Nor did he flag later: he wrote all those wonderful books with those seductive *great ideas and small nations* in their titles.

I don't know why, but when the President speaks I always have the feeling that he is addressing me, personally. A few days ago he was talking about intellectuals. Some spiteful, uninformed Western journalists had written that the President persecuted intellectuals, which, according to our newspapers, made our President laugh, 'declaring that this was a laughable accusation' and that such tales sprang from 'among the pharisees, who had not understood anything, who based their judgements on themselves, without any faith in their own nation and its intelligence', and that it was laughable that such calumnies should come from those who had 'served the old, communist and Yugo-unitarist regime'.

The President is right. I myself lived in the communist regime, did I serve it, I wonder in alarm. I must say that I am a little perplexed by the fact that our new state is only two years old and that consequently its citizens are older than it is itself, and therefore all of them, including our President himself, must have lived in the old communist, Yugo-unitarist system. Admittedly, they lived in it only physically, never in spirit. That goes some way to justifying them.

I'm glad that our President spoke so fiercely against the pharisees and quasi-people, because ever since the new Croatian state was formed, 'the new Croatian democratic authorities' gave everyone 'the freedom to write'. Those are the President's words, and that's the truth. Because when I come to think about it, before I wrote my books in 'non-freedom', and who knows who for, whereas now I write them in freedom, I write them in my family and for my family, for my nation, for President Tudjman, to please him, to convince him that I'm not one of those pharisees and quasi-people.

Many people do him down spitefully, him, that 'genius of Croatian thought', that 'man for all times', 'the architect of the defence of Croatia', as it was so well put recently in 'the cathedral of the Croatian spirit' (that's what people call Croatian television since our emergence from 'the prison of nations'). They do him down by writing against him and his ruling party, they do him down because they are envious; they are envious because the nation freely expressed its will by voting for him and his party, and not for them. There, that's what pains them, those traitors and pharisees, it pains them because they live in the most democratic regime in the world, they'd like the communism they were used to, they'd like totalitarianism, and not democracy. And those foreigners, who bluster and write that freedom of the press in Croatia is a catastrophe. What do they mean, catastrophe, we've got everything, television and newspapers, what more do they want!

I'm sorry for our President. I'm sorry for the man who dragged us out of the mire of communism, out of the 'prison of nations' into the light of freedom, independence, sovereignty and democracy. What do they all want? He's even given his guards wonderful red uniforms to wear and now it's all lovely and red outside the Assembly, like in a Denmark or an England. It's not grey any more as it was under communism. And he's bought two aeroplanes, and now he flies to and fro; it's not as it was before, when one could barely walk anywhere, let alone fly or sail.

As a writer what impresses me most is the President's sincere inclination towards art. He regularly attends first nights at the theatre, he marks the death of every artist with his personal condolences on television, and if the artist is exceptionally important then the President appears in person at the funeral.

Thanks to the President, artists, especially writers, now become members of the government, some go off to be ambassadors, in New Zealand and such distant places. I don't regret not being one of them, I've done nothing to deserve it. I'm glad when my fellow writers give him their books, when they have their photographs taken with him and when the pictures appear in the papers, I'm glad about that. Let people see the strength of the written word.

And yet there are some people who do him down from that, artistic point of view. Immediately after he came to power, the

President had a fine monument built in Istria, the 'Bird of Croatia', a symbol and a work of art, all in one monument. And then some malicious people put explosives under the bird. 'It is symptomatic that the stone bird of Croatia, with the Croatian coat of arms, should be blown up and "This is Italy", "This is Serbia", even the remnants of some sort of Yugoslav flag should be sprayed on to it,' commented the President when the sculpture of the 'Bird of Croatia' was destroyed. 'This act of barbaric destruction of a monument has its political dimension which is in keeping with the undermining of the integrity of the unity of Croatia, even this act of sabotage must be understood as the act of a criminal,' said the President. And he was right, it certainly had a political dimension, it presumably wasn't an artistic act. All those saboteurs and traitors, although they are an insignificant little group, and thank goodness they are, otherwise it would all be blown up, the freedom we've gained, and the democracy we've finally fought for and won.

That's what I'm thinking about while my plumber Jura is fixing the tap in the bathroom. I don't regret it, although the tap does cost as much as my monthly salary; I've changed the last 100 marks of my savings, but I don't regret it, I say, because from now on I want everything in my house to be orderly, I want to have the right to say in my new democratic state, not only that I am a Croat, but that I have a tap that doesn't drip as it did under communism . . .

'What would you like to drink, Jura?' I ask my plumber.

'HDZ – zna se!' says Jura cheerfully.

That good-natured 'zna se' cheers me up. Brimming with the spirit of warm, national togetherness in which everything is known, in which everything is clear and everything is foreseen, I bring Jura a beer.

'Did I guess right?' I ask Jura.

'Of course, OZNA sve dozna,'[2] says Jura, taking a swig of beer from the bottle.

Episode three. Forgetting

I don't know when I first noticed. Perhaps it was two years ago,

---

[2] Since 1945, the secret police were known by the acronym OZNA. My plumber Jura made an acoustic connection between the old catchphrase of former communist times 'OZNA sve dozna' ('OZNA gets to know everything') with the new, democratic, ruling HDZ party and its popular slogan 'zne se' ('HDZ – of course!').

when we declared our independence, perhaps last year when we actually became independent. Perhaps it was when this war began, perhaps it was far earlier than it seems to me now, I don't know. All sorts of different times have somehow got mixed up, I often can't remember what came first and what was later, I sometimes feel I'm living in a time that has already been, sometimes in one that has yet to come.

The hardest thing to bear is that I often can't remember the names of my friends, those who now live in other states, in Bosnia, in Serbia . . . If someone from Bosnia turns up in Zagreb and I want to ask them for news of my friend . . . The name is there, on the tip of my tongue, but I can't get it out, I can't remember it. 'Is he alive?' I ask. 'Who?' asks the person from Sarajevo. I blush deeply, I don't know where to look. And then I console myself: my temporary amnesia must be the result of some profound inner shame.

I walk through my city. Everything's the same, nothing's changed, the occasional new statue, the occasional new shop. The only thing that's different is that instead of the striking number of photographs of Tito there used to be, now there are pictures of the Croatian coat of arms everywhere, in the same offices, shops and restaurants, exactly the same size, in exactly the same place. It's just as well they're the same size, I tell myself, at least you can't see the dust marks, otherwise think what all that paint would cost. The streets have changed their names: the Square of the Victims of Fascism has become the Square of our Great Croatian Forebears, Republic Square is Ban Jelačić Square . . . Never mind, I'll learn, I think, but I notice with horror that I can't remember either the old or the new names. And I become very anxious: I'll have to learn, I'll buy a new map of the city, I'll learn the streets, because if I need something, a doctor, or a lawyer, how will I find them . . .

I walk through my city. I used to have a regular route and places where I always stopped: a publisher for coffee and a chat, a bookshop to browse through the latest publications . . . I feel anxious again, for a moment I think I've got lost, the editor has become the Deputy Chief of Police, and the bookseller is different. There are new people in all the old places, old people in all the new ones. I don't recognise anyone any more, I don't remember anything any more.

*

But my mother remembers things. She's a pensioner, she whiles away the time watching television. She says she remembers television programmes, the old ones, Yugoslav ones. She keeps mentioning some series or other, made in Belgrade, some actor or other, from Belgrade.

'Hush, mother, they'll say you're *a representative of the Yugo-Chetnik, Bolshevist-Communist band, a remnant of the former non-national regime!*' I say and observe with satisfaction that I have learned something.

My mother has a satellite aerial: she sometimes switches to a Belgrade channel. Only she turns the volume down. So that the neighbours don't hear. But still, a little while ago she let a neighbour into her flat without thinking, and forgot to change the channel.

'So, you're watching those dreadful Serbs!' the neighbour screamed.

'I'm just analysing the enemy propaganda machine,' my mother replied calmly.

'*The war is a black hole.*' That's what some child wrote in a piece of school work. For days I've been trying to remember various things, fragments come to the surface, gleam and vanish. Then I'm plunged again into a black hole of oblivion. The war has sucked up and carried off into the darkness not only houses, towns, people, but even remembrance of our former country. It only took two years for what was definitively destroyed to be definitively forgotten. And it's not only the war that's done it. The new masters of forgetfulness have been working at it hard. Yugoslavia was *a prison of nations*, they say, and it's natural that one should try to consign life in a *prison* to oblivion for ever. Besides, what is there to remember from a prison?

The name of the *prison* is banned now. The word *Yugoslavia* has been erased from all textbooks, readers, encyclopaedias, titles, maps . . . Even the nautical handbook has been altered in just one year! An expensive business, but well worth it.

People around me often accuse me of suffering from *Yugo-nostalgia*, or of being a *Yugo-zombie*. They're wrong, they've no idea how wrong they are. Because nostalgia implies remembrance, and I've forgotten everything, I've even forgotten the Cyrillic alphabet. *Yugo-zombie* is more like it. I've forgotten all the old things, but I haven't learned the new ones either.

'Jura, can you tell me the beginning of a Macedonian song?' I test Jura, my plumber.

He immediately comes out with a first line.

'What about a Slovene one?'

Again, not a second's hesitation.

'And a Bosnian one?'

Not a moment's pause.

'How come you know all that, and I've forgotten everything?'

'I'm an old dinosaur,' says Jura, laughing.

The builders of the new state, the new masters of oblivion, are eliminating everything that reminds people of the old country. Of course, the Serbs, our enemies, are doing most of the destroying, but our people are doing some as well. An eye for an eye, a tooth for a tooth, the black hole of oblivion will suck us all in. The Serbs are destroying towns, churches, bridges, dams; our boys are destroying Serbian villages, Serbian houses and monuments, the partisan ones of course. They mined one in Bol on the island of Brač. 'The dinosaurs died out because they couldn't adjust to the new climate. I'm confident that the last dinosaur is departing with the departure of this monument from Bol,' the local official, a man of the new times, told the newspaper.

'Jura,' I turn to my plumber, jolted suddenly, who knows by what or why, out of my permanent amnesia, 'what was the name of that dog of Tito's, the one which saved his life in that . . . war of national liberation?'

'Marx!' replies Jura instantly.

And I suddenly feel better. Not because I care at all about Tito and his dog, of course. But the dog was called Luks!

And as we drink beer from bottles, my plumber Jura and I begin quite spontaneously to sing: *'The savage has a bow and arrow – railway, city, soil – long live our country wide and narrow – long may we live to toil.'* I used to sing that song in my school choir. It's strange that Jura knows it too, though.

'Why did we remember that, Jura?' I ask.

'Because nothing has changed,' says Jura.

'Then why have we forgotten everything?'

'For the same reason,' says Jura.

March 1993

Closing. Still a time of war

'Večernji list' (Evening News), January 1994: copy of the 'bird of Croatia'

'Professor Šime Vidulin, representative of the Croatian Chamber of Commerce in the regional centre, Pula, the creator of the monument 'Bird of Croatia' which was blown up in Istria, has made contact with the stonemason Blaže Štambuk from the island of Brač, who is making a copy from the model of his work, in order to give the stonemason whatever help he needed. Professor Vidulin stresses that at this moment we need a great many 'Croatian Birds', as a message of peace and freedom. In addition, the artist from Istria notes that stone from Brač and Istria has decorated space and objects in all the continents of the world since time immemorial, and we should continue to fight for stone-work to remain a glorious tradition of the Croatian state, because stone is the real enduring material of our history.

5

Culture and Gunpowder

Because We're Just Boys

1.

If a foreigner turns up in Zagreb, the 'metropolis' of the freshly baked European state of Croatia, and particularly if he turns up on a Saturday morning, he will be startled by a scene which he would probably more readily associate with some Far Eastern city rather than a European one. On Saturday mornings the main square in Zagreb is filled with men. Men stand, often with newspapers in their hands, smoking, talking, strutting importantly up and down, smiling cheerfully at one another, patting each other on the back, the younger ones giving each other friendly shoves or hugs, all pattering about like a flock of penguins. If the foreigner directs his gaze towards one corner of the square he will see steps leading up to a flat space. That is Dolac, Zagreb's main market. Up and down the steps go women with serious expressions, carrying plastic bags of groceries. These are the female inhabitants of the new European 'metropolis', hurrying home to cook the Saturday lunch.

2.

This picture belongs to typical Yugo-imagology, and it is immaterial whether it is associated with a Zagreb, Belgrade, urban or rural, Catholic or Orthodox, 'Western' or 'Eastern' setting. It is so general and so *natural* that during a primary school sex education lesson (in the communist period, of course; nowadays they teach catechism) a teacher was stopped in her tracks by a question. As she was displaying drawings of the naked bodies of a woman and a man and explaining their sexual features, a child interrupted her anxiously:

'But where are the mummy's plastic bags?'

For the child a bag of groceries in a mother's hand was a relevant gender marker.

3.

Yugo-man, the male inhabitant of the former Yugoslavia, hardly exists in the singular. He is rarely an isolated instance, a person, an individual, he is most frequently a group of men. Yugo-man is brought up in a group, he grows in a group, he lives in a group, he dies in a group. The male group is his natural habitat, without it he flounders and expires like a fish on dry land. 'Because we're boys by the bar, meeting over a jar' goes the chorus of a popular Zagreb song. It seems that Yugo-men stroll through life mentally holding hands. And that's why contemporary supporters of masculinism, in their search for a lost male identity, need not travel to New Guinea. Tried and tested male identity is here, right in front of them.

4.

In the Yugo-male mindset one of the most important places belongs, of course, to woman. The 'image' of woman has not been tarnished by either the political changes brought by the Second World War (in which women, for the most part highly educated, participated on an equal footing with men in the partisan movement), or almost fifty years of socialism (which made men and women equal, at least in law), or the dominance of women in some fields (education, medicine), or their presence in public life (journalism, universities, the arts), or the phenomenon of feminism, or the so-called democratic changes, or even the new war. In this male mindset woman has the fixed, unchanging status of an inferior being.

5.

Women's status is securely marked by language. The colloquial synonym for a woman, and it has a long tradition and wide usage, is 'pička' (cunt). There is another colloquial expression in equally widespread use: 'pizda'. But while 'pizda' can refer to a man, a weak, unreliable person, a 'bad lot' (a man who behaves like a woman in other words!), 'pička' can be used only of women. These colloquialisms are so widespread and frequent that they have lost their offensive connotation, and are used even by women themselves.

When asked, in an interview for the *Village Voice*, what democracy meant to him, the writer and Yugo-male Milorad Pavić replied that democracy was 'pičkin dim'. As the journalist did not know what this meant, Pavić repeated bravely in his halting English:

' . . . A smoke of the cunt!'

'Cunt smoke' is the commonest Croatian and Serbian expression for nothing, for something non-existent. When people who communicate in these languages want to say that something is entirely worthless, they use the poetic image of the female sexual organ with smoke rising from it.

If Yugo-man wants to issue a serious threat to someone, he will again think of the female sex ('You'll get it in the cunt!'); if he wants to say that a person was as silent as the grave, he'll say 'He was as silent as a cunt'; and if he wants to boast that he gave someone a beating, he'll say 'I thrashed him like a cunt!'

6.

The treasury of famous Yugo-humour (where ethnic, national, cultural and religious differences play little part) is reinforced by the repetition of jokes to the point of exhaustion of teller and audience. The foreigner will interpret the telling of jokes as a form of perversion which has the technical title of 'coprology', and the status of a social game or convention in the Balkans. In these jokes woman has just one role: the role of her own sexual organ.

7.

If our foreigner wanders off to the suburbs or to a provincial town he will not be able to avoid noticing something: numerous posters advertising male and female singers of popular or traditional music. The male population seems to lie in wait for the appearance of a fresh poster. As the cursed 'homo deflorans', Yugo-man cannot resist intervening in space. The next morning the woman's face will be adorned with a moustache, attacked by masses of drawings of penises and crude comments. The posters of men's faces do not offer remotely the same satisfaction. The first thing the observer will notice will be the unconcealed self-satisfaction of the penetrating male hand.

8.

If we show our imagined foreigner some fifty films from the (former) Yugoslav cinema, he will be amazed by many things, but out of the whole accumulation of shots he will pick out the rigid and unchanging 'image' of woman. For fifty years Yugoslav films were made almost exclusively by male directors and together over the years they hammered home one single female character. Seen from that perspective Yugoslav films reveal the profound and discouraging truth about the way Yugo-man sees women. In these films women are violently raped (there is one favourite shot, used hundreds of times, of a woman's torn clothes and a woman's breast with a hairy male hand covering it), slapped (another favourite shot: a man's hand against a woman's cheek), beaten, ill-treated in various ways.[1] The old-fashioned pair of opposites – *virgin and whore* – will often be replaced by an even more old-fashioned one: *mother and whore*. Over the years, with insignificant deviations and sub-variants, the system of male stereotypes has become fixed between the 'old mother' and the 'young whore'.

9.

The foreigner, to whom we have first shown the retrospective exhibition of Yugoslav films and then documentary testimonies of women raped in the war, will, I imagine, be confused. And however hard the local men try to prove that the purpose of the appalling sexual terrorism practised by the Serbs was to humiliate 'our' women, the foreigner will more readily associate the real rapes with the general cultural attitude to women in the Balkans, exacerbated in times of war.

In the Yugoslav lands, regardless of its treatment in law, rape was never considered a serious criminal act. If they were reported and brought to trial, which rarely happened, rapists would be given a few months' jail sentence and that would be the end of the case.

It was this practice that gave rise to the popular anecdotal advice to women: '*If you are raped, it is best to relax and try to enjoy it.*' This anecdotal advice is usually related cheerfully by men and listened to with dull resignation by women.

---

[1] In a film made a few years ago by a Montenegrin director, the rural, patriarchal-pornographic tale is resolved in a scene in which the Yugo-man kills his wife by crushing her head with an enormous stone. The woman obediently lays her head under the stone.

10.

When a young Yugo-male wants to tell his male herd (and he does so often) that he made love with a girl the previous night, he will say: 'I shot her a bullet!'

11.

We could acquaint our foreigner with an anthology of selections from Yugoslav literature which are not infrequently textbook examples of misogyny and patriarchalism. We could introduce our foreigner to our mass-media culture, popular culture, cartoons, newspapers, to women's magazines, and then to statistical data. We could take him through political institutions, through editorial boards, we could oblige him to watch television, to visit publishers . . . Everywhere, both before and now, on the left and right, west and east, south and north, our foreigner would see the same scene: warm, friendly male togetherness, with the shadow of a woman somewhere in the corner: a silent secretary, a silent cleaning-woman, the silent companion of the loud Yugo-male. The one place he will meet only women is in children's playgroups. Let's add a small boy with wet trousers wailing, 'Mummmyyy . . . Look what I've done!' to the picture. Not because this little addition is necessarily authentic, but because we need it for the sake of another truth.

12.

And why have we thrown a thoughtful, ideal foreigner into the story at all? Because it seems that both the male and female inhabitants of the Yugoslav lands have become so accustomed to their cultural surroundings, their everyday reality, their unwritten rules, that they are no longer capable of registering their abnormality.

'It's your duty to write about the rapes carried out by the Serbs against your "sisters", Muslims and Croats,' said a colleague of mine recently, stressing the word *duty*.

'But wasn't it your "brothers" who did the raping?' I asked.

My colleague stared, open-mouthed. That simple thought would never have crossed his mind. I believe he is still convinced that it is my duty, because, for God's sake, rape is after all . . . 'women's business'.

13.

Talking with Yugo-men before the war, our imagined foreigner would have been amazed at the readiness with which men talked about two things. In their conversations, men always enjoyed recounting events from their army days, even if they had happened ten years earlier.[2] The other subject was sexual exploits in which Yugo-men enjoyed exaggerating their own sexual prowess and mocking the sexual impotence of others, 'fairies'. In this Yugo-mythology there was a myth that the Croats 'couldn't do it' the way the Serbs and Montenegrins 'could'. Serbian Yugo-men found support for their thesis (that Croats were 'fairies'), in language, that is in Croatian colloquial synonyms for the word 'penis'. the male pack (army, sport, pub, workplace, etc.) and sex – those were the two priority areas in the life of Yugo-men.

The war simply activated what had always existed in the male mindset. Jokes and anecdotes at the expense of the (former) army were replaced by war heroism, 'manliness', tests of courage, and stories of invincibility in the field of the bed shifted to the battlefront. War and sex were richly intertwined. Weaklings came to be called 'poofters' ('poofter' is the wartime synonym for a coward). *Hrvatski vjesnik* (*The Croatian Herald*), a provincial newspaper, is full of homosexual pornographic caricatures in which the 'poofters' are, of course, Serbs. An identical war-pornographic male slang is in use on all the warring sides. The traditional war-pornographic rhetoric is confirmed by the names of weapons (often women's names), war photographs (a fighter with his rifle sticking out, a soldier embracing the barrel of a fieldpiece) and the subculture of war (cartoons, 'literature', jokes, humour). Propaganda usually projects war as an attractive, exciting male adventure, less often as a holy, ascetic struggle for the homeland. 'War is shooting and shagging, screwing and killing,' a returnee from the front is purported to have announced.

[2] The publication *War, Patriotism, Patriarchy*, recently published by the Centre for Anti-War Action in Belgrade, the authors of which are women, is concerned with an analysis of school textbooks. The analysis of readers for primary schools shows that there are four times more texts about war than peace (66.4 per cent to 15.6 per cent). In numbers of pages this relationship is even more unfavourable (89 to 5.7 pages).

14.

In the male concept of war there is, of course, also the homeland. The homeland is, as always, a feminine gender word. On an abstract level, she is the 'mother' ('the mother country'), and on a practical level, she is a large bank for the laundering of all kinds of 'dirty money'. But that's how it is in every war.

The dusty, outmoded rhetoric of patriotism continues to demonstrate its effectiveness. No one has written so many outmoded patriotic poems as contemporary poets on all the warring sides. The homeland ('You are my love, my holy Croatia', goes one Croatian line) is still the tormented mother, the holy mother, the Virgin Mother, whom 'the murderers' (foreign men!) have dishonoured, soaked in blood, and so on and so forth. The homeland, of course, forgives everyone everything. 'Mummmyyy, look what I've done!' And the homeland smiles tenderly, takes her little boy on her lap and 'There, there, it's all right . . .'

15.

The homeland-mother is abstract, the child (now father, now child) is concrete. The day after the Serbian 'leader', Slobodan Milošević, announced in an interview that his wife was a bad cook, some 200 women offered to go and cook for him.

16.

If someone gave me the chance to select the most terrible scenes of the twentieth century, the short-list would certainly include the television broadcast of a sitting of the Serbian (rump Yugoslav) parliament. The parliament was filled with men: ageing, overweight, mostly with puffy faces, mostly pudgy, all somewhat seedy, sweaty, with loose ties and half-unbuttoned shirts. At one moment the man standing on the rostrum made a blunder, by throwing a scrap of rolled-up paper at another who was sitting in the body of the house. At that moment it was as though an invisible magnet drew the faces towards the camera. Dozens of male faces looked at the camera and . . . grinned. Those faces *must have known* that their soldiers had been destroying Sarajevo for months, that they were raping, killing, burning, they *must have known* that Croatia and Bosnia had been destroyed with their blessing. They were the faces of the democratically elected representatives of those who were killing, but also of those who were rummaging through rubbish bins to find something to eat, or at that moment burying the bodies of their sons. The 'leader' was grinning and the representatives of the people were grinning, and suddenly everything was terribly funny. 'Mummmyyy, look what I've done!' the faces gloated bravely, because they had all 'done it', and there was no reason for them to be individually ashamed, because only adults feel shame. It was a grin of relief: how easy it all is, everything is possible, and who says politics means responsibility, and who says you have to answer to anyone for anything?

For me that television shot of the meeting of the Serbian parliament was like a photograph of a football team kicking around not balls but innumerable people's heads. And the team, 'the boys', were having their picture taken with a cheery grin on their faces.

17.

The people responsible for the war in former Yugoslavia, as indeed for every war, are men. Men invented and provoked the war, men participated in the war.

In the autumn of 1991 women in Sarajevo protested against the war. 'We are women and not nationalities! Generals, murderers!' they shouted, and, in front of the television cameras, the women demonstrated a short introduction to their future deaths. One held up a metal tag with a number engraved on it, showing how they place the tag in the mouths of dead soldiers in order to identify them. A few days later hundreds of women from Croatia and Bosnia set off for Belgrade, where they were to be met by women from Serbia. They were all supposed to go together to the headquarters of the (by then already former) Yugoslav People's Army. The women had only one weapon in their hands: little photographs of their sons. The generals, realising for the first time that women after all amounted to half the population, roughly prevented them from meeting. Soldiers blocked the roads leading to Belgrade and the women returned to their homes humiliated.

The very next day Serbian television showed pictures of weeping Serbian mothers joyfully sending their sons to the army. 'This is the happiest day of my life,' said one of them, wiping away her tears. On the third day other men, Croats, convinced their wives that they had no choice but to send their sons 'to defend the homeland', for 'liberty'. On the fourth day, a group of women from Croatia was shown in a television shot in Germany, in audience with a leading German politician. Instead of little photographs of their sons, this time the women were carrying a large photograph of their President. It was a humiliating scene, no less humiliating than the one that was shown some months later when the man from the big photograph, the President, was handing out medals to the widows and mothers of *brave Croatian knights* who had *laid down their lives on the altar of the homeland*. On that occasion one of them gratefully kissed the President's hand.

18.

One of the best-known theatre and film actresses in former Yugoslavia, a woman from Zagreb married to a man from Belgrade, was accused by the Croatian media of treason against the nation. The actress had written a moving anti-war article for a newspaper. Violent attacks followed; she left the country. For months afterwards the Croatian newspapers carried offensive articles, full of lies, with nude photographs of her, deeply offensive details from her private life, tasteless political accusations. The fury of the media attack could not be quenched. Everyone fanned the flames and brought their own twigs to add to the fire. To be fair, some people came with little pails of water, including the occasional male journalist. At the same time some of the actress's friends and colleagues of a short time before (four of them) recorded a Croatian version of 'Lily Marlene' for a record company. For the boys dying at the front, of course.

19.

About ten years ago, three over-excited young men in the streets of Priština set fire to the skirt of a Gypsy woman who was carrying a child in her arms. The case was reported only in the Slovene press. When asked by a journalist whether she intended to prosecute the men, the Gypsy was surprised: 'It was only a joke,' she said.

20.

In the war, women have lost homes, children, husbands. Women have been raped. First by one lot of men, then often by their own husbands ('No one drinks from a broken glass'), then by the foreign media, and then by the local media . . . At the moment these raped and deserted women and their children are being cared for . . . by other women. Not by men. Men have more important business. I imagine that they sometimes wonder how the money reaching the women from humanitarian organisations all over the world could be diverted, in a legal, legitimate way, to be 'temporarily loaned' for more urgent purposes. For the purchase of 'defensive' weapons, for instance.

21.

The war in Yugoslavia is a masculine war. In the war, women are post-boxes used to send messages to those other men, *the enemy*. And *enemies* who were their *brothers* until a short time before, at that.

'Rape in war is quite a normal thing, it's part of the male psychology, it's irrational, I hope you won't get me wrong, but it's a kind of negative compliment to a woman, an ugly sexual blunder. But what is really monstrous, is the deliberate Serbian impregnation of Croatian and Muslim women! Not mere rape, in other words, but forced impregnation. That's a Nazi concept. And only the Serbs could do such a thing!' said my colleague, a writer, with feeling.

22.

'Only a family with four children can ensure the future of Croatia, especially in the countryside [. . .] The State must take appropriate measures to control the epidemic of abortions! In that area laws from the communist period still prevail. As far as abortion is concerned, we are still living in Serbo-communism,' one Croatian Catholic thinker announced recently.

'I have proclaimed a fatwa,' one Muslim spiritual leader said recently. 'I have told my Muslim women: a minimum of five children! Two for themselves, three for Bosnia!'

23.

When being presented to the Croatian public, one female member of the Croatian Assembly – one of the pathetic single digit percentage (3 per cent) of women in the Croatian Assembly – listed three facts, in order of importance. First, she was the mother of five children; second, she was a Croat by nationality; third, she was a pharmacist.

24.

In patriarchal and misogynist societies, women have established functions, they always *serve some purpose* (bearing children, doing housework, working in the fields); among other things, they serve as a mask of male maturity, responsibility, normality and 'sexual correctness'. I know a story about a male person of a rather unstable nervous disposition. He was not very well off. He got married and they had a child. They did not have a flat. They separated. Things immediately began to improve for his wife.

Recent political events suddenly cast our anonymous protagonist on to the surface where he was transformed into a political figure; he began to make speeches, to travel, to go to receptions, to appear on television, he was on the brink of an ambassador's position abroad. His patriotism was rewarded by a success which overwhelmed him unexpectedly like a deluge of coins from a telephone booth. And everything was perfect, apart from one thing. He didn't have a wife. He was too visible and in the new context this was too glaring a drawback. And our man hastily summoned his former wife back, they got married again, they were given a larger flat. The wife was even pleased at the abrupt change in her social status. The man continued to display his wife as required: as a ticket, a pass, a mask of his own normality. And luckily, the woman was good-looking and . . . his. Everyone liked her. 'The boys', of course. At last it was a happy marriage.

25.

The case of Herak was covered by virtually all the world's newspapers and television channels. In one documentary, in response to the journalist's question as to why he had done it all and how could he have done it, this is roughly what the Serbian rapist and murderer said: 'I never had anything . . .'

26.

One of our freshly baked Croatian politicians wrote a short diary for the Croatian weekly *Danas*, containing his reflections on the theme of the war, the difficult political situation in Croatia, the thoughts of an anxious patriot, but also, lighter, poetic observations on the theme of the town he loved and its inhabitants. So he described a stroll with a friend, the sunny day and the legs of the female passers-by.

'Well and truly shaggy . . .' concluded one of them poetically.

The sentence referred to the fact that spring had come and the women of Zagreb had not yet begun to remove the hair from their legs.

27.

In answer to the question 'What are women?', a small boy replied: 'Women are girls, and girls are rubbish.'

28.

Insofar as Yugo-men (whether the communist, post-communist or new democratic model) dare to say anything in public, they become 'dissidents', 'victims of the system', 'the wise men of the people', 'our most courageous men', 'Croatian Havels' or 'Croatian Rushdies'. If women do the same, they are labelled only . . . 'whores'.

In Croatia, women – journalists, writers, intellectuals – have written against the war, against nationalism and chauvinism, against hatred, against the infringement of human rights, against corruption, against stupidity, against the totalitarian mentality, against rape, against the undemocratic system in Croatia, against numerous mistakes of Croatian politics and the Croatian governing bodies. In 'democratic' Croatia those women have been proclaimed 'traitors', 'women who conspire against Croatia', 'a serious danger', 'women who sell their homeland for their own gain', 'amoral beings', 'a group of unhappy, frustrated women', who have become 'the organisational core of international resistance to and defamation of the Croatian patriotic war', 'women who rape Croatia', 'old maids who persecute Croatia' and finally . . . 'witches'.

The 'Croatian witches' (five selected ones, although there are more) burned for months at the Croatian media stake. Oil was poured on the flames also by some women, colleagues, but the stake was maintained mainly by men, colleagues, 'brave Croatian men' and 'Croatia's wise men'. The 'witches' were supported by very few, the occasional journalist (yes, men!), the occasional friend. And one of the local media executioners publicly expressed his surprise that the Western press had been so concerned about the burning of the 'Croatian witches', when, really, it was just a matter of a media blunder.

29.

The Croatian case has simply confirmed the frustration of Yugoman, this time supposedly transposed to the political level. The witch becomes the most precise mythic image of those frustrations. *The witch* is above all the mate of the *Devil (public enemy Serbs, foreign powers, the Western world*, etc.). She is the wrecker of comfortable male stereotypes, she mocks the male value system and calls it into question, she is a dangerous woman. The contemporary Croatian media case is not an excess but the rule, it is just a louder footnote to the history of quiet Balkan stakes at which *whores* of all kinds have burned: the excommunicated, intellectuals, writers, artists, suicides, the barren, the isolated.

30.

At a public meeting in 1987, Slobodan Milošević uttered the historic sentence: *From now on no one will dare to strike you!* With the instinct of a pedigree leader Milošević touched the infantile pulse of his people. And the children (boys!) rushed forward knowing that their blunder called war would be forgiven. Because only adults are responsible for their actions.

That, of course, is one way of looking at things. Which won't be acceptable anywhere. Because what shall we then do with the international negotiators, political forums, institutions and politicians; what shall we do with our future national histories; what shall we do with the dead, the heroes and numerous victims; what shall we do with the organisations of future states? No, blunders do not make history. And everyone will prefer to favour a different way of looking at things and maintain that they were engaged in a difficult and responsible historical task.

31.

A very popular song (whose author is a man) speaks of a worthless man-mosquito. It ends with an ironic refrain in praise of the worthless male, and a warm, conciliatory, jokey message to women: 'Whatever he's like, hang on to him, don't let him go, he's a man.'

Yugo-men and Yugo-women will go on boiling in their enchanted sado-masochistic pot for a long time. The women will mend what is broken, clear up the rubbish, remove the male shit ('Mummmyy, look what I've done!), wash everything, try to forget, and quietly, as always, withdraw into a corner. (Besides, the damage was done by . . . those other men.) Half the population, the women, will continue to be silent shadows, mummified companions, masks of male responsibility, banks for 'laundering dirty money', mothers, while the other half, the men, will continue their *historical* games. Those games will have serious names: building a state *for us all*, democracy *for us all*, making peace, a future *for us all*.

Farewell, Till the Next War, is the title of a Yugoslav film (made in the second inter-war years). The sentence lodged in my memory for ever. Naturally, I would like to erase it, but I can't because it has been indelibly reinforced by another: our children are our future!

October 1993

Postscript, four years later
The 'Alka', or 'Ring', is a traditional knightly contest played out by male competitors in the Croatian town of Sinj. Dressed in formal robes, mounted on horses and at full gallop, the competitors aim their lances at a metal ring hanging at the end of the course. The highest praise goes to the rider who hits the very centre of the ring. It is worth saying also that the Sinj 'Alka' is the only one of similar local games to have acquired the status of an annual national spectacle. In 1997, Franjo Tudjman became the second honorary 'Duke of the Ring'. The first was Josip Broz Tito.

A certain Dr Petar Vučić explained the meaning of the 'Ring', in the Croatian daily *Vjesnik* (August 1997), as follows: 'The ring is a symbol of the male principle. The basis of the Croatian being is the male ethnic principle. The Croat is a warrior, but also a farmer. The warrior is characterised by the active energy of attack and defence, while the farmer is the ploughman who fertilises the earth. The earth here is the passive, female principle [. . .] The male principle is clearly expressed in the Croatian, but not in the Serbian being. The essence of the Serbian being is self-exile, flight, wandering, which makes the Serbs similar to the Romany and Semitic peoples, nomads and herders, in other words. That part of the Serbian being is not Slav. It is, admittedly, male, but infertile, the libido is of low intensity [. . .] The relationship between the Croatian and Serbian beings may best be expressed by saying that the Croatian principle is creative, artistic and positively male, while the Serbian principle is negatively male [. . .] The Ring connects the conscious and the unconscious, reality and dream, the reality of non-freedom with the dream of freedom. The Ring is the resolution of the conflict between the Croatian 'ego' and the alienated 'super-ego'.

Balkan Blues

Sharing music? Why, can one ever be closer . . .?

B. Pasternak

Balkan Blues
Boris H. is a Bulgarian poet and by all accounts a serious person. I met him a few years ago, abroad, at an important conference about Eastern Europe. Boris laid out his modest possessions before the foreign audience: pipes, flutes . . . Boris would first recite some of his verse, and then, almost with relief, he would begin to explain his primitive instruments: this flute sounds like this, this pipe is played like this. Demonstrating them all to us as well.

I wondered why Boris H. dragged his modest possessions around the world with him, why the sound of the pipes meant more to him than his own verse. Why was this writer not prepared, like all the rest of us, to talk about democratisation in his country, about the freedom of the media, and similar interesting post- totalitarian things.

On one post-conference evening, Boris H. tried to teach me an old Bulgarian folk song. It was about a woman waiting for her husband to come back from the inn. Each line was interrupted by little cries (uuu! iiiiiii!), sighs (uh!), spoken sighs (uh, woe, ah me!). Everyone else's husband has come home, went the song, only her 'old soak' had not, uh, ih, there he is, uuuu, iiiii, stumbling, he misses the house, stretches himself out in the chicken coop, uh, woe, ah me, ishishish, ishishishooo . . .

'What do I want with this? I can't stand folklore . . .' I protested.

'Remember it . . . You never know . . .' said Boris simply.

We met once again, at a similar conference. Boris H. was laying out his pipes again. He reminded me of the modest old ladies, who can still be found in East European markets, laying out all they have to sell: a few wrinkled apples, a sprig of parsley, a bunch of garlic . . .

I can hardly stand folklore, but oddly enough I have not forgotten the song. Sometimes I pull my covers over me and let out little cries in the dark (uuuu! iiii!), I soothe vague anxiety with little sighs (uh, woe, ah me!), I turn it into modest rhythms, I wait for the husband I don't have, I chase invisible chickens (ishishish shooo . . .). It could have been a little Indian song I picked up, I think . . . But there we are, I've only got this Bulgarian one.

Sometimes I lie under my covers trembling, whimpering my Balkan Blues in the dark, driving away my Balkan fever, the fever of the Balkans, with notes I drive away my anxiety, the anxiety of notes, with rhythm I drive away my fear, my fear of rhythm . . .

Tango

One hot summer's day I stopped in the New York subway hypnotised by what I saw. A middle-aged couple was dancing an Argentinian tango, describing around them an invisible circle in which only the two of them existed, the man and the woman, and a dusty cassette player on the ground beside them. The man and the woman were neither ugly nor beautiful, neither young nor old. They were dressed in black, their clothes were tidy but worn, the man's black trousers shone with a greasy sheen. They danced seriously, modestly, without emotion, without superfluous movements, with no desire to please. The crowd around them was becoming steadily larger. I wondered what it was that had made the New Yorkers, who trip over musicians, entertainers and beggars of all kinds at every step, what it was that had made the inhabitants of a city which never stops for a second miss their train and stop by the modest Argentinian tango dancers.

The reason for the hypnotic voyeurism of the crowd, and my own, seems to me to have been the truth of the scene. The dancers carried out their dance as though it were the only thing they knew, they laid out their only possession, performing the rhythm as their deepest intimate truth. The Argentinian tango was their identity card, their fingerprint, their name and surname, their selves.

It was infernally hot in the subway. The olive faces of the dancers were dry, without a bead of sweat. For a moment I felt sweat running down my spine. Theirs, I thought.

Rere

On our way back to Zagreb from the coast, my friend and I chose the longer route. It was the summer of 1990, drivers tended to avoid the shorter route which passed through Knin. When we left Split it was late, but we hoped that we would find a restaurant somewhere along the way and have dinner. Somewhere above Split, on a road which was inexplicably empty, we spotted a village inn with lights on and stopped. The air was sharp, there were bare fields around us, a deserted road ahead, and a bright moon in the sky.

I stepped into the inn first and stopped as though pole-axed, in the doorway. There were about twenty men sitting in the thick smoke of the room. Silence reigned. Twenty pairs of eyes were fixed on mine. Then one of them, the one sitting closest to the door, feeling perhaps that he had the logical right to go first, slowly raised his beer bottle and took a swig. It lasted a long time; the sound of the beer pouring down his throat could be heard. The man set the bottle down just as slowly without lowering his gaze. As though the contact of the bottle against the table had hit a gong, he tightened the veins on his neck, plunged his gaze still more deeply into mine and . . . began to sing. It was a strong, throaty voice which was coming from who knows where, resembling a wolf's howl. The howl was taken up by others as well, staring me straight in the eyes, just like their leader. Their looks did not express anything, it was a dark, unblinking stare.

My friend and I continued our drive. A little further on, out of the dark there loomed, beached beside the road, a large white illuminated boat. It was called *Mirko*. In that deserted, unearthly landscape, on the empty road, the sky with its bright, sharp moon, the men's wolf howl, the boat standing by the road, in that nocturnal journey through my homeland, I sensed madness (real madness was yet to come), that silence when everything congeals in anticipation of the first shot.

It was not until we reached Zagreb that I realised that what I had heard in the inn above Split was the famous 'rere', the men's wordless intoning, the most primitive form of folklore which has survived in the Dalmatian hinterland, in Lika and Krajina. One form of intoning with words is called the 'ganga', this kind of singing is called 'ganganje', and is performed to this day most frequently by men, Serbs and Croats, in Hercegovina. The men sing in a group, their arms round each other's shoulders, the veins on their necks swollen, their faces red, their legs placed wide apart, letting out throaty, strong sounds in a range of two or three notes. One such 'ganga' goes:

> Ganga of mine,
> I would not have you, ganga,
> Had I not been
> Born in you.

As far as the boat was concerned, I did not feel at all better when I discovered that the white vision was not a product of my nocturnal hallucination. Some local really had dragged up an old boat and renovated it like a house. That was its name: *Mirko*.

My personal experience of things identifies the episode described above as the beginning of the war. The montage of disparate scenes ranging from the deeply primitive (the men's wolf howling) and the highly sophisticated (the boat in the deserted fields) simply could not support its component parts. And the image soon burst, the madness boiled over, shattered into sound and rhythm!

Rhythms

In a little note published in the Zagreb *Evening News* on 21 December 1993, I read that there was an exhibition of Croatian national costume in a wine bar in Munich. On that occasion, said the note, the organiser announced that in its own way the exhibition was 'a presentation of what had been suppressed in former Yugoslavia', something with a specifically Croatian flavour. The note did not attract my attention because of the new-style regime speak, nor because of its obvious untruth, nor because of the information that the costumes for the exhibition had been lent by the (formerly Yugoslav and now Croatian!) 'Ivan Goran Kovačić' folklore group. The innocent little text pressed a button in my memory and the whole fifty-year history of Yugoslav daily life dissolved in front of me like a musical text book!

If anything in former Yugoslavia can really be described as abundantly stressed (rather than *repressed*), then it was folklore. For some fifty years, the Yugoslav peoples capered and pranced, tripped and jigged in their brightly coloured national costumes in various formations (*of the songs and dances of the nations and nationalities of Yugoslavia!*), indeed it seems to me now that they did nothing else. And the difference was only in the fact that up to now they had capered together and now each one is capering on his own. The newly proclaimed democratic regimes have fought for the right for nationally and territorially delimited notes and rhythms; the 'repressive' Yugoslav federal regime emphasised a *community* of popular notes and rhythms.

I remember how the teachers in primary school used to madden us with a potpourri of popular songs. We all had to move from north to south: from Slovenia ('My little pony, on paths steep and stony . . .') to Macedonia ('Biljana weeeaaaves white cloth . . .'). *The songs and dances of the nations and nationalities of Yugoslavia* were an integral part of our so-called physical education. Hard-hearted teachers drove us into school folklore groups and choirs. Ethnic identities were forged by stamping, skipping, whirling, twirling, choral singing, pipes, lutes, harmonicas and drums. And we all knew everything: the sound of the 'bajs' from Zagorje, the tune of ballads from Medjimurje, the songs of Dalmatian groups, the words of Slavonian jigs and Bosnian 'sevdalinke', the beat of Albanian drums, the sound of the Serbian trumpet and the rhythm of the Slovene polka . . .

It was as though the whole fifty-year history of Yugoslav everyday life had passed in folklore displays, in the inter-republican exchange of folklore groups, in news of performances by our folklore groups throughout the world. All the socialist countries used folklore as an innocent, parallel ideological strategy which it was hard to resist: the strategy was directed at everyone and everything, the literate and the illiterate (the deaf are after all an insignificant statistic!'). So, for some fifty years, under the cupola of Yugoslavia, that 'repressive' community of nations, the variety of national identities was drummed into its soil through folklore. Probably in order that it should not occur to those same nations to seek something other than folklore – their own state

---

[1] During the national homogenisation of the Serbian people (which was carried out in large part with the help of organised national spectacles, so-called meetings), the political manipulators did not forget the deaf. There was one placard which proclaimed: even the deaf hear the voice of the nation!

or geographical identity for instance. The new states, which promptly proclaimed democracy on the ruins of the old, make use of the same strategic device. First they assured their peoples that their national identity was *repressed* under the *Yugo-communist regime* (the 'musical' phrase of the new age!), and then in return gave them (again!) the freedom of folklore, always an effective opiate. Because the citizens of the new states might have recalled that they were not merely merry nationally autochtonous folklore groups but . . . citizens, political subjects. They might have recalled that thousands of corpses, refugees and cripples were the price they had paid for the right finally to dance 'on their own land' (the 'musical' phrase of the moment!), and the most depressing thing about it is that for the time being all they may do is dance!

The area where music really did forge *brotherhood and unity* (the phrase of former times!) was the broad and democratic stage of pop music. While folklore drummed variety into us, pop music forged unity. That is why the whole country rang with cheerful sound, like a music box!

Today, when ex-Yugoslavs meet – crushed by the amnesiac steamrollers of war and thoroughly rinsed in national brainwashing machines – the most frequent common ground, that still warm terrain of common references, is the history of popular music! They no longer remember party congresses, or years of change, or the replacement of political terminology every ten years, or the years of 'self-management', or the names of political leaders; they hardly remember their common geography and history: they have all become Yugo-zombies! But what they do most often and most gladly recall are the years of festivals of pop music, the names of singers and songs. In other words, they remember the history of triviality poured into verses, rhythm and sound; they remember their common 'musical idiots'. And it is just this culture of the everyday – and not a state or a political system! – that is the source of Yugo-nostalgia, if such a thing exists today. Nostalgia belongs to the sphere of competence of the heart. Just like pop music.

Musical virus

Immediately after Tito's death, the Yugoslav community was crowned with a 'masterpiece' (even 'musical idiots' produce masterpieces!), in the new-style 'folk song' 'Yugoslavia' which the entire country sang ad nauseum, just as though it sensed its forthcoming disintegration. The song gushed out of all the radio stations, television screens, out of the remotest village inns, people hummed it on the street, it resounded at football stadia. The lethargic pulse of the Yugoslav community was quickened by the adrenalin shot of the cheap, folksy anthem.

An acquaintance of mine, an English woman who works in a tourist agency, described a scene she had witnessed. She went to meet a group of English tourists whose trip to Yugoslavia she had organised and was greeted by an unusual sight. Sunburnt, with burning eyes and strained veins on their necks, the English tourists were singing at the top of their voices, 'Jugoslavijoooo, Jugoslavijoooo', joyfully stumbling over such refrains as 'Od Triglavaaaaa, do Vardaraaaa' (which, of course, described the beauties of Yugoslavia and its geographic unity). Enchanted with Yugoslavia, the English tourists promised that they would come again the following year, they demanded that my acquaintance supply them with cassettes and before they left they danced the traditional ring dance![2]

The Rolex watch rhythm
The popular Bosnian singer of new-style folk songs, Nazif Gljiva, contested the first democratic elections in Bosnia as an independent candidate and won a considerable number of votes. 'When I come to power, everyone will wear Lurex suits and Rolex watches,' he proclaimed in the election campaign. Nazif Gljiva did not win. Louder 'singers' won. Now in the ruling bodies of the newly elected governments sit the owners of Lurex suits and Rolex watches. While the people are naked and musical.

---

[2] I recently received a letter from an acquaintance of mine in Belgrade, L.M. Among other things, she mentions a friend of hers who had managed to get her husband out of Sarajevo. *They are of different ethnic origins, they have two children and it was only as a 'mixed marriage' that they were able to get a visa to emigrate to Canada,* writes my acquaintance. *The Canadian Embassy made all the travel arrangements, by bus to Budapest, and then on by plane. That night, in March 1994, it was very cold, the bus set off at 9 p.m. from central Belgrade. There were about fifty of them in the bus, many of them with children, and outside were their relations and friends who had come to see them off, and the inquisitive. When the engine was heard revving up, something caught in their throats. At that moment a voice began to sing 'From Triglav to the Vardar . . . Yugoslavia . . .' And suddenly all of them, in the bus and outside, burst into tears.*

Folksies

What are 'Folksies'? They are the new-style, 'newly composed' folk music, an endemic musical virus. 'Folksies' are the glue of the nations of the former Yugo-space, a common ailment, a mark of mutual recognition, a shared reason for simultaneous sympathy and hatred. 'Folksies' are the bared 'soul of the nation', the heart, the weak spot, a genetic code, collective remembrance reduced to sound.

Today, when the former Yugo-nations are frenziedly cleaning their cultural space of everything *construed* as alien and putting their little, national cultural homes in order; when, for fear of anyone snatching from them what they have acquired, they are founding special commissions for the preservation of the 'national essence', the 'national spirit'; when they are designing that 'essence' in frenzy because they don't really know what it should be, the 'folksies' are, it seems, ours, our *common* trash, ineradicable as desert dust. 'Folksies' are our common hereditary cultural disease, an ironic cultural grimace, they are, perhaps, just that . . . *essence*.

Let us now replace the term 'folksy' with the more refined: 'newly composed folk music'. Let us use the abbreviation NM, gender: feminine. (In the Slovene and Croatian and Serbian and Macedonian and Bosnian languages the word 'music' is feminine.)

So, NM was born in Yugoslavia, she grew up with Yugoslavia, humbly to start with; she entered homes with the first radios, the first fridge, the first television. For years NM and the so-called 'ordinary man' (a verbal mask for the so-called 'people') practised their rhythm of love. NM spoke His language, she sang of His everyday reality, together they established their values. NM suited Him, and He suited her. She sang of His pains: erotic-gastronomic ones ('You left me to cry, you didn't taste my apple pie . . .' wails one line of a folksy); erotic-residential ones ('When at last my mother goes, I can live here with my Rose . . .'); erotic-cultural ones ('On the sheet two red drops appear, proof that you were the first, my dear . . .'). NM did not show off, she didn't speak some high-falutin' language, she did not humiliate Him, her 'ordinary man', nor did she mock Him. She kept her hand faithfully on His pulse and adapted her musical rhythm to the beating of His heart. NM faithfully accompanied His death and burial, His departure to the army, His assignations with His beloved and His breaking-up with His beloved, His marriage, the birth of His children, the death of His parents. NM didn't get involved in politics – why cut off the branch she sat on? In her way she supported the values of the system in which she flourished. Indeed, the loyalty known as patriotism was always His theme. She sang of His region, His village and mountains, individually and locally, and then of His Yugoslavia, globally. NM was thematically wide-ranging, but she made sure that the basic words were the same, comprehensible and dear to Him: heart, mother, dear, home, love, fate, life, friends. NM 'opened her heart', NM was His freedom, He felt most at ease in her company.

The singers, male and female, of newly composed folk music were His idols: the Yugo-dream, a fairy-tale of glory and wealth come true. From the sleeves of gramophone records and cassettes, from TV items, from posters, from the front pages of newspapers and magazines – all around His gods smiled at Him. The female singers, Yugo-Barbie-Dolls, with their tight skirts, cleavages, and high-heeled shoes, were exactly what they actually were: their own preconception of an enticing woman and the fulfilment of His preconception of a 'real' woman. The male singers – with open collars, gold chains round their necks and thick gold signet rings on their fingers – they too lived in perfect, authentic harmony with their 'ordinary men'. They realised their own idea of a successful man (in every sense!) and fulfilled His idea of a successful man (in every sense!). The gods and goddesses of Yugo-mass-culture were His golden reflection. They sprang up in remote village inns, in provincial workers' cafés, at cheap lorry drivers' coffee stops beside trunk roads, they sprang up from the very depths – and were transformed overnight into 'stars'. From being café 'whores' – into whose bras the intoxicated male crowd thrust their monthly wages – the female singers became the unattainable queens of Yugo-pop. It was the 'folksy' singers (and not the communists!) who were powerful, they were the golden raspberry of the regime, of any regime, including the Yugoslav one. Why didn't they leave, if they were so rich? Because of the market. It was only in their 'homeland' that they could sustain Him with their songs, and it was only He, the people, who could sustain them.

NM, that faithful companion of the so-called 'ordinary man' quickly adapted to the political changes and was transformed into a political propaganda, war industry. Like a powerful transformer, NM turned the political ideas of the national leaders into sung synopses accessible to the 'ordinary man'. The mutual permeation of the political and the popular has reached its legitimate height today: the mass cultural stage has become the loudest, and therefore also the most potent means for sending political (war) messages, and political life exactly resembles a stage.

Among those responsible for the war in former Yugoslavia, one of the most important places belongs to . . . the media. One thinks of course of newspapers, television and radio. The newly composed folk music is not to be found on the list of war criminals. The accusation would sound flippant.

Today, when all sorts of things have been destroyed – lives, libraries, schools, priceless cultural monuments – among the ruins, like plastic flowers in a cemetery, the indestructible NM blooms. She, who contributed to the destruction, is now weeping over the ruins; she, who drove sons to war with war cries, now weeps over their graves; in songs sung in refugee camps (at home and abroad), she who produced hatred, now blames 'unhappy fate' for everything. Yes, NM is indestructible!

Our fate is song
Suada Bećirović, alias Suada from Bosnia, who has been living in Western Europe for six years already, has had a hit with her first album. The songs 'A girl from Bosnia', 'I'm coming home, mother dear' and 'What's got into you' are in all the charts, announces *Bosnia Press*.

'Our fate is song,' said Suada for that paper.

A portrait of the king of all the 'gusle'[3] players
Paul Pawlikowski, who made a documentary film about Radovan Karadžić (BBC, 1992), follows the development of the madness of disparate elements with his precise editing. The musical theme of that madness is song, and its representative is the leader of the Bosnian Serbs, Radovan Karadžić. In the film we see the psychiatrist, a doctor of science, a poet and a murderer, holding a 'gusle'

---

[3] The 'gusle' is a single-stringed lute played by folk singers to accompany heroic and epic song. (Translator's note)

and chanting monotonously ('Thirteen captains sit down to drink wine . . .'), and then, gazing sorrowfully over half-ruined Sarajevo, he recites his own poem ('It is still and clear as before death . . .'). We see an authentic highwaymen's lair after a dance of knives (slaughtering sheep!), the intoxicated murderers passionately trip a Serbian ring-dance. We see a natural editorial juxtaposition: the Russian poet Eduard Limonov firing a few shots at Sarajevo, and a warm Serbo-Russian drinking bout. The two poets, Karadžić and Limonov, toast one another and their respective peoples. In one shot we see the fat fingers of another murderer, General Ratko Mladić, drumming on the table, in rhythmic accompaniment to Karadžić's stammering folk rhetoric ('Secret suffering symbolises Serbian faith . . .' says Karadžić poetically into the camera). In just such a 'natural' musical combination we hear a blend of the sounds of gunfire and cheap 'folksies' ('Who is saying, who is lying that Serbia is small . . .'), church bells and mortars.

Karadžić promotes personal madness almost as though it were a common value of the end of the twentieth century. The murderer has himself photographed flying in a helicopter over the Bosnian mountains (with fashionable designer sunglasses on his nose!), telephoning ostentatiously ('Hello, Eagle . . .'); he exchanges his highwaymen's lair naturally for a luxury clothes shop somewhere in Geneva. ('No,' says Karadžić, trying on one coat, 'this makes me look like a policeman.') The murderer exchanges the worn-out iconography of communist leaders at their desks, with the requisite pen or book in their hands, for a more attractive image: the image of the psychiatrist-leader, a doctor of science who does not read or write, but chants in Serbian, recites in English, drums his fingers, chews his own fingers till they bleed and brutally kills.

The ring dance in Pawlowski's documentary film is a symbolic leitmotiv of the Serbian siege of Sarajevo. Karadžić and his murderers – that brotherhood of emphatic rhythms – hold the city in a tight ring ('O lovely Turkish lass/Monks will christen you/Sarajevo in the valley/Surrounded by the Serbs') so that the stamping of their feet should wipe out all trace of other rhythms (Muslim, Jewish, Croatian, but also Serbian). In the end they will tread their ring dance to the glory of the 'heavenly people'. But in order for the people to rise, they will have to be able to liberate themselves of the heavy burden of other people's deaths. That is why the hypnotic 'gusle' will be there to sing of Serbian heroism and heroes for the 'n'th time on the smoking ruins. Among them will of course be Radovan Karadžić, king of all the 'gusle' players.

Radovan Karadžić could not have chosen a more accurate instrument. In regions, especially in Serbia and Montenegro, where the 'gusle' symbolises only 'the heart of the people', Karadžić is, metaphorically speaking, a 'gusle' player who plays on the aforementioned heart.

Today's 'gusle' playing, which has been aimed from time immemorial at the illiterate – so-called 'gusle journalism' – sings of contemporary events, summoning the memory of glorious forebears, with whom the new men stand in an unbroken necrophiliac connection. The heroic forebears are not, of course, anything other than a musical-mythic bank for 'laundering dirty money'. Passing through the 'gusle laundering', contemporary Serbian war criminals gleam with the pure glow of national heroes!

The process of passing through this 'gusle laundering' – i.e. the transformation of a murderer into a hero – is most obvious in the 'gusle' songs about Radovan Karadžić himself. Karadžić is presented as *a man of steel (Oh, Radovan, man of steel, first leader since Karadjordje)*, who has defended *freedom and the faith (You defended our freedom and our faith)*. But where? The location has been changed on this occasion and defence is not currently carried out on the 'field of Kosovo' but . . . on 'the lake of Geneva'!

The singer and the President

In his novel *The Book of Laughter and Forgetting* Milan Kundera writes:

'When Karel Gott, the Czech pop singer, went abroad in 1972, Husak got scared. He sat right down and wrote him a personal letter (it was August 1972 and Gott was in Frankfurt). The following is a verbatim quote from it. I have invented nothing. *Dear Karel, We are not angry with you. Please come back. We will do everything you ask. We will help you if you help us . . .* Think it over. Without batting an eyelid Husak let doctors, scholars, astronomers, athletes, directors, cameramen, workers, engineers, architects, historians, journalists, writers and painters go into emigration, but he could not stand the thought of Karel Gott leaving the country. Because Karel Gott represents music minus memory, the music in which the bones of Beethoven and Ellington, the dust of Palestrina and Schönberg, lie buried.'

The President of forgetting and the idiot of music deserve one another. They are working for the same cause. 'We will help you if you help us.' You can't have one without the other.

The episode Kundera describes is typical and belongs to the common memory of citizens of the former East European social-ist countries. Each of us had his own 'idiots of music', we even shared some of them, such as Karel Gott, in the early days of socialist pop.

The episode which follows occurred twenty-one years later, in the small, independent and democratic country of Croatia. A popular pop singer, who had affirmed herself as a passionate patriot in the political changes and days of war, announced that she would kneel in public before the President and beg him not to give the Serbs her native Konavle. (The Serbs really had plun-dered that area, burned it and aimed their guns at Dubrovnik from the Konavle hills). It was just at that time that the President was snapping furiously at intellectuals, 'enemies of the people'. The Croatian media were burning 'five Croatian witches' at the media stake.

In the case of the singer, the President immediately hurried to write her a nice, warm, open letter. She should not worry, he would not allow it, he would not let it happen, and so on and so forth. The President acted correctly. He replied to the one who deserved it: the woman who sings, the woman who kneels and begs. 'We will help you if you help us . . .'

I add a detail to this episode. At that time, the Croatian (and world) media were brimming with articles about the rape of Bosnian and Croatian women, victims of Serbian gratification. And at the same moment, Croatian music stalls were selling a cassette featuring a cheap 'folksy' with the title 'punish me like a woman'. The aforementioned singer was not the performer of that song. That would have been too much.

The death of a singer

In Croatia in 1993 the pop singer T. I. was killed. He died because he was driving too fast. He hit another car, and killed two other people. At the height of the most dramatic events of the war in Croatia, the newspapers were flooded with the tragic death of the popular singer, composer of the most popular patriotic pop song.

The two other people who were killed by his speeding car were mentioned in passing by their initials in the newspaper reports, and by the second day they had ceased to appear in newspaper comments. The singer and his death were condensed into the honourable formulation: he had laid down his life on the altar of the homeland. The funeral which was broadcast on state television was a true state musical spectacular. Shots of small girls singing, dressed in national costume, were followed by young girls singing Dalmatian songs; Dalmatian male ensembles alternated with a pop group performing a potpourri of songs by the 'genius of Croatian pop music, whose life was so tragically cut short', and these were followed by arias sung by opera singers. In the front row stood the President, overcome by sorrow, together with almost all the members of the Croatian Assembly. The direct transmission of the magnificent funeral had the entire state in tears. The sweet collective emotion transformed the unwitting murderer into a victim who had died a tragic death. After the funeral a group of citizens from the town of Z. wrote in with a request to the Commission for Naming Streets and Squares proposing that a street (which had recently changed its name from that of a national hero to become the street of one of the historical 'illustrious' Croats) now be named after 'the great pop musician'. T. I., ran the proposal, was 'the most eminent promoter of his town which he celebrated in his songs; his compositions had drawn the attention of the whole justice-loving world to the aggression of the Serbs against our homeland and in that way made an enormous contribution to the emergence of the truth among all people who care about justice, honesty and democracy'.

Musical divorce

Neda U. was one of the first stars of the Yugo-pop scene. Her cheap, half-folksy hits echoed 'throughout our lovely homeland'. Neda U. came from Sarajevo, and her songwriter, N., came from Zagreb. In the course of the war, Neda U. became . . . a Serb.

After its regular report from the war zones, the Croatian television screen showed a young singer dressed and made-up like Neda U.

'We've re-recorded all Neda's hits. So that we can restore all our great composer N.'s wonderful compositions to Croatian popular music. So that his music will belong to the corpus of Croatian pop,' said the singer, emphasising the word 'corpus'!

'But you sing just like Neda!' said the TV reporter.

'That's the way to make N.'s music Croatian again,' said the Croatian singer, herself for a moment confused by the complex logic. 'I'll work on developing my own identity later,' she added.

That's the kind of song which torments

'That's the kind of song which torments with its caress. And the more we surrender to that caress, the harder it becomes to part from its torment. The sharp edge cuts ever deeper; just as steel chains dig more deeply into the body the more it resists.

'The finale here is the beginning, nowhere completed, always open. A projection into the unmeasurable. In their initial arrangement these songs cannot "end" at all, and one feels that they ought not to end, to "become what they are". It's the kind of song that gives that special impression: that "after it there is nothing", no life – an inexpressible and indescribable impression. In their monotony and eternal inner sameness, in their plumbing of eternally the same depths, they become ever stronger, deeper, more powerful. That lack of completion is their very essence. And that is why it is inevitable that there should be that constant sense of something "remaining" which can never be experienced but which unavoidably remains.' (Vladimir Dvorniković, *The Psychology of Yugoslav Melancholy*, 1917)

Whine

Sometimes I wonder whether what drove me out of my country was in fact music. That is, the reasons for going into exile are often far less serious than one imagines. After all, if someone can go mad because of their sensitivity to sounds, I don't see why a similar kind of sensitivity (a sense of taste, for instance) could not be the reason for someone to leave their homeland. Be that as it may, every exile often feels that the state of exile is a special kind of constant sensitivity to sound; sometimes I feel that exile is nothing but a state of unconscious musical recollection (which may be agreeable or disagreeable).

One day I went into the centre of Munich to meet my acquaintance Igor, but some distance away from Marienplatz I stopped, drawn to the sound of music. An elderly Gypsy was playing Hungarian Gypsy songs on a violin. He caught my passing glance, gave me a smile that was both deferential and brazen at the same time, recognising me as 'one of his kind'. Something caught in my throat, for a moment I couldn't breathe, and then I lowered my eyes and hurried on, realising a second later that I had set off in the wrong direction. A couple of paces further on I caught sight of a life-saving telephone box and joined the queue, pretending that I had to make a phone call, what else. There was a young man standing in front of me. Tight black leather jacket, tight jeans, high-heeled boots, a kind of insecurity and impudence simultaneously on his face, like colours running into each other. A second later I knew that he was 'one of us', 'my countryman'. The way he slowly and persistently dialled the number – looking neither to right nor left, like a waiter in a cheap restaurant – filled me with a mixture of anger and pity and put me on the side of the people in the queue. And then the young man finally got through (yes, 'one of us', of course!). My countrymen's habit of talking for a long time about nothing, as though coddling, pampering, mutually patting each other's backs and jollying each other along, that habit filled me again with a sudden mixture of anger and pity. The violin was still whining sorrowfully, the young man was talking to a certain Milica, and in my head, as at an editing table, I was joining the whine with the young man's babbling. The black-eyed violinist was staring persistently in my direction. For a moment I wanted to leave the queue, but I didn't, that would have given me away, I thought. That is why, when the young man finished his conversation and smoothed his hair with his hand (a gesture which filled me with the same mixed feelings as before because of its unexpectedness), I telephoned Hannelore, who was the only person I could have telephoned, thinking up some urgent, practical question.

I was late for my meeting with Igor. We went to a Chinese restaurant and as we chatted while waiting to be served, I observed that I was restless, absent, that my eyes were wandering, I felt as though I was covered with a fine film, like spectacles on a winter's day. At one moment I was conscious of a sound which I had not registered at first. There was Chinese or Korean pop music playing, or at any rate pop music from some Eastern part of the world. It was a soft, elegiac, sweet crooning, a love song, presumably, which could have been from my home, or from Igor's Russian home. Just then there was a sudden downpour of rain which streamed down the restaurant window behind Igor, and finally I broke, let myself go, reacted properly, exactly, according to an ancient, well-practised reflex, of which I had not been conscious until that moment. In a word, I salivated at the sound of the bell, that universal, sweet whine, the same whine no matter where it came from . . . I struggled inwardly, resisted, complained, almost glad that I was in its power, almost physically satisfied. Quite softened, I splashed about in the warm invisible puddle of tears . . .

'What's happening, Igor . . .?' I asked him as though apologising.

'I quite understand,' he replied. 'I myself belong to a provincial, tango culture,' explained my friend, a Russian Jew from Chernovitsa, an exile.

The magic qualities of the circle

'I too once danced in a ring,' admitted the Czech writer and long-term exile Milan Kundera in *The Book of Laughter and Forgetting*. 'It was in the spring of 1948. The Communists had just taken power in my country, the Socialist and Christian Democrat ministers had fled abroad, and I took other Communist students by the hand, I put my arms around their shoulders, and we took two steps in place, one step forward, lifted first one leg and then the other, and we did it just about every month, there being always something to celebrate, an anniversary here, a special event there, old wrongs were righted, new wrongs perpetrated, factories were nationalized, thousands of people went to jail, medical care became free of charge, small shopkeepers lost their shops, aged workers took their first vacations ever in confiscated country houses, and we smiled the smile of happiness. Then one day I said something I would better have left unsaid. I was expelled from the Party and had to leave the circle. That is when I became aware of the magic qualities of the circle. Leave a row and you can always go back to it. The row is an open formation. But once a circle closes, there is no return. It is no accident that the planets move in a circle and when a stone breaks loose from one of them it is drawn inexorably away by centrifugal force. Like a meteorite broken loose from a planet, I too fell from the circle and have been falling ever since.'

Ring dance

In the autumn of 1993 my Munich acquaintance Fridel asked me to hold a reading in the 'Yugoslav' centre for mothers and children. There were more women than men at the meeting, given the nature of the venue, and they were all from different parts of the former Yugoslavia.

The evening began late, we had to wait for everyone to arrive, people were at work, you know how it is, the kindly organiser explained. Women arrived with trays and dishes, each had prepared something: cakes, meat, salads, home-made bread . . .

It was in the genre of a small village event: a young man with a guitar sat beside me, I would read an extract, and he would pluck the strings mournfully. Women in the audience shed tears. Then one of them read a poem herself, cursing the criminals who had destroyed her homeland, then another about her native village, her mother and the warm home to which she would never return. The women wept more copiously this time. The young man plucked at his guitar, less mournfully now. The organiser gave me a bouquet. The women clapped and wiped their eyes.

Someone led me away for a moment into another room, I was supposed to talk with goodness knows whom about goodness knows what, and when I came back, the room – where a moment ago there had been the table where I had sat and the chairs for the audience – had been transformed. In the little hall music was now blaring: in addition to the guitarist, an accordion and a 'tambura' player had appeared from somewhere. The women (who had been wiping their eyes a moment before) and some men began to dance the ring dance, the 'kolo'. I looked at those smiling faces, their feet were stamping ever more quickly, their chins were jiggling, their arms firmly gripping each other, as though they were afraid that one of them might fly out of the happy circle. The ring dance, as far as I could judge, was Serbian, but it could have been Romanian, Bulgarian or Macedonian. The choice of national tunes (which were Serbian, Slavonian, Slovene and Macedonian) was incomplete and did not respect the 'Yugoslav principle'. The musical deselection of songs from Dalmatia, Montenegro, Kosovo, Zagorje, Lika and Bosnia was not made according to the 'national key' (the musical phrase of the old days) but was a rhythmical one. The rhythm of those others was simply too slow. Only the rapid rhythm of the 'kolo' could provoke that blank stupor in the eyes of the dancers, which is the result of physical satisfaction.

What it was that my countrymen were driving away with their stamping feet, I don't know. I think that they simply stamped. It was an adrenalin 'kolo', a supernational 'kolo', it was a display of the brotherhood of strong rhythms, as my acquaintance K. puts it. My countrymen used the rhythm to wipe away all meanings and all borders, including national ones and emotional ones (which was frightening). It was an adrenalin 'kolo' danced by dancers with distracted expressions, a 'kolo' in which the rhythm could at any second tip the scale one way or the other, turning into an emotion with a name (shame, joy, tears, laughter, despair, hatred, love) or into an action with a name (an embrace, a murder, a kiss, a rape . . .).

'You know,' said my acquaintance Fridel on the way home, 'they dance more and more often. They get together just to dance. As though *that* is what they need increasingly. As though they can't do without *that*. *That* is something quite incomprehensible . . .' concluded Fridel, and we stopped talking about *that*.

The minor key

'People in our southern areas sing plaintively and always equally plaintively, even for "joy"; not in the "kolo" nor in a jig nor in the most animated wedding dance does the minor key quite disappear, as a musical theorist would say. That inexpressible ballast in the depths of the music will never escape anyone with a musical ear and sensitivity. Even without "sorrow", sorrow is always present, even without lament the elegiac note may still be heard. Why is this so? What is it that these people are experiencing, even if it is *unconsciously*? [. . .] And that this experience of the Yugoslav race really is unconscious may be seen in the fact that it is physiologically built into the very rhythm of the "kolo", and into the wildest drinking song. [. . .] Whether Orthodox or Muslim or Catholic, it is always and everywhere the same, monotonous and desperate in its tedium, always the same song, always verging on . . . sobbing.' (Vladimir Dvorniković, *The Psychology of Yugoslav Melancholy*, 1917)

Weapons peal

The Bosnian paper *Exile* which recently began to appear in Frankfurt publishes pieces by Bosnian refugee children placed in the German town of Viernheim. It includes a poem called 'My homeland of Bosnia and Hercegovina' by a little girl called Amira Osmanović. The last verse goes like this:

> And still Bosnia cannot heal,
> Because you still hear weapons peal,
> They peal, tearing at her heart
> While Bosnia sighs, blasted apart.

The hurdy-gurdy and the drum

Ivan Bunin wrote a poem, 'With a monkey' ('S obez'yanoy'). The poem is about a hurdy-gurdy player and his monkey, and the little scene takes place in a hot Odessa square in summer. In Bunin's poem, for some unknown reason the hurdy-gurdy player is a Croat. All we know about him (because Bunin is more impressed by the monkey) is that he is 'thin and bent, drunk with thirst'. The Croat asks for water and gives it to the monkey (incidentally, Bunin rhymes the word 'horvat'/Croat with the word 'zad'/rear, meaning the monkey's rear, of course!). While the monkey drinks, 'raising his eyebrows', the Croat 'chews dry white bread' and slowly walks to the shade of a plane tree. Bunin ends his poem, written in 1906–7, with the line 'Zagreb, you are far away!'

In 1918, another Russian poet, V. Hodasevich, wrote a poem with an almost identical title, 'Monkey' ('Obez'yana'), completing it in 1919. The little scene, described in Bunin's poem, takes place further north, in the town of Tomilino, on the outskirts of Moscow. The same intolerable heat as in Bunin's poem. The narrator of the poem goes out on to a porch and there, on the steps, leaning against the fence, dozes 'a wandering Serb, thin and dark'. The narrator notices a heavy silver cross hanging on his bare chest where beads of sweat are coursing. The Serb in Hodasevich's poem walks away, beating on a drum. On his shoulder the monkey sways like 'an Indian maharajah on an elephant'. And Hodasevich ends his poem with the simple line: 'It was on that day that war was declared.'[4]

Why Bunin had to make his poor hurdy-gurdy player a Croat and why Hodasevich needed to camouflage his obvious plagiarism with a Serb drummer, I do not know and at the moment I do

---

[4] My attention was drawn to Hodashevich's and Bunin's poems and the similarity of their subjects by Igor Pomorantsev, a Russian poet and essayist.

not care. At the end of this century, I read the poems by two Russian poets from its beginning in my own way. My country-men, 'thin and dark' with their only possessions (a hurdy-gurdy! and a drum!), 'drunk with thirst' serve their master, a monkey; they serve the aggressive and ironic human replica, a grimace of cunning and deceit, an animal in human clothes, which 'raises its rear comically' (Bunin); they both serve a master who rides on them, swaying like 'an Indian maharajah on an elephant' (Hodasevich).

Musical foam

'Do you have any bedtime stories that aren't about the former Yugoslavia?' asked the little boy in bed. His mother was sitting beside his bed, reading to him from the newspaper. This cartoon was published in the weekly, *New Yorker*, on 22 November 1993.

We've travelled our road, and now, from being victims, we've become the heroes of bedtime stories, entertainers of the indifferent world, hurdy-gurdy players, drummers, dark-skinned swindlers, selling our misfortune like street attractions, our misfortune is sold around the world by the managers of pornography like moral and emotional vibrators. We only supply the goods. The only thing we have all failed to notice is that the batteries are running out . . .

In a mere three years we've become the new gladiators, we have sprung up again at the end of the twentieth century to advance technology, it is enough to turn on the television or to buy a newspaper. From the screen 'thin, dark' people pour, performing their misfortune, and, look, they won't stop, there's not a bead of sweat on their brow, how do they have the energy? We beat our drums to the point of exhaustion, we turn the handle of the hurdy-gurdy of our suffering without rest. At first people stop, and then they walk away, bored. What can one do, the effect is lost with repetition: the music is always the same, and the monkey goes on gulping water without ceasing . . .

We massage the weary world's heart, rouse it with increased doses of adrenalin, but we can't get it going. Our pictures are on the front pages of newspapers, we enter the TV screens, they sell us on videocassettes like a life-show: the rapes are real, the tears are salt, the massacres are fresh. What do we not do to acquaint the world with our skill at dying? Like that of Oskar Matzerath, our voice breaks the panes of our own and other people's windows. The heart of the world, a tired sack, rattles dully like a beached whale. And the more real and more perfect our death, the more persistently the world perceives it as a provincial spectacle. The greater our unhappiness, the more persistently the world experiences it as a little village event. The more of us die, the more tedious we become. Now we feature in jokes, we have become 'material', but we've made it to the top: to the *New Yorker*! The height of our rise is equal to the depth of the *New Yorker*'s current fall. We have ended up as street entertainers at the end of the twentieth century, but the twentieth century too is ending as *our* stage. The artistic defeat is two-sided: ours and that of the audience.

But they, the audience, by the very logic of things, will remain, and we shall disappear. For they are deaf, while our hearing is perfect. What is it that has occurred and where is the artistic, if not the human, justice? Perhaps we really have moved (like cartoon characters!) into another dimension, into a fourth world? Perhaps we are no longer alive, as it seems consistently to us, perhaps we are ghosts, spectres who appear at crossroads in Geneva, Paris, London, New York and perform our 'national substance', twanging on the last remaining string, letting out our primitive wail decanted into a 'gusle', pipe or 'tambura' . . . Perhaps we all belong to the brotherhood of strong rhythms, yes, sound and rhythm, that is all we know . . . We spring up like serpent's teeth in all the corners of the world. 'Thin and dark' we tread our phantom ring-dance, our feet stamp out the energy for the continuation of the species, but there is no continuation; we keep sending out our sound signals, but no ear recognises our message. Behind us, up there, nothing but foam remains. Musical foam.

Balkan Blues. Refrain

Boris H., the Bulgarian poet, taught me an old Bulgarian folk song. I can't stand folklore, but the song has stuck to my memory like a musical burr and won't leave me alone . . .

Sometimes I pull my covers over me and let out little cries in the dark (Uuuu! Iiiiii!); I pour my loneliness into short sighs (Uh! Eh!); I howl my Balkan Blues in the dark (Uh, woe! Ah me!); driving away my Balkan fever, the fever of the Balkans, with musical notes I drive away my anxiety, the anxiety of musical notes, with rhythm I drive away my fear, my fear of rhythm . . .

Sometimes I suddenly seem to feel a monkey's paw cold with moisture on my shoulder. And then 'terror engulfs me like a wave . . .'

December 1993

The Tale of the Bomb and the Book

1. The death of the book

A few years ago, when I saw my first real book-eating moths in the glass display case of a museum in Antwerp, I began to think about the death of the book. It was only a fleeting, indifferent thought, I was more attracted by the devourers of books with their dusty wings and beautiful names: *Periplaneta americana, Anobium punctatum, Lepisma saccharina.* My indifference stemmed perhaps from the fact that a book is an object. And objects do not die because they can be replaced.

The passing thought about the death of the book provoked by the museum exhibits with their beautiful names soon vanished. We are living at the end of the twentieth century, curiosity about the transience of human life is no longer relevant in either artistic or human terms. Such an old-fashioned idea may still be found in the occasional pop song, where a line may cross over the decades and end up in this, deathless, one of ours, to be transformed into a parody of itself.

We are living at the end of the twentieth century, a time of forgetting, *the dance of death*, that genre has been forgotten long ago, death itself seems to have been banished somewhere. All that we have is the face, the other side of the coin seems to have disappeared. 'The beginning was when I was born, and there's no end,' said a child once.

In an essay a colleague from Sarajevo, the writer Dževad Karahasan, describes an episode from the Sarajevo autumn of 1992. A large shell came through the window of his flat and cut through the books on his shelf like a knife, or to be exact (the writer

151

assesses the damage precisely), through a book of Faulkner's stories, Nadezhda Mandelshtam's *Hope against Hope*, and Keller's *Green Heinrich*. Establishing that at that precise moment he and his wife had been walking towards the bookshelf, my Sarajevo colleague concludes that once again, 'this time in a quite concrete way, literature had saved him from reality and from those who sought to dictate that reality'.

Reading this fragment from the Yugoslav landscape of misery – death, rape, murder, exile and destruction – for the first time I saw the clear outline of the book as an object which is itself physically mortal.

'You know,' said an acquaintance of mine, who had succeeded in getting out of Sarajevo after a year of the siege, 'in Sarajevo, communism disappeared in the nicest, warmest and noblest way.'

'What do you mean . . .?' I asked.

It turned out that during the winter the inhabitants of Sarajevo had warmed themselves with their own collections of books. The people who did best were those who had kept among their books the works of the communist leaders. When books like that are tied tightly with wire, they burn slowly, with no rush, like the best coal. At first the people of Sarajevo warmed themselves with 'communist' briquettes, and finally it was Shakespeare's turn. Radovan Karadžić – the supervisor of work on the project of the destruction of Sarajevo – had himself written a little volume of verse, of inferior calorific value, unfortunately.

If one looks more carefully at the chaotic and still unfinished map of destruction, a precise plan may be discerned underlying the chaos. The small baroque town of Vukovar, where people of different nationalities lived together, has been razed to the ground. Multinational and multicultural Sarajevo is being destroyed. Sarajevo is not a symbol of the 'Yugoslav Utopia' (*'Everything is a symbol for you,'* observed a foreign journalist, rightly) but a city. If the very concept of the city implies ideas such as multiculturality and multinationality, then it is urban life that is being destroyed. If churches (the cathedral in Šibenik), old cities (Dubrovnik, Zadar, Šibenik), valuable libraries (The National and University Library in Sarajevo,[1] the Oriental Institute in Sarajevo

---

[1] 'When the State Library was burning in August, snow smothered Sarajevo for three days. For three days I could not find a single pencil in the house and if I did find one it didn't have any lead. Even erasers left a black mark. My homeland was burning

with some 700,000 irreplaceable documents, the old and exceptionally valuable library in Dubrovnik), if these things are symbols of culture, then it is culture that is being destroyed. If culture is being destroyed, then a crucial item in the project of destruction is the annihilation of memory. Those responsible for the assaults listed above are the Serbian military hordes; but Croatian soldiers in Bosnia were not in this sense mistaken when they destroyed the famous bridge in Mostar. Mostar too is an old urban centre: a crossroads of various cultures and nationalities.

It is only now that I feel I know something about destruction. An object that has been destroyed, like a life, is not replaceable; it disappears for ever. Devastation is never solely material, it has multiple aspects, multiple meanings, but it is always final. We shall build new libraries, publish new books, announce the optimists, accustomed to a regular rhythm of destruction and rebuilding. But the idea of reconstruction contains the notion of future destruction.

The devastation caused by the war in Croatia and Bosnia coincides not only with the disappearance of the general Yugoslav cultural context – a culture which existed without any doubt and which everyone now zealously denies – but also with the disappearance of 'East European culture', or rather with the end of the political complex which gave a common imprint to the cultures of Eastern and Central Europe. Many things have been definitively changed: the context and the author, the recipient and the communicative code. And the times are completely different.

---

sorrowfully. Freed from their bodies, characters from novels roamed through the city mingling with the passers-by and the souls of dead fighters. I saw Werther sitting on the broken wall of the cemetery, Quasimodo on the minarets of mosques, Raskolnikov and Mersault talked quietly for days in the cellar. Gavroche walked about in a camouflage uniform and Yossarian was already trading in a big way with the enemy. Not to mention young Sawyer who would jump into the river from Princip Bridge for a few coins.

'For three days I lived in a ghost town with the terrible suspicion that there were fewer and fewer living people in the town and that the shells were falling only because of me. I shut myself in the house and leafed through tourist guides. I went outside on the day when the radio announced that people had carried ten tons of clinkers out of the library cellar. And there was lead in my pencil again.' (Goran Simić, *Sarajevska tuga*, Ljubljana, 1993)

The war, the dismantling of one state and the establishment of new ones, the destruction of one identity and the construction of a new one, changes in language, the end of one ideological value system and the establishment of a new one – this is the millstone which has been grinding down the citizen of former Yugoslavia for the last three years. Let us now imagine that this citizen is an inhabitant of Zagreb, that he lived through the war peacefully, that he lost none of his relatives, and that he even kept the roof over his head. The changes at first seem easy, manageable, he needs only to alter his personal documents and his passport, of course. He has to get used to the fact that there is a new state just fifty kilometres from Zagreb, with a proper border and passport control. He has to get used to the fact that his new country is called Croatia, but that's easy as well, that's what he voted for, for heaven's sake. But he must take care that he does not happen to utter the word Yugoslavia (politically undesirable, often also dangerous), which is just a bit more difficult, he referred to it every day for fifty years. He has to get used to removing some words, 'Serbian' ones, from his vocabulary, and learning new, 'Croatian' ones – oh these languages, they've got so mixed up! Oh, yes, and he has to learn the new street names (he has to be careful to call the main square Ban Jelačić Square, and not Republic Square as it was up to now). He has to accept that there are none of the old newspapers, and it's a good thing there are fewer of them, he wouldn't have bought them anyway. He has to get used to the new money . . . Let us now imagine this citizen of the former and citizen of the new state sitting in an armchair and reading a book. Our imagined reader suddenly feels that he no longer recognises the letters, that he no longer understands anything. Either the book is no longer that book, or he is no longer that reader. And how is it possible, in just three years . . . ! Our imagined reader suddenly feels that he no longer remembers what belongs to before, and what to afterwards. Suddenly he is tired. Too many things have happened at once. There's a new time outside, he has to learn it. His own, the one that has passed, will have to be forgotten as soon as possible.

The history of the book, the object, is the dramatic history of ink, lead and fire. In the thirties the smell of quality fuel hung over Germany. They were burning books. 'As you watch the fire devour these un-German books, may the flame of love for your

Homeland catch light in your hearts,' said the burners of books to the pupils gathered round the pyre in Munich, on 9 May 1933. What they were burning were some of the finest pages of German literature.

In Croatia, books written in the Cyrillic script are put to one side. The Cyrillic script offends Croats, they say. Serbian writers are being thrown out of the school curriculum. In Serbia, books in Latin script are put to one side. The Latin script offends Serbs, they say. Croatian writers are being thrown out of the school curriculum.

Croato-Serbian (or Serbo-Croatian), until recently a single common language, has been divided into two hostile ones: Croatian and Serbian. The struggle for the emergence of a third, *Bosnian*, is still being waged.

The history of the creation and destruction of books runs parallel to the history of mankind, its path is long, from the library of Alexandria to that of Sarajevo. One of the most famous burners of books was the Chinese Emperor Shih Huang Ti who in 213 BC ordered that all written documents in China be burned, so that history would begin with him. Dreaming of his eternal dynasty, the Chinese Emperor began at the same time to build the Great Wall of China. Jorge Luis Borges wrote a story about this, 'The Wall and the books', trying to guess the secret connection between these two apparently logical actions: the burning of books and the erection of a wall.

I am reading Borges's story in my temporary abode, a city in which one wall has been brought down, but the traces of which may still be seen. In Berlin I am surrounded by a dozen precious books in the Croatian and Serbian language. I couldn't carry any more.

2. The death of the model

Leafing long ago through an anthology of science-fantasy stories, in which authors from many countries were represented, I stumbled across an unusual sentence; 'I stayed at a girl friend's house till the small hours drinking "the best quality whisky".' The sentence was inappropriate for the genre of SF, which does not as a rule go in for comparisons of this kind. Apart from that, I wondered, what kind of a hero stays at a girl friend's house until the small hours drinking, and in fact what is 'the best quality whisky'? The author's name seemed to confirm the 'justification' of the sentence. The author was a Czech.

I taught contemporary Russian prose at an American university. In one lecture I talked about the Russian writer Yury Trifonov and his short story 'The exchange'. The Moscow intellectual in Trifonov's story is in a dilemma: his wife persuades him to exchange his flat with his own dying mother so as to increase their living space. My American students could not begin to understand why the Russian writer should have wasted paper in describing an ordinary housing transaction. Secondly, my students could not grasp the essence of that housing transaction. Why didn't that man from Moscow and his wife simply rent a larger apartment? Why did the old lady have to move in with them, if neither she nor they wanted it? And why use up so many pages soaked in moral suffering over such a trivial matter as . . . an apartment? And I found myself in an uncomfortable position: in contact with another culture, the text of a Russian writer who was at the time popular suddenly lost its literary value, and instead of a lecturer in literature I became an interpreter of Soviet daily life.

My American friends very much enjoyed the film by the Yugoslav director Emir Kusturica, *When father was away on business*. As there was a scene at the beginning of the film in which the father was reading a newspaper with a photograph of Stalin on which the father commented aloud, my friends quite correctly concluded that after that the father went 'away on business, i.e. to prison'. It took a long time before I succeeded in explaining that the father, 'a victim of the Stalinist regime', had spent a few years in prison because of his warm commentary and apparent sympathy for Stalin, and not the opposite. And our discussion of the film turned into a lecture on post-war Yugoslav history.

Although it has been destroyed, the Berlin wall still exists. Westerners are still 'Wessies', Easterners are 'Ossies', and the term 'Eastern Europe' is still in wide usage. The term is reinforced by books with Eastern Europe on the cover; it is used, as are all other concepts from the East-European dictionary, for the most part, by 'Westerners'. 'Eastern Europe' – a concept which is today completely emptied of its original geopolitical meaning – has not disappeared. The concept insists on a border and on difference, it suggests a world that is different from the Western one, a culture that is different from the Western one, an identity that is different from the Western one.

'Easterners', of course, do not agree with a common appellation which so crudely eliminates cultural distinguishing features. Central Europeans will quite rightly insist on the fact that they are different from the so very 'Eastern' Russians, and hesitate to accept into their midst the equally 'Eastern' Bulgarians, Romanians and Serbs. For their part, the Russians will regularly point to the example of Peter the Great and rightly demand their place in Europe. Western Europe, of course.

Why do 'Westerners' keep assiduously shoving 'Easterners' into 'Eastern' Europe? And why, when 'Easterners' pronounce the word 'Europe', do they usually imply its 'Western' half, passing over their own as though it did not exist? Let us remember, the Berlin wall was pulled down exactly five years ago.

Different cultural traditions, different cultural centres and different creative individualities cannot, of course, be simply placed under the heading 'Eastern Europe'. Let us try for a moment to accept the justly or unjustly established term without resistance and start from the assumption that the point at which the different cultures of Eastern Europe come together is the point at which they differ from Western Europe.

That point of difference is above all the ideological-political system (communism or socialism, according to taste), which prevailed for some decades in countries such as Poland, Bulgaria, Romania, Czechoslovakia, Hungary, Yugoslavia (yes, Yugoslavia too), as well as in the former empire of the Soviet Union. That system stamped its mark on everyone and everything, including culture, whether it developed in tune with ideological-political demands or in opposition to them. But no one denies that there were variations: for example, socialism of the Yugoslav type differed from the Soviet brand, and thanks, among other things, to that difference, Yugoslav culture and its mechanisms were different from Soviet culture. Within that common framework, Poland had its own story, as did Czechoslovakia, as did Hungary . . .

What is the distinguishing feature of 'East European' literature, on which cultural texts can East Europeans justifiably stick the label 'Made in Eastern Europe', what is it that constitutes the

East European copyright? For instance, if the English writer Julian Barnes can publish an 'East European' novel (*Porcupine*, 1992), which could just as well have been an article of Bulgarian literary manufacture, does that mean that there is a model that can be copied? If there is such a model, what constitutes the unique nature of the original production? And, as we seek for the 'Easternness' of East European culture, will we be unconsciously dealing in assumptions from an East European mindset constructed by 'Westerners', or the cultural reality which was, after all, built up by 'Easterners' in the course of their socialist years?

Beside the Brandenburg Gate in Berlin, there are souvenirs for sale: a little piece of the Berlin wall in a transparent plastic box, Russian fur hats with a red star, sickles and hammers, flags, medals. The souvenirs are not sold by Russian émigrés any more, as we might at first have thought. I saw a Pakistani. The Pakistani standing in the place where the wall stood a short time ago selling cheap souvenirs of a vanished epoch is perhaps the most precise and condensed metaphor of the times in which we are living.

Any serious literary theoretician or historian of literature is reluctant to get involved in constructions on shaky ground. But nevertheless, perhaps one day someone will take on the cultural-commemorative task of building a more acceptable construct, an 'anti-formative' model which will articulate the *common* features of the *different* cultures which functioned under the cupola of a more or less common ideological system.

'The character X is one of those typical East European characters . . .' I read these words recently in a literary review written by an American. I would not myself be able to say what constitutes a 'typical East European character', and nor, I assume, would the author of the review. But as an inhabitant of a former Central European (or East European or even South-East European, whatever) country, I do know something about disappearance: the disappearance of colours, smells, contact with objects and signs which surrounded us for years. What has disappeared, without doubt existed. But what it is that makes that special substance, that specific colour, that particular smell, is as hard to explain as the substance, colour and smell themselves. And all I can do is for a moment try to consider the matter from the point of view of the seller of literary souvenirs.

The first point which makes East European literary texts different from West European ones is the system of everyday life, 'byt' (an untranslatable Russian word, which means a great deal more than its translation into any foreign language), everyday life imbued with an ideological system, with established habits, rituals, mechanisms, signs. Without an understanding of the system of everyday life, without recognition of its rules (and absurdity), but also its smells, tastes and colours, many East European texts would be incomprehensible, as Trifonov's short story was to my American students. In that sense, by changing their readers and cultural context, many texts will disappear like frescoes suddenly exposed to the air. The Russian writer Venyamin Yerofeyev's short novel *Moskva-Petushki* is not a novel about a Russian alcoholic, it is far more than that, a novel of 'byt' and about 'byt', a novel of untranslatable substance. But translated into the language of a different cultural climate, it is simply a novel about a Russian alcoholic.

In conjunction with the political system, literary everyday reality (the 'byt' of literature) set up rituals which Western culture did not know. East European culture (in some places more, in some less, in some cases for a shorter time, in others longer) was characterised by a system of aesthetic and ideological rules. East European culture developed the phenomena of censorship, repression, self-censorship, special functions of literature and of the author; the phenomena of 'samizdat' and 'tamizdat', alternative institutions ('drawing-room theatre', 'drawing-room exhibitions', 'drawing-room books'); the whole phenomenon of 'alternative culture' altogether, that is the division into 'official' and 'parallel' ('alternative', 'other', 'underground') culture, with the accompanying concept of 'dissidence', and connected with that . . . a long and rich 'culture of exile'.

Literary life, therefore, was one of the fundamental specific features of East European culture; without knowing and understanding it, a reading of the texts which came into being in that cultural habitat will be at the very least impoverished. Because that kind of literary life determined far more than the destiny of writers. It determined also the thematic corpus (that whole specific thematic menu which characterises East European texts!), literary forms and genres, language and style. The whole of East European culture is marked by a lengthy history of accepting the political regime, but also opposing it. In that sense it is a culture of hidden or open polemic, a culture of questioning the imposed models of thought, aesthetic and political, of cultural subversion, escapism, inner and outer exile.

The culture of socialist realism (which, if it were alive, would this year be celebrating its seventieth anniversary!), or the alternative culture which questions the official aesthetic-ideological assumptions, is at the same time what most clearly articulates the specific nature of the East European cultural model. Such texts are the core of the hypothetical model and they came into being precisely where the assumptions were most tenacious, in Russian literature and art. Artistic exploration of Soviet mythology which fashioned the consciousness of generations, the exploration of 'byt', the ideological-aesthetic habitat, is the field of the autonomous artistic phenomenon of 'soc-art', which came into being on the border between sociology, 'archaeology' and art, and was realised in texts which themselves eliminate the borders between art, literature, painting, theatre. In that sense, the entire ideological-aesthetic habitat is the artistic material of the 'soc-art' artist: textbooks, readers, pioneer songs, posters, products of Soviet mass culture, language, political slogans, design (for instance, to confirm his idea that 'the Soviet Union did not sell biscuits but ideas', even the semiotician A. Zholkovsky took the wrapping of 'October' biscuits as the object of his analysis). The most varied representatives, painters (Kabakov, Komar and Melamid, Bulatov and others), prose writers and poets (Sorokin, Prigov and others) created an autonomous and unique artistic movement. The same type of 'polit-art', whose fundamental assumption is alienation from the ideological habitat and articulation of the socialist/communist collective unconscious, sprang up in other East European cultural centres as well (the films of Dušan Makavejev, the Slovene 'Neue Slovenische Kunst' and the like).

Central Europe is an artificial construct (and at the same time the third point of difference) on which East European writers (Kundera, Konrad, Kiš, and others) articulate the essence of 'Central Europeanness' in a rich corpus of works, in essays, novels and stories. The creation of a cultural construct is conditioned above all by the cultural sovietisation of the majority of the Eastern Bloc countries, and it came into being not only as the result of a search for the specific nature of their own cultural identity, but in part also out of a need to escape the narrow framework of small xenophobic national cultures, to discover the general, unifying cultural components of the small languages and small literatures of Central Europe, of all of those, that is, which shared 'the same memories, the same problems and conflicts, the same common tradition' (Kundera).

The East European cultural model no longer exists, and it has still not been either constructed or articulated, because that may not be possible. The imagology of 'Eastern Europe' is still kept alive by texts (films, painting, literature) which are more present than ever before on the 'Western' market. The majority of those texts, however, came into being in a former age and give the impression of extinguished stars shining with their full brightness as they fall on a different cultural soil. East European artists and writers today are in fact selling souvenirs of a vanished culture. What kind of culture comes into being on the ruins of a system – and, in an age which likes cultural labels, will it be called 'post-communist' or 'post-totalitarian'? It is hard to say. The East European cultural dossier is in any case closed, whatever its contents mean and however it might be re-evaluated one day.

In a short note written in 1979, Danilo Kiš, the last 'Yugoslav' writer, clearly stresses: 'Because for the intellectual of this century, of this age of ours, there is only one test of the conscience, and there are only two subjects which if one fails them mean not only the loss of one year, but lose one the right to a (moral) voice once and for all: fascism and Stalinism.' Today I read this sentence, which sounded moralistic and severe some fifteen years ago, whose simple pamphletism did not fit with Kiš's literary elegance; now I read it from a quite different perspective and with due respect. Danilo Kiš, who in his essays favours a Yugoslav cultural identity, a Central European cultural identity – who seems to have done so, conscious of the nationalistic, self-satisfied, provincial mentality of his own country, virtually as a programme – would be astonished by the alarming speed with which cultural and moral regression has overwhelmed many former Yugoslav centres. The common cultural heritage – the works of Ivo Andrić, Miroslav Krleža, Meša Selimović, Danilo Kiš, which long ago articulated the assumptions of the reality confronting us today – this heritage is now dead, just as its authors are. The former Yugoslav cultural centres have sunk into a torpor of cultural autism, the air there is heavy not only with aggressive misery but with stupidity and banality 'indestructible as a plastic bottle' (Kiš).

In Croatia, for example, fragments of the totalitarian cultural past suddenly spring up as in a nightmare. Dusty quotations from the museum of totalitarianism appear on the cultural scene: state exhibitions which send us straight back to the time of socialist realism with the zeal of a new discovery;[2] monuments, made long ago, then destroyed, to be immediately replaced by stylistically identical ones; projects emerge, the grotesque quality of which was confirmed long ago in the already forgotten days of totalitarianism; black and white texts of literary propaganda appear, although similar ones would have been considered a short time ago as a literary-museum rarity and mocked by critics; the occasional 'state' writer springs up, a role which writers used to take on in the distant days of state culture;[3] cultural phenomena are being revitalised which we believed belonged to the early childhood of communism and would remain there, in the museum; once again, like a persistent virus, the mechanisms of censorship, self-censorship, collective censorship, begin to function, familiar to us from the dusty 'handbooks' of the culture of totalitarianism; projects of 'national' culture and 'spiritual renewal', which we know from the yellowing pages of the 'handbooks' of Nazism, reappear. A kind of amnesia prevails in the cultural scene, the participants themselves seem no longer to recognise either the scene or the meaning of the cultural symbols.

At this moment, the Croatian cultural scene is characterised by a kind of retrospective, fragmentary, referential totalitarianism. The Serbian cultural scene is dominated by a tendency which swings like a pendulum between two poles of the same

[2] An amusing example is the exhibition of works by the Croatian sculptor Kruno Bošnjak 'People for all Croatian times' (Zagreb, 1992). The sculptor cast seven bronze figures of people 'to whom it was given', as it said in the catalogue, 'to help the thousand-year dream become reality'. The dream of creating the Croatian state was helped by Hans-Dietrich Genscher, Helmut Kohl, Margaret Thatcher, Alois Mock, Pope John Paul II, Franjo Tudjman and an unknown Croatian soldier with a child in his arms.

[3] 'Ivan Aralica wrote what he wrote as though he were with me every day, and I have not seen him once in these last two years,' are the words of President Franjo Tudjman. The Croatian President went on to recommend that everyone should write like Aralica, the Croatian 'state' writer.

thing: nationalistic populism and élitist intellectualistic neo-fascism.[4] Nationalistic populism followed the growth of the concept of Greater Serbia and was a kind of introduction to the war. This second tendency has grown up in the course of the war, and its newly manufactured cultural concept serves to confirm and affirm the evil which has already been done.

Thinking that they are closing their doors only to their immediate neighbours, both cultural milieus are paying a heavy price – or so it seems from outside: today they receive visitors from their own provinces, from the ethno-museums and political museums of past epochs. At the same time both milieus warmly welcome cultural ghosts as a long awaited encounter with their own identity.

3. The life and death of the writer

In one of his articles, the Sarajevo journalist Miljenko Jergović tries to calculate the trajectory of the bullets fired from Pale at

[4] The journal *Naše idejé* (*Our Ideas*, June 1993) describes a conception that opposes the virtues of eternal Europe to 'the new world order', that is to say, I quote: it opposes faith to rationalism; the primacy of the spirit over matter, to materialism; the rule of order to disorder and anarchy conceived of as 'freedom'; idealism to sensualism; love of power to a search for wealth; the hierarchy of authority as opposed to equality; discipline to 'laissez faire'; respect of authority and the elder to parliamentarism; aristocracy, the rule of the élite and the nobility to plutocracy and the rule of the wealthy; stability to constant oscillation; the cult of duty as opposed to the search for happiness; society as an organic whole to society as a collection of individuals; the state as harmonising social strata to class struggle; the restoration of authority to liberalism and the tyranny of human rights; the ideal of knighthood and faith to systematic hypocrisy; the cult of military virtues to the cult of bourgeois values; the open affirmation of war and conquest to pacifism; military and political expansion to economic expansion; the impulse of prosperity and strength to decadence; the absolute will to biological fertility to birth control; the absolute will to power to the voluntary rejection of European hegemony; and so on and so forth . . .

This political and cultural mish-mash becomes clearer in the context of the whole journal in which the former fascist movements in Europe (German, Romanian and the Serbian Chetnik movement) are unambiguously affirmed; which prints texts by the classic spokesmen of fascism alongside texts by contemporary Russian and Serbian neo-fascist thinkers. The ideas quoted are endorsed through their contributions to the journal by a substantial number of public figures (film directors, painters, writers). They are all participating in the process of creating a new combination of the prevailing politics and culture, a combination in which Russo-Serbian Orthodoxy is mixed up with militaristic exhibitionism, monarchism, cheap folklorism, fascism, aesthetics and the aestheticisation of evil, something which for the time being has the narrow title of the 'new Serbian right'. Let us in addition point out that the 'left' does not exist, and the 'ideas' referred to have their origin in the bloody reality of Bosnia.

Sarajevo by Eduard Limonov, and concludes quite correctly that the Russian writer's bullets were intended precisely for him, a Sarajevo writer.

One of the latest shameful 'literary' episodes is certainly the one in which, at a meeting of the Bosnian Serbs at Pale (at the moment when the Serbs were to vote on whether to continue the war – and they continued it), the 'Yugoslav Tolstoy', the President of the false Yugoslavia and writer Dobrica Ćosić uttered the sentence: 'I am here to serve you.'

The writer spoke the words in a quiet, deferential voice. In front of him was a crowd of maddened nationalists, the product of his imagination which had become reality, in fact. He stood before them, their broken God. His books can be found in every Serbian village house. In every 'honourable' Serbian household, even illiterate ones, this writer's books are a cult object, along with the Orthodox icon. Now, here were his own characters, in front of him, quite real, the local leader with burning eyes, warriors, murderers and their instigators. 'I am here to serve you,' the writer said in a quiet voice to those who would soon set off again to murder and destroy.

And here our tale connects with its beginning. If their trajectory is correctly calculated, the shells that destroyed the books in Sarajevo homes, the bombs that annihilated the Sarajevo libraries all originated with the writer who had come to serve his living characters. Some will say that this was how the writer died, others will say that he bought a ticket to a new life, by consistently taking on the role of waiter to Serbian fascism. Both will be right.

Living in a stable system, the WEW, the West European writer, realises his right to a peaceful and stable biography. The history of East European literatures is at the same time the history of dramatic personal biographies. Exile, inner and outer, repression, compromise with the authorities, the experience of the 'homo duplex', censorship and self-censorship, and so on and so forth, are not only the literary-historical specialities of East European literatures but also real lives, autobiographies.

Our WEW rarely has the opportunity to observe his own death as a writer. Such an exclusive experience belongs on the whole to the EEW, the East European Writer. In the general break-up of a system, or in a war such as that being waged in former Yugoslavia, it is hard to imagine that writers will be a protected human species. They die, really or symbolically, disappear, for ever or for a while, they hibernate, and come back to life. That is why the EEW undoubtedly surpasses the WEW at least in one respect: in his elasticity. In the art of adaptation and survival. In the art of refusal to adapt and death. In accepting his new writer's 'destiny', which in the West is called so undramatically his 'career'.

The EEW, the East European writer, has lost his cultural base. That base was the system which he accepted or opposed. Whatever it was called – official or alternative literature, internal or external exile, an ivory tower or life in his own literary milieu, political dissidence or conformism, one or the other – that base no longer exists. The dissident is no longer a dissident, exile is no longer exile, even reality is not that reality. Even his right to a subject, his last copyright, has been taken from him. There is no iron curtain any more, cultural nomadism is now the fashion, and the EEW, as he reads the numerous pages written about him by WEWs, feels for a moment or for longer, more or less . . . robbed.

As far as the ex-Yugoslav writer is concerned, he barely feels alive. He, the Yugo-writer, has been deprived of his homeland, the literary life he was used to, his readership, market, libraries, publishers, the culture of dialogue, cultural exchanges, critics, literary journals, even books themselves. The Yugo-writer has become what he always was, just a Slovene, Croatian, Bosnian (there he has divided himself into three!), Serbian, Albanian, Macedonian writer. But nevertheless, the greatest drama is being played out on the territory of the language which was shared until a short time ago. In this sense, Slovene, Albanian and Macedonian writers get by relatively unscathed.

In order to survive, the ex-Yugo-writer has to commit suicide (things are easy and joyful for the majority, hard for the minority), he has to carry out an enormous mental task, go through a kind of 'brain-change', transform himself, throw off one skin in order to earn the right to another.

At this moment, the drama of many citizens of former Yugoslavia, including writers, is (literally and metaphorically) the drama of their biography. Many writers, artists, intellectuals sweat over the reconstitution of their own biographies. The novels of M. K., a Belgrade writer, one of the loudest and most zealous warmongers, are published in Zagreb. B. D., a Croatian literary critic, considers his own books published in Belgrade as ugly blots in his bibliography. I know a certain Slobodan from Belgrade, at this moment a refugee in some West European country, who speaks nothing but English and insists that his name is Bob.

The former Yugoslav writer has three options: transformation and adaptation; inner exile, in the hope that it won't last long; real exile, in the hope that it is temporary. All three options are a kind of conscious passage through death in order to earn the right to a new life. As he jumps to his death, the writer is led by the hope that he will resurface, this time as simply . . . a writer.

The majority will adapt and conform, some of them will accept their new skin as their own, authentic one, others will simply accept the rules of mimicry. The writer who settles for the first, least painful option for survival will nevertheless have to accept some things (with more or less pleasure). He will have to get used to the fact that his market has shrunk, that his readership is smaller and nationally more homogeneous; he will have to get used to long-term shortage of books (fewer publishers, fewer books, fewer translations). He will have to watch his language: the one in Croatia must not use 'Serbisms', the one in Serbia must not use 'Croatisms' (every use of one or the other will mean far more than the author's choice of a nicer or more precise word), the one in Bosnia will have to protect his 'Turkisms', the one in Montenegro will have to replace his 'ijekavian' dialect with 'ekavian' if he does not wish to be accused of secessionism. He will have to accept a new kind of self-censorship so as not to be exposed to censorship from outside; he will have, finally, to accept the fact that he is now a builder, defender and representative of his national culture, the guardian of a fuzzy 'national essence'. He will have to get used to the fact that he is an attractive target for political manipulation (from either one side or the other). He will have to get used to the fact that young national states, especially small ones, are fond of writers, that they demand of them love and loyalty, and to the fact that his writing has a social function, whether he likes it or not. He will have to get used to a new system of values, including literary ones. He will have to get used to tolerance. Writers in Serbia will have to get used to the fact that at this moment the editor of the most expensive, most exclusive, best produced literary journal is a murderer, a war criminal and profiteer, that one journal with numerous contributors openly propagates neo-fascism (their

money, their ideas); he will have in that case also to get used to
accepting the terrible and very real consequences of neo-fascism.
The writer in Serbia will have to get used to the fact that many of
his colleagues openly support the war, to the fact that he shares
his language with murderers. And the writer in Croatia will have
to get used to a new system of values as well. He will have, for
instance, to overlook the fact that an old man – the author of two
or three patriotic pamphlets, the former copier of Nazi concepts
of culture and the creator of the concept of 'Ustasha Literature',
albeit unrealised – has today, a whole fifty years later, been
promoted to 'doyen of Croatian poetry'. They will all have to get
used to a new cultural standard. A little touching-up here, a little
remake there, a little forgetting on one side, a little deceit on the
other, we've opened up a bit to the left, moved a bit to the right,
broadened a bit at the top, closed up a bit towards the bottom,
and, here we are, we are alive, with smooth new skin, we crawl,
breathe, write.

What happens when the ex-Yugo-writer, coming out of his
cultural milieu, finds that his books are beginning to communicate with a different cultural milieu? Emerging into the world in
many cases destroys the illusion of cultural (literary) communication which, they say, does not recognise national borders.
Borders do not exist only so long as we don't travel anywhere.
That is why writers often feel, when they cross borders (regardless of where they come from), like their own books peppered
with critical shot.

In one West European centre a reviewer stressed the literary
value of my book, but he wondered in all seriousness whether
that was 'what we needed', implying that my book did not
correspond to his (their) expectations. It was not that I had
betrayed his literary expectations (that was all right), but my
book did not fit in with his assumptions about the country I came
from. Is that what *we* need, the critic wondered. What bothered
me most about the whole thing was that little pronoun *we*. I had
previously believed that it existed only in countries of highly
developed collectivism.

In another West European literary centre a critic accused me of
writing 'satirical novels' while my country was 'swimming in
blood'. The point is that my books were accepted for publication
before the war and, unfortunately, began to appear during the
war. If he showed no literary compassion, the critic betrayed no

human compassion either. It was hard for him to verify the original date of publication of the book, to imagine how long it would have taken for it to be translated, and then be published in his country. And then the war came and I betrayed his expectations. What bothered me about the whole thing was his expression of moral accusation. It seemed, all in all, that I had not gone away anywhere. The language of accusation was so familiar. By going away, I had arrived home.

In a third literary centre, a reviewer emphasised with profound understanding that there was a problem of *bad timing*, which wasn't my fault of course, but that that would not prevent him from trying to find in the book at least a hint of the future bloody conflict in the Balkans. Since he did not succeed in finding such hints (because there were none), the reviewer was a little disappointed, and seemed not to know what to do with the book as a result.

In a fourth literary centre, a friendly editor finally advised me to write a novel about a little Serb and a little Croat to show, through an account of their growing-up together: a) the origins of Yugoslavia; b) the history of the break-up of Yugoslavia; c) the essence of the bloody conflict in the Balkans. In this case I was genuinely delighted to have crossed the border. Because I had travelled into literature, or rather into a literary work, or rather into a story by Ilf and Petrov, 'How Robinson was created'! Naturally I didn't accept the invitation. Later I wondered whether the difference between a WEW and an EEW wasn't just in that self-confident word 'naturally'?

And the other way round. I know a writer whose wrong timing gave him a whole new life. His books about the Second World War, already forgotten in his own country, were resurrected in a foreign setting as books about the new war. The novels of Ivo Andrić, the only Yugoslav Nobel prize-winner, are today read with interest by foreign politicians and negotiators, like a tourist guide through an ethnic characterology. The substantial opus of the greatest Croatian writer, Miroslav Krleža, has been condensed into two or three quotations which are happily repeated by people who have never read a line of Krleža. In the context of war, the famous literary mammoth has gained the right to a new life – in the form of a fly. The name of Miloš Crnjanski, the great Serbian writer, is today used as the trademark of an élite intellectual contingent of new Serbian fascists.

When he crosses the border, the ex-Yugo-writer arrives in territory which he does not recognise: the West European literary market-place. All the traps he had succeeded in avoiding in his own cultural milieu – guarding his sacred right to literary autonomy as his most precious possession – now lie in wait for him. He becomes everything he had never been until that moment. Like it or not, he becomes the representative of his country, whether the old one or the new one (which he had never been, because he was neither a diplomat nor a politician, but at a given moment he is an exile from his own cultural milieu); like it or not, he becomes a reporter of reality (which he had never been, because he was not a journalist, but a writer); like it or not, he becomes a new kind of tourist guide, an ethno-writer (something that had never entered his life). All in all, he becomes a kind of interpreter, psychologist, anthropologist, sociologist, political analyst, ethnologist – in other words, a translator of his own reality and the reality of his own country into a language comprehensible to West European readers. He feels caught in a trap which he had so far managed to avoid, in a system abounding in traps. Literature, his exit-light, the field of his freedom, is now in real danger of being read as a report about his country, the war, the Balkans, ethno-mentalities, the everyday reality of post-communism, God alone knows what. He is himself in constant danger of being reduced to a mere translator of that reality into words.

And our writer ends up feeling bitterly confused. Instead of being glad that he (who comes from a small country, a small culture) has the chance of having his work cross the border, of communicating with other literary centres, he complains, the ungrateful creature! Our writer feels terribly isolated, he has no cultural context behind him to call on (not because there is none, but because no one knows him), he has no firm, well-known literary shoulder to lean on. He has to keep producing his literary ID all over again and proving all over again that he is a full and equal member of the international literary family, that he has his entry visa. And he becomes more and more confused, he suddenly feels that he is defending something that does not in fact exist, or rather that what he is defending exists only in communication, however poor. And our writer settles for communication. Because he's a writer.

The EEW, the East European writer, who has now been joined

by the ex-Yugoslav writer, suffers from a not over-attractive syndrome: he tends not to know his place. He is a megalomaniac, greedy, eternally dissatisfied and a grumbler. He always feels that he deserves something more. If he was neglected in his own milieu, he will blame the communist system; it won't for a moment occur to him that he was neglected simply because he was not of much interest. But if he was famous, that is of course because of his literary qualities and the milieu had nothing to do with it. In so far as he succeeds in achieving a certain standing in the Western market, he will attribute it to his undoubted literary talent (which is of course acknowledged abroad and overlooked at home), but if he does not succeed, he will blame the cold Western market which does not recognise true literary qualities. He will resent it if his books are not treated as literature but as a means of discovering more about the political situation where he originated. And if they are indifferent to that political situation, he will hurry to remind them of the unfortunate political context in which his books came into being.

Russian writers who slid into the Western literary market-place on political waves of varying strength – first on waves of bloc politics and dissidence, and then on the last powerful wave of perestroika – will attribute their literary export to the high literary value of their work. Hungarians, Poles, Romanians will complain that they were unable to get into 'Europe' because of the cultural and political domination of the Russians, and they will be right to some extent. And so on and so forth.

The ex-Yugoslav writer, like all his East European colleagues, is for the most part distinguished by intolerance towards others. The Slovene writer will not miss an opportunity of stressing that he lived under the oppressive dominance of Serbian culture and he will overlook the fact that his books were published in Serbia, as well as in Slovenia. The Croatian writer will complain that during the 'Yugo-Bolshevik regime' it was impossible for him to be published in the West because they only published Serbs. If they still don't publish his works now, as an 'independent' Croatian writer, he will be convinced that it's because the West hates Croats. The Serbian writer will complain that he is not published in the West for political reasons; if he is published, then he will complain that they only publish him for political reasons. The writer from Sarajevo will accept the fact that his work is translated into several languages as something quite normal (it's translated because he's a good writer) and will be genuinely surprised at the possibility that his books have made it into the world – just because he's from Sarajevo. If they don't make it, he will be upset that they don't and pull out his trump card, his personal misfortune, Sarajevo.

The EEW will respond quickly to the need for any autobiographical 'touching-up': he will keep quiet about the fact that his books were abundantly published during 'communism', but if one of them was not, he will gladly make a fuss about it and accuse the former regime of interfering with his artistic freedom. The EEW has retained the habit of always blaming others for everything, it will not occur to him to confront his real literary worth (which I know is difficult), or at least his real place in his own literary context and abroad. He prefers to carry himself and his unfortunate 'destiny' across borders like something precious. It will never occur to him to wonder how a Danish, Dutch, Norwegian or Belgian writer lives and works. Because if an East European says that he wants to 'go to Europe' and insists that he is its inhabitant with equal rights, on the whole he is thinking of himself in 'Western Europe' and not of the European in himself.

If at some literary gathering we catch sight of a person with a haughty expression of unhappiness and dissatisfaction on his face – which its owner wears as an exclusive ornament, but also as a reminder to others, the cheerful – we won't generally be mistaken when we guess who he is. The person with the unique expression on his face is sure to be an EEW, an East European writer.

The most painful point for the ex-Yugo writer, if he is truly a writer, is not at this moment communication with his own or a foreign literary milieu. If that were the case, things would be simpler. His real torment is the war. He, who deals in words because that is all he knows, is now caught in the ultimate trap. Everything he writes suddenly seems profoundly inappropriate. If he writes about the war, deeply affected by its horrors, in a frighteningly short time what he writes becomes a kind of pornography of suffering. If he is naive enough to believe for a moment that his words can save human lives, his paper protest becomes a pale pamphlet. The authentic account of an anonymous victim has far greater human and literary value. It doesn't seem possible to write about the war itself because (he had forgotten for a moment) it is all but impossible. It is even more terrible to keep quiet. For the first time the ex-Yugo writer, if he is really a writer, feels real impotence, as a human being and as a writer. In his torment he seems to have forgotten that books and literature belong to the culture of peace and not to the culture of war. His impotence merely demonstrates that simple truth once again.

Just as the East European is not an altogether *normal being* (as G. Konrad says of Central Europeans), neither is the EEW, our East European writer. At this moment, he is living without a firm roof over his head, his literary house (whatever that meant) has been destroyed, and with it his personal and literary biography. We can imagine him with a bundle in his hand. In the bundle are the things he chose to take with him, a pencil and paper – the tools with which he will rebuild what has been destroyed or restore what has been taken away – and a few books in languages whose names are barely remembered (Croatian? Slovak? Ukrainian?). He is a museum item, a new cultural nomad, no longer at home in his own country, and just a guest abroad. He is the representative of a world which no longer exists, a tragi-comic being, a tightrope-walker overloaded with mental baggage, the citizen of a ruin, an eternal exile, neither here nor there, homeless, stateless, a nostalgic, a zombie, a writer without readers, a travelling salesman selling goods nibbled by moths or peppered by shells, always for too much or too little, a fool who still believes that he is either admired or reviled for what he has written, a poor hoodwinker who thinks he will outwit his new foreign milieu, a swindler who thinks he will outwit his own, home-grown milieu, while it, the milieu, is no longer his or home-grown. He is a loser, a seller of souvenirs of a vanished epoch and vanished landscapes, an incompatible being, both despairing and deceiving at the same time, former, from every point of view.

Long ago, in 1975, I found myself in Moscow for the first time. I cheerfully related my own experiences of my first encounter with the everyday reality of Moscow to my Moscow acquaintances. I often lamented out loud on the theme of *my* encounter with *their* totalitarianism. I thought I was terribly witty, I entertained them with my tale of how I was obliged to steal toilet paper in the 'Intourist' Hotel in Gorky Street. Having first shown his passport, a foreigner could have a reasonable meal in that hotel and at the same time secretly supply himself in the toilet with an otherwise inaccessible roll of paper. I cheerfully related my encounters with Moscow bureaucracy, with people; I observed aloud that some still had grey metal crowns, oh those people with 'lead teeth', comic clothes, with eternal string bags in their hands, comic caps on their heads, oh those queues, oh those empty shop windows, oh that terrible daily life . . . My Moscow friends nodded, smiled, agreed, praised the 'freshness' of my 'observations'. And then at a certain moment I realised what I was doing and stopped talking, overcome with shame. I wondered how I could so easily have taken on myself the right to explain their own life to them. I soon had the opportunity of seeing my own reflection in the mirror: from time to time I would meet my own countrymen, Yugoslavs. Two things – a passport and foreign currency – gave my countrymen a sense of security, a sense of superiority. In those years, my countrymen felt like 'someone' in Moscow, Budapest, Prague, Sofia . . . They felt superior because they were surrounded by people who were worse off. With clothes bought in Trieste, with a passport and hard currency, my countrymen were 'Wessies'. And I myself, after all, was a 'Wessie'.

A short time ago, I was with some people in (West) Berlin. Among other things, the conversation turned to toilet paper, someone mentioned the fact that some toilets in East Berlin still look 'Eastern', imagine, they still have the roll hanging on a rusty wire. The wall has come down and there are no more borders, but, for some unknown reason, the stubborn 'Ossies' still steadfastly refuse a change for the better!

And suddenly I caught a whiff of the distant smell of that same arrogance with which my Yugoslavs (now ex!) used to walk through the streets of Moscow, Prague, Budapest . . . And all at once, instead of feeling sorry for the 'Easterners' (for whom things are always worse), I felt sorry for the 'Westerners', seeing how flimsy were the foundations of their self-assurance: toilet paper, passport, hard currency. All at once I recalled all those pages which 'Westerners' had assiduously written about the sad and ugly East; pages in which, priding themselves on their own powers of observation, they discovered for themselves again and again, what was entirely obvious: the queues, the empty shops, the grey people, ugly everyday life. All at once, it seemed to me that the 'Westerners' needed that border, that symbolic roll of toilet paper as large and firm as the Great Wall of China, far more at this moment, because it showed, if nothing else, that they belonged to a softer, more fragrant and cleaner world. And, what do you know, at that moment I was an 'Ossie'!

In March 1994, in the Berlin 'Podewil', the Russian artist Ilja Kabakov put on an unusual performance. On the stage, reading from a music-stand, lit by a small reading-light, Kabakov repeated the sentences of anonymous participants in the spoken marathon which had taken place in the 'communal kitchen'. Kabakov's project, 'Olga Georgievna, your saucepan's boiling!', evoked the Soviet everyday reality, the world of so-called 'communal apartments'. From another music-stand, another male voice (that of the drummer Tarasov) read the anonymous responses. It was a kind of duet, an unsynchronised canon. From somewhere came radio music, the typical Soviet radio repertoire: sentimental verse, patriotic poems, classical music, *Swan Lake*, of course . . . The reading was occasionally accompanied by kitchen noises: banging pans, forks, spoons . . . It was a kind of requiem for a vanished epoch, its sad résumé, the very heart of the system. Kabakov's exhausting verbal flagellation made me feel physically sick, it was a kind of assault on the memory tattooed with sentences, a kind of aural hallucination, the painful noise of a vanished culture . . . That evening the audience had bought an authentic fragment, a souvenir, or at least so it seemed to me.

I knew Kabakov's project from the time of his Moscow life. The artist never imagined then that his long screen with the remarks of the inhabitants of the communal kitchen written on it would ever see 'the light of the stage'. Seeing Kabakov's performance on a Berlin stage after all those years, I was moved. And I cannot, in fact, say for certain what it was that moved me. The 'communal kitchen' was not a part of my experience. But nevertheless, I cried. And it seemed to me that I had an exclusive right to my tears. Whatever the reason, Kabakov's show rang a bell of some vague sorrow, a general East European trauma. 'Traumas acquired in the formative years are never forgotten,' says my friend V. K. and adds: 'Some people call that nostalgia.'

In this tale about books and writers, at this moment the ex-Yugoslav writer stands out from the general East European landscape through his exclusive right to unhappiness. If the customs officers of culture were to search his baggage they would be astonished at its contents. His mental baggage consists of traumas. They would find in it the heritage of the Second World

War (whether he experienced the war himself or had been told about it); then the experience of life in a system teetering between 'East' and 'West', the experience of socialism, the experience of nationalism and fascism, the experience of historical oblivion. They would find also a happier experience of multinational and multicultural life, the experience of cultural community. Out of his baggage peers the experience of soft totalitarianism, the experience of a dictatorship in which life was, if nothing else, supportable, and the new experience of post-communist democracy in which life is barely supportable. They would find the experience of mixed cultures, rural and urban, the experience of cultural cosmopolitanism and cordial xenomania, but also cultural autism and frenzied xenophobia. They would find the experience of a new war, of division and the creation of new states, the experience of chaos, blood, death and devastation, the experience of deceit, all in all the experience of multiple exile. At this time, the ex-Yugoslav writer, if he is really a writer, feels a sense of multiple exile. The contents of his mental baggage are revealed as the 'drama of non-authenticity'. Even the writers of the new states of former Yugoslavia – the ones who swear that they have finally acquired their true identity – only confirm the schizophrenic nature of the situation in which they are living. Passionate adherence to an exclusively national identity is just another form of alienation.

Writing some ten years ago about the Central European writer, Danilo Kiš said: 'Exile, which is merely a collective name for all forms of alienation, is the final act of a drama, the drama of "inauthenticity". Central European writers have long been caught between two kinds of reductionism: ideological and nationalistic. Though tempted by both, they have learned that the ideals of an "open society" lie in neither, and find their ultimate legitimacy exclusively in language and literature – the "strange, mysterious consolation", spoken of by Kafka. Dangerous yet liberating attachments: "a leap beyond the killer's ranks". Yet the commitment is not untainted by doubt: no one abandons a community without regret. Betting on eternity is as vain as betting on the present. Hence the constant sense of "inauthenticity".'[5]

[5] Danilo Kiš, *Homo poeticus*, Carcanet, 1996, p. 113.

Epilogue

In Berlin, at the beginning of 1994, I found myself at an exhibition by the Chinese artist Choi Yan-Chi. The show was called 'Swimming in the Dark'. A small room with improvised walls (which did not reach the ceiling) was painted bright red. In the middle of it were two tables with shallow basins built into them. In the basins, filled with water, lay books, spine up, as on bookshelves. The basins were connected by plastic tubes to glass jars placed on the top of the walls. The jars were half-filled with water and covered over with transparent black veils, like widows. There was a gurgling noise coming from the jars, disturbing and soothing at the same time.

I cast my eye over the titles of the drowned books. The selection was arbitrary and random. Among the books was a Croatian one, in Latin script. Marin Držić, *Dundo Maroje*. And a Serbian one, in Cyrillic. Bora Stanković, *Nečista krv*.

For a moment, I felt as though I was in a mysterious test-tube. I wondered whether the gesture of the Chinese artist Choi Yan-Chi had some secret connection with the grandiose pyromania of the Chinese Emperor Shih Huang Ti, the inventor of historical amnesia; was the artist not the descendant of those who, when they were found hiding books, were branded and sentenced to build the Great Wall of China until their death? And if so, in what kind of symbolic relationship were the Emperor's fire and the artist's water? And what place in that mysterious web of symbols had Držić and Stanković?! Am I not right now in a city in which they first burned books and then erected a wall? And have I not come here from a country in which they burn books, and where they are now erecting a wall, for the time being invisible, in a ruined city?

The question was too much. I was swimming in the dark, just like Choi Yan-Chi's books. When I came out, I was accompanied by the disturbing and at the same time soothing gurgling of the water.

April 1994

Profession: Intellectual

1. Who is to blame?

From time to time I agree to participate in some foreign event concerned with the war in former Yugoslavia. It is hard to resist the beguiling call of a righteous gathering of my colleagues.

I take the microphone, the applause is restrained. A colleague from Sarajevo appears, the applause is frenetic. My colleagues wipe tears from their eyes, fall into a passionate clinch with the Sarajevan, they dance a sorrowful tango, patting him long and tenderly on the back. I wipe my eyes as well. Our colleague is suddenly no longer a colleague but a living metaphor of the sufferings of Sarajevo. I see him straightening his shoulders, his step becomes proud, his movements dignified, his face ennobled with collective suffering. It is true that our colleague has left Sarajevo, that he is enjoying the hospitality of a foreign European country, but it doesn't matter. Now he is Sarajevo-man.

Two years ago, I met Dubrovnik-woman in Copenhagen. Admittedly, she had been married to a Dane for twenty years, but it didn't matter. I mean that detail did not affect the face of the woman from Dubrovnik. Her face was marinaded in incalculable collective suffering. The face of Dubrovnik-woman looked accusingly at the Danish audience with their impassive, ironed faces, and especially so at me. 'What have you, as a writer and intellectual, done for Dubrovnik?' shrieked the woman in a righteous voice. I was daunted by the face of suffering, the woman-city. It would have been awkward at that moment to have countered with the banal question: and what have you done yourself?

At our foreign literary meeting I notice also a Serbian colleague in the corner. He has a tic. He keeps wiping invisible spittle from his face. My colleagues – both my Sarajevan, decorated with his invisible medal, and my reviled Serb – have no idea that things are changeable and that the friendly intellectual crowd might at any moment ask us all the same question. What did you all do to prevent the war from happening?

The war in Yugoslavia is a life-show: a living retrospective of an already forgotten European repertoire of evil. Among other things, the war has brought to life a forgotten museum treasure, a profession: *intellectual*. And the related ideas of *the politically committed intellectual, the role and responsibility of the intellectual in historical events*, have been resurrected. The war has quickened the moral pulse of intellectual Europe, verbal battles *for* and *against* rage once more, intellectuals hurl mutual accusations at one another, they put all the blame on intellectuals, they work on the genre of the moral roll-call, they wage a struggle for *right* and *wrong*, for the *correct* intellectual image, to restore the lost dignity of the profession: *intellectual*. The intellectual has become a desired commodity in media terms, he keeps being asked what he *thinks* about it all, he never misses an opportunity of *thinking* about it all; on the contrary, he is convinced that it is now his *duty* to do so. He who had preferred to abandon that duty (in Eastern Europe at least) – having got to know the whole range of manipulation that this chosen duty might entail (from state intellectual to dissident, and back). Now he has suddenly forgotten his acquired 'knowledge' and he leaps into his old role with fresh conviction.

Meanwhile, neither the *victim* nor the *executioner* has any need of the intellectual. The victim would rather buy a cheap cassette and weep over his *unhappy fate* with his favourite folk singer than listen to the intellectual prattling on about why he is a *victim*. The *executioner* knows why he is an *executioner*, and indeed he has intellectuals of his own: a psychiatrist, a poet, a Shakespearologist and a philosopher. It seems that in the terrible embrace of the *executioner* and the *victim* our intellectual is redundant.

Our Yugo-intellectual (let's call him that, as shorthand, out of consideration for the typesetters) is a goodie. Let us disregard the bulk of them who perform an intellectual service to their governments, rulers and executives. Articles and books will be written about them, after all: the din they have made, beating diligently on their war drums, is too loud not to be remembered.

Our hero is different, he corresponds to the somewhat old-fashioned, but still attractive preconception of the committed intellectual. He is a pacifist by conviction, against every kind of evil, he is freedom-loving and truth-seeking, a democrat, a humanist. But still, in so far as he has accepted commitment, and commitment always entails a message, our intellectual has to consider two rational questions: where is he sending his message from and for whom is it intended.

The Yugo-intellectual has been deprived of an initial assumption in the communication chain: he has lost his centre, his place, the point from where. That is, in so far as his message originates from a convinced anti-war position, he will very soon be accused by all three sides of in fact advocating a return to the generally hated *Yugoslavism*. Because in the local interpretation codes, the war is a struggle for national survival, for liberty, against Serbian domination. In the new vocabulary of the former Yugo-nations, Yugoslavism means nothing other than a return to communism. Advocacy of peace will be interpreted from the Croatian or Bosnian perspective as advocacy of Yugoslavism, in other words the Serbian conquest option. From the Serbian perspective advocacy of peace will be interpreted as questioning the right of Serbs to their 'longing' all to live in one state. Media practice shows that all Yugo-intellectuals who have advocated peace have been accused of betraying their nation and portrayed as apologists for a return to . . . communism!

Hence our committed Yugo-intellectual takes the side of the statistically verified victim. The Serbian intellectual who publicly protests against the Serbian policy of conquest, will be attacked (or ignored) in his own milieu but readily accepted in Croatia and Bosnia. The Croats will publish his work and celebrate him as the *only honourable Serb* they know. Our intellectual is, of course, flattered by the idea of being the only honourable Serb to have risen out of the quagmire of Serbian evil. But, to whom does he address his message? To *the victim*. By directing his message to *the victim*, he has not only missed the target (it was actually aimed at the *executioner*), but he has agreed to be a Serb. And he never was a Serb. Now, however, by agreeing to the role of an honourable Serb, he no longer has the right to reproach the *victim*. And, to be perfectly honest, the *victim* does not appeal to him over much. Suddenly that victim, who had until recently been his kinsman (in the common homeland), is no longer his, but foreign. Suddenly he has found himself on the side of the *executioner*, who had never been his kinsman, but has now become so. The Yugo-intellectual knows that he has been manipulated, but he holds his tongue, he doesn't have time for subtleties, the wave of sweet commitment on the side of 'good' bears him onward.

The commitment of the Croatian intellectual has also tragically missed its target. In so far as he protests publicly against Serbian aggression, he becomes nothing other than a petty civil servant in the plenteous intellectual-political service of his Croatian government. However, if he protests also against the obvious negative aspects of his *victim-state* (which has in the meantime changed roles and become one of the *executioners* in Bosnia), he tragically misses his target once again. He too will be unable to send a message to those for whom it is intended. 'His' people won't listen to him, but he will be promptly taken up by the Serbs. He becomes *the only honourable Croat* who has dared to speak openly about the *victim's* darker side. At the same time, our intellectual has no particular desire to be a Croat, nor does he wish his righteous commitment to be used as a sponge for temporarily assuaging Serbian guilt. But, like it or not, that's how it will be used.

That is why our Yugo-intellectual usually directs his message to foreigners. It seems that only foreigners need him, or at least they listen attentively to his message. Besides, as long as it stays abroad, his message is protected from manipulation, at least for a time. However, now his failure is even more obvious. Our committed intellectual is playing his part in the wrong place, waging his struggle far from the battlefield.

And, like it or not, through the very ritual of *commitment*, our intellectual becomes a kind of public animal. He receives invitations, he accepts them more and more often, he makes more and more speeches, more and more authoritatively, not noticing that he is directing his message . . . to his colleagues. He becomes a kind of moral psychotherapist to people the same as himself. Together they hone their attitudes, multiply misunderstandings, shake their fists, and they are all firmly convinced that they are fighting against evil.

Not noticing the difference, our intellectual ceases to be the leader of the moral intellectualistic séance and becomes its object. All at once he hears foreign colleagues explaining with aggressive zeal that he had been living in an artificial creation, Yugoslavia (Who says it was artificial? *Everyone! Besides, had it been natural it wouldn't have fallen apart!* So what is a natural creation? *We won't go into that now, you're taking us on to thin ice . . .*); all that had happened was the natural (natural!) consequence of an unnatural state construct. The French assure him that there is no greater happiness than to wake up one morning in one's own national state. (Why don't you go there and wake up? *Why should we, we've got our state in which we do wake up every morning.*) The Germans assure him that Serbian intellectuals are to blame for the war. (And what about the generals? The soldiers? The criminals? *They are just carrying out the ideas of the Serbian intellectuals.*) The English explain that the Yugo-intellectual had spent his life asleep, in a dream, that Balkan hatred had been seething for years waiting to explode. (But how come I didn't see it myself? *Intellectuals are always the last to open their eyes!*) A young man approaches and shouts into the speaker's face: *It's all Susan Sontag's fault!* Why Susan Sontag all of a sudden? *She should have stayed in Sarajevo!* Why didn't *you* go there and stay? *I'm not Susan Sontag!*

All these foreign colleagues – promoters of other people's misfortune, supporters of justice in other people's lands, intellectual fighters for the truth, intellectual philanthropists, participants in debates and round-tables and bearers of media moral charisma – they all seem to him suddenly equally lost. The terrible maelstrom of the war has sucked them too into its jaws, it will suck in both those on the right side and those on the wrong one, they will all find themselves there together, although they cannot imagine it.

Finally, as crowning proof that they are in the right, they show their paper swords: their articles, their published books, their TV reports (where they lay their own lives on the line to bring the truth to the world), their photographs.

Our Yugo-intellectual is confused, he no longer knows what to think, he no longer knows where his own point of identification is, one that would be his alone, one that will give him the strength for his commitment to the side of good. Our intellectual sits wearily leafing through a book by a famous foreign writer. A book about Sarajevo. There's a photograph on the cover. The photograph shows the author in a flak-jacket, in animated conversation with Susan Sontag. 'The author and the American writer Susan Sontag during a visit to Sarajevo', runs the inscription. Sarajevo cannot be seen.

Our Yugo-intellectual suddenly feels that he is surrounded by the same nightmare from which he had fled, he sees the same multiplication of stereotypes (Can he offer any better ones?) about the origins and causes of the war and who is to blame, he seems to recognise the same war cries, the same transformation of clichés into general truths, the same transformation of truths into cliché . . . He hears the pompous voices of his countrymen, his colleagues (*I warned people that this was all going to happen as long ago as . . .*), more concerned about the copyright on their predictions than the suffering itself. Our goodie interrogates himself (How come I didn't see it? How come I didn't warn anyone of anything? And if they knew, why did they let it happen?). Suddenly our intellectual sees clearly that human unhappiness can easily be transformed into intellectualistic and artistic porn, he sees his colleagues, the bearers of truth, fighting for their media second (for their sound-bite!) in which they will salvage what may still be saved, and (or) incidentally refresh their media image. All at once he feels that instead of promoting commitment to good he is just one of the participants in a general process of transforming living human misery into media trash . . . He is even visited, for an instant, by the terrible and inadmissible thought that it, misery, is not waiting any longer for the assistance of professionally equipped masters of make-up (writers, poets, artists, intellectuals) but itself rushing headlong into the media war carnival!

And our Yugo-intellectual ponders, sweats, mumbles Hamlet-style . . . What should he do? Speak? Write? Massage the tear ducts of the reading public with war stories? Stop speaking for ever and let his silence condone the war? Donate books, the only possessions he has, to the libraries in Sarajevo? Go to Sarajevo, help to rebuild what has been destroyed? Get a job as a teacher in a village school, teach children to love their neighbour whoever he may be?

And then our intellectual suddenly seems to know what he has to do in the general media hullabaloo of the war. Indeed, he is suddenly firmly convinced that it is the only thing still worth doing. Yes, one has to adapt to the technique of the brief, loud, sound-bite. And our Yugo-intellectual buys a revolver and shoots . . .

. . . He shoots Radovan Karadžić! Him first, and then all the rest of them, one after the other . . . In the second that he fires his gun our 'goodie' is convinced that his action is breaking the long chain of evil. But then he is suddenly struck by the new thought that his previous action had achieved nothing at all, and he slowly raises the revolver to his own temple and fires another shot.

Our committed Yugo-intellectual is nothing but the author's invention. I leave him to expire, he's my alter ego, after all. That is, I don't want him to have to face the headlines in tomorrow's newspapers. Because they might run: *Yet another bloody feud in the Balkans! Colleague shoots colleague!*[1]

2. I am!

I often wonder how it happened that I changed from being a writer into a PE, a 'public enemy'. Although I'm not certain that this is the case. I mean that I was a writer first and only then a PE. Perhaps I was always a PE? Perhaps the PE was hibernating in me all those years and now it's woken up. And in the meantime I became a writer. But let's start from the beginning.

My mother is Bulgarian. Of course I would not have mentioned this unimportant detail if I had not wanted to say something else. In my earliest childhood three little girls from our road used to exercise a sweet childish terrorism over me. As soon as they caught sight of me, they would shout at the top of their voices: 'Bulgie! Bulgie!' Instead of 'Bulgarian' they would pronounce the word 'Bulgie', stressing the pointed sound 'ie'. The 'ie' pierced my child's heart like a thorn. When Romany women came down our street, the three little girls would shout: 'Gypsy! Gypsy!' And again they would shift the stress to the sharp final 'y'. The little girls had no idea what a 'Bulgie' was. That made the word seem even more offensive to them. I didn't know myself, and that's why their teasing was so hurtful. I must admit, I adored them. They were nimble, spry, and they had long plaits. I had an enormous ribbon as a substitute. The ribbon used to slip sadly sideways on my short hair, like a broken helicopter. 'Bulgie! Bulgie!' I longed passionately for their company. They didn't

---

[1] Radovan Karadžić, war criminal, recently became the winner of the Mikhail Sholokhov prize, awarded him by one of the unions of Russian writers for his outstanding poetic, humanistic and moral achievements.

want me. I was something else, a being called a 'Bulgie'. I resorted to cunning and bribed my would-be friends with chocolate. The sweet togetherness would be brief. As soon as they had eaten the chocolate, they'd start shouting: 'Bulgie! Bulgie!' The hypnotic power of my would-be friends lasted until I went to school. No one there knew that I was a 'Bulgie'. The wounds healed, like all children's wounds; the childish traumas were soon forgotten.

But was it all forgotten, in fact? Today when I try to remember how I became a PE, it turns out that I never belonged to any group, clan, society, I was never a member of any commission, editorial board (I once served on an artistic jury!). In the career of a writer in a small literary milieu, that sounds almost incredible. In small circles everyone has a turn, if nothing else then as chairman of the house committee. Like it or not, my biography persistently confirms the simple fact: I was always a . . . 'Bulgie'! And it was as though it was not in my hands, it just happened somehow, and it would not be honest now to interpret that minus as a conscious, moral choice.

It is perfectly possible that that distant childish terrorism determined the coordinates of my horoscope. Perhaps the jingling of Pavlov's bells settled permanently in my childish subconscious even then. Perhaps the cause of my unconscious refusal of (any) collectivity was the distant humiliation of bribing the three little girls with chocolate: you have to give something for the collective, you have to be the same, as part of the collective you must yourself have the nerve to exclude some unsuitable individual . . . Did this early defect (my lack of plaits) lodge in my consciousness as an enduring realisation that I was different and that mimicry did not help (the enormous ribbon would always slip sadly sideways)? Perhaps any summons to a collective awakens an unconscious fear in me? And is that childish humiliation really the reason I am a renegade today? That is, I am aware of my stubborn refusal to understand the importance of the national collective, and I recognise in myself a kind of secret, enduring sympathy for 'Gypsies' of every kind. I myself was a 'Bulgie-Gypsy'.

So why did I wait all these years and have only now become a PE? It seems that a public enemy needs above all to have a nation which can be betrayed; there has to be the correct constellation which at a given moment will turn a particular individual into an . . . enemy.

One of the proverbs I remember from my earliest childhood and which always filled me with fear goes: *Whoever aims high, falls low.* I used to hear it from my parents, later from other people around me. The moral of the proverb was that it was not advisable to be better than other people. This was my first lesson in socialisation, my first instruction that it is best to stick to the 'golden mean'. I recall that as a child I was less concerned about the high flying. I was more afraid of falling low.

At secondary school I read my way through Croatian literature avidly. I remember being amazed at the number of novels in which the main character was an educated man and . . . an outcast. These novels usually began with the hero returning to Croatia, having been studying in Prague or Vienna. The novels always ended the same way: after a certain time spent in his own milieu the hero would a) go mad; b) resort to drink; c) kill himself. Often all three. All in all, the hero paid for his high flight (to Vienna or Prague) with a low fall.

One of my favourite novels, which follows the same narrative and thematic line, is the Croatian writer Miroslav Krleža's *On the Edge of Reason*. In this novel the main character spends his whole life in 'our stinking burrow, virtually deaf and dumb, hidden and withdrawn into himself like a snail', and then at a certain moment, at a certain dinner party, reacting to an anecdote told by one of the guests, he announces that 'it's all criminal, bloody, morally sick'. And the hero loses all that he had achieved: family, friends, home, job, possessions, reputation, homeland.

Croatian writers (Serbian ones too, for that matter) have written numerous angry pages about the destructive power of their own surroundings. They wrote about it more than a hundred years ago, and again sixty years ago, and twenty years ago. All these writers have long since died. The surroundings remained.

The Dubrovnik-woman, who asked me at the literary evening in Copenhagan, in a self-righteous voice, what I had done 'as a writer and intellectual for Croatia', was no exception. Dubrovnik-woman is the norm. By naming others, in this case me, the woman in the audience had deftly demonstrated several things. First, she had absolved herself of any personal responsibility (because she represented 'the man in the street', her city, her country). Secondly, she had made use of the opportunity to confirm out loud her own political acceptability, again by naming others (which is not an individual act, but a widespread genre of declaring loyalty to the state). Thirdly, although it might not at first have seemed so, our woman from the audience had expressed a widespread and deeply rooted anti-intellectualism. Let us add the picturesque detail that the next day my anonymous countrywoman sent a letter to the Croatian academies, the Croatian writers' union, the PEN Centre, the Lexicographical Foundation, all institutions in other words, informing these institutions of the way a Croatian writer in Copenhagen 'was slandering Croatia'. I had not been 'slandering' anything, but that's not important. I imagine that in sending her letters, the anonymous woman was firmly convinced that she had 'done something for Croatia'.[2]

Why do I mention these lengthy details? In order to say something very brief. Notably, Croatian intellectuals (and Serbian and Slovenian ones, and so on and so forth) quickly learn historical lessons about survival in their own cultural milieu.

Through the experience of others and in his own flesh, he learns that an individual act is costly and unreasonable. That is, individualism as a way of behaving is a blurred area for him, a foreign country, a dangerous adventure for which one pays dearly, and which is not much fun; in his head individualism means defection, shame, isolation, a high aim and a low fall.

In his own flesh and through the experience of others, he further learns that in a provincial culture institutions are the safest protection, the institution is impenetrable protective clothing, a flak-jacket. That is why the Croatian intellectual (and the Serbian and the Slovene, and so on and so forth) hastens under the roof of an institution: an academy, a society, an organisation, a function, a doctorate, 'honour' ('He is an honourable Croatian intellectual', that's a phrase which explains a great deal). The institution is proof of his true faith.

---

[2] The phrase 'doing something for Croatia' is recent. It is exceptionally widespread ('He has done a lot for Croatia') and has become a kind of verbal medal which, naturally, never seeks proof.

Thanks to the fact that he did a lot for Croatia, one former Croatian émigré from Canada has progressed to . . . Croatian minister. In the list of acts which the present minister performed for Croatia a prominent place is occupied by the information that he had painted the word 'Tito' in red on a Canadian pig and walked it around in front of the then Yugoslav embassy in Canada. The event was noted in the Canadian press, because a Canadian society for the protection of animals had protested.

Through the experience of others and in his own flesh, he learns further that publicly proclaimed patriotism is the best protection against everything. Patriotism is a protective magic circle: a bad book, conformity, careerism, foolish statements, all will be forgiven, if we have publicly proclaimed our love for our homeland.

So it happened that recently, when asked by a reporter why there were no dissidents in Croatia, the president of the Croatian PEN centre replied: 'It's because we are all of us in fact in love with Croatia.'[3] This Croatian intellectual had uttered the magic, protective-spray formula. He had cut others off from the possibility of individual choice (by not allowing anyone not to be 'in love'). Convinced that his noble pronouncement was *protecting* the few renegades, he placed everyone under the same sticky, protective pronoun we. We are children, our acts are innocent, even when we are wrong, we are forgiven because we are in love with Croatia.

Who is that terrible Invisible Someone to whom the current dance master of Croatian intellectuals was directing his glib, conciliatory sentence? Who is it that our intellectual – president of the Croatian PEN, editor of a renowned journal and a renowned cultural newspaper, university professor and author of several books – fears? He is afraid of the Holy Majority. He is afraid of the milieu: government, institutions, police, ministers, colleagues, neighbours, us. To say something unpleasant to the milieu, is the same as saying it to oneself (for we are the milieu); to say that something is after all 'bloody, criminal and morally sick' would mean to condemn oneself to exile, to the naked, individual I. That is why our intellectual readily blows his kiss to

[3] Our Croatian intellectual, a professor of Croatian literature at Zagreb university, did not realise that he was actually quoting a sentence of Mato Hanžeković's which had some sixty years earlier inspired the greatest Croatian writer, Miroslav Krleža, unfortunately deceased, to write an essay on 'Petit-bourgeois love for what is Croatian'. In that essay – still unsurpassed in its relevance as an analysis of the Croatian patriot – Krleža says, among other things: 'This self-absorbed "besottedness" with what is Croatian is tedious, and when it is drunken (which it most frequently is), then it is provocative. Petit-bourgeois, somewhat reactionary Croatianness, "in love" with itself, is incapable of doing anything other than wail over its destiny. [. . .] This "love" of theirs for their nation is nothing but comical, false ranting. In the numerous complexes of the Croatian darkness it is the brightly lit window of a Croatian inn, through which one hears the song of drunkards and the echo of an indistinct, fragmented chant that "a Croat loves his Nation" . . .'

the homeland, thinking the while of the Holy Majority. Kisses are blown simultaneously by the intellectual and the war criminal and the warlord and the master of the written word. They are all equally 'in love' with their homelands, and who can deny them the right to love?

Homeland, Institution, We, those are the magic formulae which cancel out the danger of the individual act. And where there is no individual act, there is no individual responsibility either.

'He's certainly not going to die of shame' is the colloquial comment about a person with a weak set of moral rules. The citizens of the country which no longer exists die from bullets, knives, shells, but not one of the twenty or so million inhabitants of that former country has yet died of shame, and nor will they. For shame is a profoundly personal emotion.

And so, when I am asked who is to blame for everything, I reply: I am! And I mean it quite seriously: I am to blame, because I did nothing to stop the war. Just as I did nothing when some ten or so years ago I watched television shots of the police beating up Kosovo Albanians. Just as I did nothing when I saw the first god of war coming on to the scene a few years ago, to be followed by the second . . . I did not react to the permanent production of lies; I let them wash over me like dirty water. I did not throw myself under the first tank as it set out for Slovenia. I did not pour petrol over myself in protest at the war and set myself alight in the city square. The list of my omissions is long. My actions are negligible, on the whole they had a written character. And I did not even manage to die of shame. The fact that others did not either is no excuse. Yes, I am to blame.

September 1994

6

Footnotes

1.

Books like this one do not have a proper end. The footnote – the writer's self-defensive gesture – becomes an exhausting race in which the runner never reaches the finish. Every full stop demands the status of a comma, every sentence fights for a footnote.

The footnote thus becomes a multiple metaphor, for the defeat of the writer and the human being. Everything that the author has written is just a footnote to the long lists of names of people who have lost their lives, families, friends, homes or the homeland which was until recently shared, a footnote to the texts written by the warlords. One such text is the Sarajevo *Book of the Dead*.

Terrible reality carries off the victory and the author, aware of her defeat, must willy nilly accept an arbitrary end. The only thing left for her to do is to leave behind her fragile markers, dates.

2.

The end of the book is composed of chance fragments of text: two little newspaper items, some genuine pieces of homework, the report of the success of a book, some statements printed in a newspaper, the impressions of a refugee . . . All of these fragments, contrasted and concordant, serve once again, from a new angle, to ask the question raised by all the texts in this book.

3.

In the Zagreb daily newspaper, *Vjesnik*, of 17 March 1994, there were two small news items. The first was about a Benetton poster, under the headline 'Benetton's Advertisement for Death'. It shows a photograph of a T-shirt (with a bullet hole in the chest!) and a soldier's trousers, and the text in Croatian: *I, Gojko Gagro, the father of the deceased Marinko Gagro, born 1963 in Blatnica, district of Čitluk, agree that the particulars of my dead Marinko*

should be used for a poster for peace in the struggle against war.
And, of course, the Benetton slogan: *United Colours of Benetton.*

The other item, under the headline 'How to recognise Croatian identity', advertises an exhibition, 'The Visual Identity of Croatia', to be held in Munich, and writes about the project of a Croatian designer 'which contains the visual effects of our country – its public, cultural and economic distinguishing features'. The fundamental characteristics of the exhibition are 'the recognisably modern lines of the Croatian identity with historical elements: changing squares and combinations of colour'. The latest contribution of the Croatian designer, it says in the note, is a new necktie or cravat, *Croata-International*, to be used to promote Croatia in the world as the *Home of the First Cravat.*

Both newspaper items, placed next to one another, alongside the reality of war, are a deeply ironic digest of a tale of war, a tale of identity or . . . a tale of design. And if we add to this the fact that a new perfume, called *Serb* has recently been produced in Serbia, in the shape of a bomb,[1] then a relationship between design and meaning, i.e. a battlefield, is established between *The T-Shirt*, *The Cravat* and *The Perfume-Bomb*.

4.

Identity, national, this is the key word of the war. A war for something (it is always for something!) gives war the status if not of an acceptable human activity, then at least of an *understandable* one. Without realising it, interpreters – politicians and political scientists, journalists and political commentators, historians and sociologists – play into the hands of the warlords. The warlords are eager to assist their interpreters.

5.

War is an organised, collective criminal act waged by *chieftains*, *leaders* and warriors for very tangible things: for political power,

---

[1] The whole world has become, essentially, aggressive, from film and painting, to war on the whole planet. The bomb is the symbol of that negative energy. By stylising a beautiful woman's body embracing a bomb and not permitting it to explode, we have made this energy positive. 'Our "bomb" is a symbol of peace', explains the perfume's designer, Jovan Nježić. The subheading of the article informing us about this fashion novelty is: 'Serb perfume – between originality and provocation'.

for territory, for this or that kind of profit. Wars are never waged for people. Wars are waged by one kind of people against others. And since the crazed majority cannot be condemned, the criminality of war is wrapped in a package of reasons, causes and arguments, into something 'comprehensible' to all. Thus we all become accomplices in the war – ordinary citizens, international political forums, political negotiators and observers. Thus the criminal madness of the minority, which passed skilfully through the so-called institutions of *the will of the people*, becomes as a result our 'common destiny', 'the destiny of the people', an 'historic moment' and so on.

6.

Responsibility for the war in former Yugoslavia does not lie with former Yugoslavia as a 'repressive' federative community, nor with the 'fall of communism', but with people: the generals (first *Yugoslav*, then Serbian), power-seeking leaders, political dilettantes (local and foreign), political manipulators (local and foreign), the manipulated people, murderers, criminals and their followers. In all of this, *identity*, national, is the key reason and fuse, the key error and defeat.

'The war has also destroyed my biography. The two states in which I lived – the SFRY (Socialist Federal Republic of Yugoslavia) and BiH (Bosnia and Hercegovina) – no longer exist, and I have not found a new one. The school I went to no longer exists, nor do the documents and diploma I achieved. All I can prove is where I was born and what my name is,' writes a Sarajevo journalist.

7.

The *struggle for national identity* becomes acceptable in the newly established value system. It gives political legitimacy to war criminality, madness, hatred, collective and individual pathological behaviour, pleasure in killing, profiteering, territorial ambitions, as well as to patriotism and the right to self-defence. So that the irony should be complete, the same notion has been used by both the stronger, who were conquering, and the weaker, who were defending themselves. Thousands upon thousands of citizens of Bosnia and Hercegovina, but also of Serbia, are today nomads, deprived of identity. Their homeland has been taken from all of them, equally. And the topography of war terror – towns and ancient monuments of Bosnia and Croatia transformed into ruins, dead and living people all equally reduced to numbers – bears witness to the destruction of every identity.

8.

In the general chaos it does not occur to anyone to make simple connections between things. From the Second World War till today, generations of Yugoslavs were brought up in the conviction that the partisans had fought a just war against the enemy: German and Italian fascists, and local *Chetniks* and *Ustashas*. Propaganda teams in the new national states have crushed the 'partisan myth' or the 'partisan truth', assuring their peoples that all sides in the war carried out the same crimes. In the process of redesigning *historical truth*, the partisans, the 'goodies', have lost their place of honour and the fifty-year-old *historical truth* of the Yugo-peoples has become an *historical lie*. Today, fifty years later, with almost exactly the same ideological repertoire, national teams are convincing their peoples that they are waging war for justice (for *freedom*, against *fascists*!). And a new *historical truth* is being designed in which the people are once again dying for the same things. Only, many people have overlooked the fact that the times are different.

9.

Anonymous human flesh has served in the battle for territorial, national and state designs. One of a thousand dead – the T-shirt with a bullet hole – happened to achieve the right to a brief life after death. Marinko Gagro. *United Colours of Benetton*. On the ruins of the former state (in war, while it is still warm), new states are hastily building their own identities. One of them is endeavouring to be *recognised* in the international market-place as *the homeland of the first cravat*.

10.

In a time of designing and redesigning, the only thing there is no place for is shame. The orgy of destruction is sold under the designer label 'struggle for liberation'. Places which ought to be a point of complete moral defeat and shame, are designed as places of collective triumph and pride. 'I was glad to watch Sarajevo burn,' announced Dragoš Kalajić, an artist, one of the spiritual designers of the new Serbian fascism.

There is a story going round that it is possible to go from Belgrade on a day trip organised by a tourist agency to Vukovar (a former Croatian and Yugoslav town, now just a Serbian ruin). Tourists can look at the ruins, sit with the destroyers eating soldiers' beans from a communal pot and take photographs, as souvenirs. In the Serbian media Vukovar is called 'liberated Vukovar'. There is also a story going round that the Belgrade Institute of Architecture has designed a project for the reconstruction of Vukovar in the Byzantine style. Vukovar was a baroque town.

The Croatian army destroyed the famous ancient bridge in Mostar. The action was commanded by a general, otherwise a film director. 'A bridge is a strategic point, so its destruction is a normal thing,' commented a Croatian intellectual, also a film director.

'We shall build Dubrovnik again, even lovelier, even older,' is allegedly the statement of a Serbian 'designer' after several months of Montenegrin-Serbian shelling of the city.

And so on and so forth, day after day.

II.

And while in one place the brutal savagery of destruction is sold as a victory, in another the result of that savagery, human tragedy, is sold as a tasteful product which will provoke agreeable and short-lived tears. Zlata Filipović wrote a diary about everyday life in Sarajevo, knowing that the diary would be published abroad. As was predicted, the book became a best-seller. The world media designed a child's product as the diary of a 'Sarajevo Anne Frank'. The little girl from Sarajevo was chosen to take the world a message. The message contained just as much unhappiness as the general consumer is capable of consuming. The message stimulates a lukewarm reminder that some fifty years ago, oh, 'terrible things' happened (Anne Frank), and that, oh, 'terrible things' are happening today as well (Sarajevo). Except that the media 'happy end' of today's story (at the end the little poor girl is bathed in fame and riches) legitimately cancels out the horror of what has happened. So evil has moved into fairy-tale. In this sense the product of the little girl from Sarajevo is perfectly compatible with the moral and emotional market-place of our times.

12.

Let us add to the media fairy-tale the footnote that the destroyed Vukovar immediately served as a cheap location for a Belgrade director's 'anti-war' film, while the survivors of Vukovar served as extras in a Zagreb director's 'anti-war' film.

Let us add to the footnote the fact that – while the inhabitants of Sarajevo were dying, and the inhabitants of Dubrovnik were holding their breath as they listened attentively to the silence – a luxurious ship set sail for Dubrovnik from Venice. On the PEN-ship were writers from all over the world, the largest number being Croatian. The writers oiled their throats with Adriatic lobsters and wine while they prepared for the forthcoming verbal battle against fascism. The newspapers gave daily reports of their struggle on the sea, and later on dry land.

Let us add to the footnote a new note: that the hit song by the singer of newly composed folk music, the Bosnian Muslim Fikret Kujundžić, entitled 'Manjača' has earned huge sums in Germany. The design of the cassette reminds one of posters for third-rate horror films: blood drips from the letters 'Manjača'. Several tens of thousands of refugees from Bosnia are living in Germany. Let us remember that Manjača was a Serbian concentration camp for Bosnian Muslims.

13.

And while in one place the greedy battle for power and territory is sold as a battle for great ideas, in another, protected by the label of great ideas, ordinary, nameless people are conquering their own 'brighter' future.

Thus one Bosnian (Muslim) was first exposed to torture by his countryman, a Serb (who amused himself by aiming knives at him, like a living dummy), and then forced into exile. Now, as a refugee in Berlin, he is constantly pursued by one image: the image of his closest neighbour and long-standing friend carrying plates, which his friend had always liked, out of the house (quick, quick, before someone else moves in!).

Thus another Bosnian, today a refugee in Berlin, fled from his small Bosnian town by paying a hard-currency travel-tax to warriors of various emblems, including foreigners, yes: 'UNPROFOR' soldiers, and Serbian and Croatian and Muslim soldiers . . . Abandoning his flat with a few essential things, he realised that he was leaving for ever and that he had left his family photographs behind. He went back for a moment, but the flat was already occupied by other people. 'We live here now,' they said, resolutely not opening the door. The people behind the door used the vital verb 'we live', instead of the neutral 'we reside'.

14.

And while in one place the war in former Yugoslavia is sold as the result of the 'unnatural' federative creation of Yugoslavia, as a postmodern necessity, as the liberation of nation states from the 'prison of nations', in another, protected by the labels of political interpretations, men in uniforms fight for their right to prolonged life. Twenty-six-year-old Damir, a professional Serbian killer, reports to a journalist from *Le Monde*: 'I hope that the conflict will go on for a long time yet. What would I do in peacetime? I don't know how to do anything but fight. [. . .] If the Muslims finally disappear from the planet, then I hope that the Serbs will declare war on some other states. I've lost all my friends in this struggle. My life is a failure. Just let it go on . . . The Serbs are not stupid, they know that the West is letting them do its dirty work: exterminating the Muslims. The Serbs will always be alone, and that suits me. [. . .] There's no hatred on the battlefield, there's no one there but madmen. Yes, I'm mad. Last year a journalist suggested that I go with him to Paris. The poor Frenchman . . . All I could have done was to become a gangster or a hired killer. My only profession is sowing death around me. That's why I want the war to go on. If peace comes, my own people will kill me, no state needs lunatics. Normal people will never understand us, they don't know what it means to kill a man!'

15.

A little girl from Bosnia, whose parents had been killed in front of her by Serbian soldiers, was in hospital, in the psychiatric wing. When the psychologists asked her what she was most afraid of, the little girl replied: 'People . . .'

16.

At least 85 per cent of the 200,000 killed in the three years of war in Bosnia were civilians, it says in *Time* of 20 June 1994. According to *Time*, 4 million people have become refugees, the majority driven out by ethnic cleansing. The documentation collected by government and private organisations bears witness to at least 5,000 crimes. For the time being there are 3,500 names of perpetrators on the lists. In the great majority of cases, the crimes were carried out by Serbs, but some were carried out also by Croats and Muslims.

Cherif Bassiouni, chief of the UN expert commission for war crimes, has announced that 65,000 documents about 5,000 crimes have been collected. Ten teams, each made up of three women (a prosecutor, a psychiatrist and an interpreter) have interviewed 200 raped women, and collected information about a further 800 cases. The victims are aged from five to eighty-one. The commission estimates that there are about 20,000 unreported cases.

The Bush administration, writes *Time*, compiled a list of names of alleged war criminals, which includes those of the Serbian leader Slobodan Milošević, the leader of the Bosnian Serbs, Radovan Karadžić, and the commander-in-chief of the army of the Bosnian Serbs, General Ratko Mladić.

17.

Slobodan Milošević – surrounded by the obedient dogs of war, loyal intellectuals, media servants and a devoted police force – is the first criminal on the list. Milošević succeeded in destroying Yugoslavia (all in the name of a struggle for Yugoslavia), bringing world diplomacy to its knees (its representatives crawl assiduously in front of him in the hope of placating him), and turning the majority of the Serbian population into hostages of his personal madness. With the propaganda slogan 'If we do not know how to work at least we know how to fight', Milošević opened up hitherto unknown scope for freedom, by restoring 'human dignity' (the words of a well-known Serbian writer!) to criminals, murderers, mafiosi and all those who secretly wished for just such 'freedom'.

In the end it will be difficult for anyone to maintain that he did not know: under the slogan of a struggle against fascism (Croatian 'fascism' and Muslim 'fundamentalism') Milošević has produced a post-communist mutant, a fascistic state, which sells the world a 'bomb', its symbol of peace.

18.

In the state which has been transformed into a madhouse, N., an unfortunate lonely Belgrade woman, in a moment of insanity, during Sunday lunch, plunged her blunt knife, not into her meal, but into her mother's stomach. The old woman survived, and N. found herself in the psychiatric wing of a Belgrade hospital.

An acquaintance who told me of the case, sought out the head of the department, a psychiatrist, and found him in the middle of a conversation in which he was explaining to someone that he had been in Vukovar.

'In Vukovar we cleansed house by house. We simply threw a grenade into each one. My only regret is that we did not know who was in the houses and we probably killed some of our own people,' blabbered the doctor, meaning local Serbs.

To my acquaintance's worried question as to what would become of the patient, N., and whether she would be put on trial, the psychiatrist replied: 'Of course. It was attempted murder.'

19.

Let us repeat the advertising cynicism of the 'Serb' perfume designer. Our bomb is a symbol of peace! The sentence is certainly an historic slogan: never before has a *bomb* been a *symbol of peace*. The sentence belongs to a new language, the language of a postmodern hell, and is perhaps the most exact expression of its essence. Perhaps that is why Europe is so ready to inhale the stench of death, taking it to be the scent of perfume.

20.

'In the last few decades, imagology has gained a historic victory over ideology,' writes Milan Kundera in his novel *Immortality*.

Two Western journalists found themselves in a small Bosnian town. In the local inn, a drunken Serbian warrior, the local warlord, understanding them to be journalists from Japanese television, drove his parents, two terrified old people, at pistol-point, to make a statement for Japanese television. The journalists repeated in vain that they were not Japanese and they were not television reporters.

The image of the two old people uttering sentences in front of a non-existent Japanese television camera and their drunken, crazed son is just one of innumerable fragments of the postmodern hell.

'Ideology belonged to history,' writes Kundera, 'while the reign of imagology begins where history ends.'

21.

At the end of the century, Europeans appear to be preoccupied with a collective 'spring cleaning'. Out of their cupboards they take their nightmares, exterminations, wars, fascisms, concentration camps, totalitarianisms, repressions, old hatreds, victims; they air the historical repertoire of evil. Europeans are cleaning their house for their entry into the twenty-first century. The work is pleasant, it doesn't hurt, the nightmares have long ago been emptied of their meaning. The swastika and the hammer and sickle lie reconciled in a drawer, their owners have already forgotten the symbolism of their old badges.

Unpredictable reality brought Europeans at the end of the century an unexpected collective psychotherapeutic gift: the repetition of their historical nightmares in the flesh. The live-show, the war in Bosnia, quickens the collective metabolism, cleanses moral and intellectual attitudes, revives forgotten traumas, stimulates re-interpretations. The war in Bosnia is a collective healing séance, a grandiose spectacle of virtual reality, a live hallucination, a virtual encounter with forgotten evil.

That is why at this moment many Europeans are rushing to Sarajevo to place flowers on their own grave. 'Europe died in Sarajevo', this is the truth that has been transformed into a beautiful and sad slogan. We are sorry that we have died, they say, our condolences, they say, and they return beneficially cleansed to their homes.

22.

'Maybe after all the year 2000 will never occur [. . .] for the simple reason that the curve of History will have become so accentuated as to create a reverse trajectory, with the result that that temporal horizon will never be attained. History would in that case turn out to have been an asymptote: an infinite curved line tending towards its own end, yet never reaching that end, and at the last moment veering off from it in the opposite direction,' writes the French philosopher Jean Baudrillard.[2]

23.

In the general chaos of our times and values, among the crazed clocks at the end of the century which instead of the present are

[2] Jean Baudrillard, *Transparency of Evil*, Verso, New York, 1993.

ticking out the past, ticking out the past as though it were the future, which have perhaps stopped, a child is moving the hands on the face. At a time which like an enormous recycling machine is transforming living human misery, at the very moment it occurs, into dead matter – into a photograph, an 'image', a newly composed popular hit, a design, a statistical datum, a story, a media-second, a sound-bite, a slogan – a child, a small ten-year-old friend of mine in Zagreb, is trying to wind his watch. I keep his *homework* as a precious possession. Sometimes I wonder whether it wouldn't be wise to synchronise my watch with his.

24. Homework
A decade is a length of time lasting ten years. We live in the twentieth century. A century is a length of time lasting a hundred years. The twentieth century began on 1 January 1901 and ends on 31 December 2000. I was born in the ninth decade of the twentieth century. My mother was born in the sixth decade of the twentieth century. Children are the descendants of their parents. Parents, grandfathers and grandmothers are their forebears. The past is the time that has gone by. What will happen and what will be is the future. History tells us what people did in the past, how they entertained themselves and how they dressed.

25.
Nedžad Begović from Sarajevo ended his diary – which encompasses a whole year of war in Sarajevo, and covers just one page – with the sentence: 'I shall never be able to tell anyone anything about any of this . . .'

September 1994

7

In Ruins

'What are you guarding?' I ask the guard.
'Nothing. Ruins.'

Vlado Mrkić, *Nikad više zajedno*

Life as a Soap Opera

It's better to use tearjerkers than teargas!
Emilio Azcarraga, Mexican media tycoon.

1.

The destruction of the communist systems in the former communist countries gave rise to numerous common phenomena. These have been discussed by historians, political scientists and writers. Books and essays about them are still being written and will go on being written.

However, I am sure that none of them will mention *Isaura the Slavegirl*! This Brazilian television soap opera, which was shown simultaneously on the television screens of many different communist countries, was the last connecting link in the worn-out communist chain. *Isaura the Slavegirl* was a brief-lived common glue, the last identification tag, a kind of obituary to the dying mammoth of communism. No one is going to believe me. But even if they did, it would make no difference. A Brazilian soap opera, no less!

Alyosha Kopytok from Novosibirsk, whom I met in Middletown, USA, entertained me one evening by relating episodes about the slavegirl Isaura, surely, we both agreed, the silliest soap opera of all time. Alyosha assured me that there was a Russian secret society of 'devotees' of Isaura. And he gave me a taste of the local Novosibirsk humour that Isaura had inspired.

Studies will be written about Milošević's national-homogenising rallies, and the prominence at them of a television cameras. The placards carried by the massed millions will serve as evidence in the theory of the rise of Serbian fascism. And perhaps one day a still photograph will show a figure bearing a placard with a surprising message: Save Isaura the Slavegirl! They say that the Yugoslav rock singer Djordje Balašević carried such a placard at one rally. That was his gesture of protest at the encroaching stupidity.

Thanks to harsh strategies of enforced oblivion, the 'Yugoslav' culture of the everyday has been entirely wiped out. It is hard to see how it could one day nevertheless find its place in a museum of the history of the everyday. Because there won't be any museums either. Because the country itself has disappeared, and with it its history, and with its history so have the memories of some 20 million citizens. And consequently, for instance, no one will ever ask how it was that after the war (the Second World War!) Yugoslavs watched Mexican films and sang Mexican songs, or why, in poor post-war Yugo-everyday life, there had been that warm inclination towards remote Mexico? Similar entertaining questions may occur to people who live in more peaceful times, in more stable and richer cultures. But the lives of the Yugo peoples are harsh, they are concerned only with questions of death and survival.

2.

One of my favourite books as an adolescent was *The Psychiatrist*, a textbook for medical students. I no longer remember how it came into my hands and remained in my possession, but I do remember the pleasure with which I read it. First I would look at the case-studies, they were more entertaining than any other material. Later I would add diagnoses to the case-studies.

I shall never forget one of the patients. He persuaded the others to dig a tunnel under the hospital so that they could all run away to the seaside. He used to pat them on the shoulder in a stupor, shouting: 'Come on, get going, don't look so flabbergasted!'

This joker was suffering from an acute mania.

So it was that as a very young woman I learned about neuroses, psychoses, schizophrenia, manic-depressive psychosis, paranoia and hysteria. I learned to distinguish lasting from short-term dementia, and how to recognise reactive psychoses, because the unusual, crackpot stories about people were accompanied by professional explanations.

I mention this reader's youthful inclination because I often feel that I am reading the 'Yugoslav tragedy' through a whole bundle of knowledge gleaned in the course of my adolescence.

3.

Recently I made a short trip to America. Whether it was because of the brevity of the visit, or because of my insomnia (because I could not sleep I spent several nights running watching the television documentary series *Divided Memory*), or because of the bundle I have already mentioned – in any case, I suddenly experienced America as a traumatised nation at a psychotherapy session. The screen showed dozens upon dozens of grown women (and some men), under hypnosis, in either collective or individual sessions, weeping as they recalled scenes of sexual abuse in their early childhood. In the majority of cases they were abused by their own fathers. They were followed by rows of appalled fathers some of whom denied it, others maintained, confused, that they did not remember, while others admitted that they might have forgotten such a thing. Child abuse is the current top, one could almost say collective, trauma in America. That is, the percentage of people who maintain that they were sexually abused is phenomenally high. According to the rules of their profession, psychiatrists and psychoanalysts are obliged to believe their patients, nothing can convince the patients that their trauma is not genuine, the parents cannot prove to anyone that they did not do anything of the kind. This attractive topic has produced a whole industry: books, discussions, newspaper articles, films, television series, documentary programmes, plays, public debates, its own terminology ('false memory syndrome') and variants, of course. Recently a female secondary school teacher was accused of sexually abusing her pupils. The boys all testified in court.

Where traumas are concerned the possibilities of manipulation are enormous. Personal traumas (which rapidly become collective) may be manipulated by psychoanalysts or psychiatrists (because of their bank accounts or professional advancement), by the media (because of ratings and earnings), by the publishing industry (for the same reasons), by the film industry (for the same reasons), by politicians (to denigrate their opponents), by grown-up children (to get their own back on their parents) and the traumatised (because of their acquired right to their own trauma).

At the same time everything affects everything else, and it becomes hard to establish what is true and what is a lie.

4.

Radovan Karadžić, the leader of the Bosnian Serbs, is a psychiatrist; Jovan Rašković, a Serb nationalist who, they say, committed suicide, was a psychiatrist; Slobodan Milošević, the Serbian President, is, they say, a potential suicide. All of them, and many of their followers, have induced a collective madness, transforming first the former and then the new states into madhouses and the citizens of their states into patients. Democracy is interpreted as the creation of the right to individual and collective trauma. Digging up bones buried during the Second World War, the new leaders bestowed on their peoples the right to trauma. And there were plenty of bones. Communism as trauma, Goli Otok (the Yugoslav Gulag) as trauma, Tito as trauma, the Chetniks as trauma, the Ustashas as trauma (the Second World War ones, of course), Yugoslavia as trauma, the borders between the republics as trauma, brotherhood and unity as trauma, and so on and so forth.

'I see my father's big hairy hands reaching towards me . . .' is a sentence, soaked in floods of tears, frequently spoken by the traumatised American patients during their psychotherapy sessions.

The new leaders, the 'doctors', the directors of the state madhouses, have induced traumas (or perhaps only released them, no one knows any more), and then taught their patients to identify them. The Serbs have named theirs: Croats, Muslims, Albanians . . . The Croats have identified theirs: Serbs and former Yugoslavia. No one asks the Bosnians: they just die.

5.

Seen from such a perspective, it could be said that it was the right to personal trauma that brought Hitler to power. Major changes in power systems, in themselves traumatic, are always accompanied by the phenomenon of magicians, hypnotists, illusionists, hastily trained psychiatrists, 'doctors', all kinds of manipulators. In the Soviet Union 'perestroika' produced Koshpirovsky, the great hypnotist who succeeded in hypnotising millions of then still Soviet viewers, through the television screen. Today Koshpirovsky stands by the side of another great hypnotiser, Vladimir Zhirinovsky. We can imagine Karadžić and Milošević as street illusionists manipulating little balls around in front of the world and the local community. And everyone joins in fascinated, hoping that they will outwit them. And they always lose. All that is guaranteed with tricksters is that you lose. At the same time no one notices that the little balls they are playing with are human corpses. Because the tricksters are skilful, the balls move too rapidly through their fingers and disappear.

6.

In the chapter about reactive psychoses, my old psychiatry textbook states that there are several factors which drive a stable personality into a state of reactive psychosis. These are: the intensity of the psychotrauma, the accumulation and frequency of similar psychotraumas and their unexpectedness, their effect on the most vulnerable place in the structure of the personality, damage to the 'ego' and various predetermining elements. These elements include psychological and physical exhaustion, convalescent states, chronic intoxication, a sense of personal insecurity, enduring states of anxiety, and so on and so forth.

All forms of reactive psychosis, my textbook goes on, may be divided into primitive defence mechanisms and complex psychogenic reactions. Primitive reactions include *pseudodementia*, *Ganzer's psychosis* (the patient gives imbecilic answers, his consciousness is disturbed, and he has a tendency to amnesia), then *pseudocatatonic stupor* and *puerilism* (an adult person behaving like a child). Complex forms can be *schizophrenic reactions*, *paranoid reactions*, depression and *induced psychosis*.

For all of the last group, my textbook asserts, there must exist both an *inducer* and an *induced*. Inducers are usually psychopathic, paranoid and manic-depressive patients, while the induced are usually people who are emotionally or intellectually immature, culturally backward and inadequately educated. They blindly accept the ideas, thoughts, behaviour and attitudes of the inducers and support them in everything.

7.

If someone were to make a dictionary of the 'great ideas' which have sprung up among 'small nations',[1] that is to say in the states

---

[1] *Velike ideje i mali narodi* (Great Ideas and Small Nations) is the title of a book by the Croatian President Franjo Tudjman.

which came into being with the collapse of Yugoslavia, if anyone were to make a dictionary of the ideas put forward in statements, interviews, speeches, books, measures and laws – whose authors are local politicians, people in power, intellectuals, 'thinkers' – the reader of such a book would be astonished by the intensity and sheer amount of general madness and stupidity. Such a quantity of stupidity could even be entertaining if it were not that beneath it, as its product, there were heaps of corpses, destroyed cities and shattered lives.

The collapse of multinational Yugoslavia, the war and the creation of new nation states have been accompanied by a parallel process: the process of the idiotisation of its peoples. There have always been factors ready to take on the role of inducers: the media (television, newspapers, radio), ministers and ministries of culture, various state commissions (for monitoring the purity of the Croatian language, for instance), censors and entertainers, old and newly baked writers (such as Mirjana Marković, the wife of Slobodan Milošević, for instance), newly elected university deans, and many others. And, of course, the new state apparatus, which has replaced the stupid in all posts, releasing them for the even more stupid. Or the voluntarily stupid.

The process of successful idiotisation is possible only in conditions of isolation. The commonest metaphors for isolation are the prison and the hospital. The post-communist states beat the breasts of their new democracy proudly, as we abandon the prison and opt for . . . the hospital.

8.

It has taken just five years (and all possible repressive measures!), to create the first precondition for the final idiotisation of the nation. That first precondition is collective amnesia. And truly, the citizens of the new states, including Croatia, have forgotten both their own personal history and history in general. They have burned their party membership cards, thrown their own aunt from Smederovo (a town in Serbia) on the rubbish heap – some have done this with their Serbian husbands, wives and other relatives – they have forgotten that they were ever in the partisans (that is, today it is better to have had a father who was an Ustasha, a Second World War one), they have forgotten all they said, did and wrote before, they have forgotten all they ever learned, they have forgotten their former life. And the only thing they can do now is to be born again, this time in the new Croatian state. This means that the citizens of Croatia are now just five years old. Behind them lies a past that has been wiped out, and before them . . . an ever better future.

9.

That this future is better is already confirmed by the short memory of the Croatian citizen. Two years ago television screens showed pictures of Croatian corpses and ruined Croatian houses. Now on television new hospitals and factories are being built, ribbons cut, Croatian mothers keep giving birth to quins, delighted foreign statesmen visit us, foreign investors rush to invest their capital, foreign tourists dash to our beautiful coast, our currency, the *kuna*, is stable, Europe respects and esteems us, the flame on the Altar of the Homeland shines eternally and steadily.[2]

As for the outside world, not much is happening there, and what is does not really make suitable viewing. That is why news from Sarajevo is the last item in the evening news bulletin and very short. After all, Bosnia is a foreign country, isn't it?

And what of the present? The reality that surrounds the Croatian citizen has become so opaque that our citizen no longer understands anything (do not forget, he has been reduced, or he has reduced himself, to the mental age of a five-year-old). Reality no longer exists.

10.

Infantilism (or in the vocabulary of my psychiatric textbook, puerilism), cultural autism and regression are the dominant features of Croatian cultural everyday life.

There have never been more stupid television programmes, there have never been so many children grimacing precociously,

[2] On the ruins of the medieval town of Medvedgrad, on one of the slopes of Sljeme, a hill outside Zagreb, the new Croatian state has built a monumental concrete shrine, called 'The Altar of the Homeland'. On this altar an eternal flame burns, and the place is used in the main for political and diplomatic rituals. Foreign statesmen are usually taken there in the course of their state visits to Croatia to place a wreath for the Croatian fighters who fell in defence of the homeland.

as they imitate grown-ups (singers and entertainers), and there have never been so many adults imitating children.

Croatian newspapers are filled with stupefying texts. Many of them are dedicated to the President and the new Croatian state. For, in the collective consciousness, the President and the new Croatian state are one and the same. Numerous interviews with the President's shoemakers, gardeners, tailors, barbers, private photographers and chauffeurs express the stuttering awe felt by the so-called ordinary people towards the President and the state itself.[3]

Life has begun all over again for the newly born people. That is why the newspapers often feature irresistible educational articles intended for the 'ordinary man'. The kind of thing our parents read after the war (the Second World War!). They belonged to the socialist genre, to columns usually entitled 'Knowledge is Power'.

That is why it is quite possible for an otherwise serious Zagreb theoretician of literature to fill her column in a literary magazine regularly with texts which are a mixture of *bon ton* and idiosyncratic training, in which readers are taught in a delicate literary manner not to spit on the ground, not to shove each other in trams, how to be agreeable, how to enhance everyday life.

That is, presumably, why a general moralising, instructive tone has entered writers' and journalists' texts. It is, presumably, because the reading public is only five years old.

Croatian television shows shots of the President in sumptuous marshal's uniforms, parades of powerful Croatian tanks and the invincible Croatian army. There is a story going round that during one such recent Croatian military parade some viewers – some of those who have become thoroughly dizzy – became so excited by the sight that they began to chant 'Tito! Tito!'

II.

The state lacquer, so like a cheap soap opera, veneers over opaque reality, brushing a shiny layer over the real face of the new mutant states which have sprung up in place of the former,

---

[3] On Croatian television there are often shots of President Tudjman meeting the 'common people'. The common people frequently address Dr Franjo Tudjman as 'Doctor', which simply confirms our metaphors of the state as asylum and the President as doctor.

communist ones. The thick, shiny lacquer covers over the 'democratorships', the democratic dictatorships, which are perhaps also mafia systems for laundering money, for trading arms, perhaps a legalised opportunity for those in power to steal private property, to set up family dynasties; for murders which will never be reached by the hand of justice . . . We know nothing of all of that, we never shall and it is not our business to know. Our life, the life of the 'ordinary Croatian man',[4] has in any case been reduced to bare survival. Outside are the 'terrible' Serbs, inside are lies. And the 'ordinary Croatian man' reaches for the proffered sedative.

12.

Narcotherapy is one method of treating psychiatric patients. In poor countries television is the cheapest narcotic, accessible to everyone. Soap opera is a narcotherapeutic genre for adults. Children have fairy-tales.

Zagreb state television (there is no other) offers several therapeutic sessions every day. The stupid *Santa Barbara* is currently surpassed by even stupider Mexican and Venezuelan soaps. The title of one of them is *The Wealthy Also Weep*.

In more than 200 episodes, a Mexican television soap opera tells the story of a poor girl, Marianna, who, after many convolutions, trials and suffering finally finds happiness. And her happiness is, of course, her beloved husband Alberto, a luxurious home and children. Thus, in the consciousness of the collective audience, Marianna has become a fairy-tale about the 'ordinary man' (a woman!) against whom the forces of evil conspire. It is well known that it is impossible to avoid or control evil in soap operas, it happens to us, and lasts as long as possible. Because it is only bad guys who ensure the continuation of the serials. When they get to the happy end they stop.

Overcoming obstacles from day to day, shoulder to shoulder with poor Marianna, the viewer learns, therefore, that he is not responsible for his life, for his destiny is in any case determined by others. He also learns, presumably, patience.

---

[4] The phrase 'ordinary man' came into use when the Croatian President introduced the term 'common people', i.e. the rabble, mob, simple folk. This innovation brought with it as a matter of course the appearance of new hierarchical terms previously used to designate feudal class hierarchies (such as 'knight', 'rank' and the like).

13.

Just as in a real psychoanalytical session, thanks to the Mexican soap opera, the 'ordinary Croatian citizens' (on the whole female citizens) who exhaust themselves daily in front of the television screen, have found themselves at the very centre of their own traumatic reality. Reality, in other words, does exist, real life is a soap opera.

For the first time, images from the screen are completely (and completely by chance) synchronised with everyday life, hence the exceptional popularity of the series. There are the *same* people on the screen, look, they are dressed like us; the poor resemble *our* poor, the rich are like *our* rich. The women (the poor women) wear the same flowery chintz housecoats (ah! don't they take us back to the fifties!), they sit in exactly the same kitchens, make the same coffee, gossip, pronounce exactly the same sentences that we would. There are identical pictures on the walls, identical little vases and tablecloths on the table . . . The homes of the rich are furnished exactly as we would furnish them if we were rich, with the same three-piece suites, the same bedroom sets. The heroes of the soaps live inside, just as we do, never outside, that's too expensive. The only difference is that the categories of good and evil are more transparent, the bad are bad, and the good are good, there's no doubt or confusion as in real life.

14.

It has therefore happened by chance that everything the repressive media had twisted into a tangled knot – isolation, war, induced madness, a repressive system of government – is being gently unravelled by innocent soap opera. All at once we find that the genre itself, whose fundamental assumption is that it is different from our daily lives, is in fact portraying our very own life. In the general chaos of values and time, in a traumatically repressive era, soap opera, however paradoxical it may sound, returns us to ourselves. Yes, that is really what our daily life looks like. We have gone backwards, back to the fifties again. The country was definitely just as destroyed, we remember. And we were just as poor, we remember . . . We remember.

They say that the soap *The Wealthy Also Weep* has been bought in China, in the Arab world, in the former socialist countries, in Bulgaria, Romania, Hungary . . . They say that in

Russian factories work is interrupted when Marianna is on television. They say that billions of people throughout the world weep as they follow the fortunes of the poor Mexican woman.

Somewhere, therefore, memory does exist, a little confused, a little vague, a little pale, but still it is a picture of *our* lives. And we are not alone in front of the television screen. Somewhere an invisible media internationalism is being established, a soap-international, a warm media brotherhood. How did it go . . .? Proletarians of the world . . .? Proletarians of the whole world, let us unite once more! Save Marianna! What about Bosnia, Sarajevo? Let them wait . . . Until there is another repeat of the soap *Isaura the Slavegirl*. Then we shall remember everything clearly. Then we shall know exactly where we stand.

June 1995

Postscript

And, while, in a paradoxical way, the marathon Mexican soap opera restores to the traumatised citizens of former Yugoslavia a lost sense of everyday reality, so everyday life (and death) are gradually being transformed into soap opera. In the late autumn of 1996 I ran into an acquaintance from Sarajevo. 'Sarajevo is echoing with the sound of gunfire and grenades from dozens of feature films being shot there,' she said. 'Steven Spielberg is coming soon as well,' she said.

'If Karadžić and Mladić haven't yet managed to destroy Sarajevo entirely, then Spielberg will,' joked my acquaintance.

People talk about a play in a New York theatre in which Meryl Streep plays a raped Bosnian woman. If this is not true, it will be; if not Meryl Streep, then someone else.

Right now the people of Sarajevo – those same people who have just survived the siege of their city – are earning a few coins as film extras. 'They lie covered in red paint, they play shattered corpses in the Sarajevo Markale market,' says my acquaintance. Anyone who omitted to cry over the real victims, will cry over the acted ones. And those acted ones will be more genuine than the real ones, because the real ones were too real to be genuine.

The film rights for the story about the Sarajevo Romeo and Juliet who died on the bridge have been bought and resold several times. Ruined Vukovar plays ruined Vukovar in some film, the Sarajevo ruins play Sarajevo ruins in another, *pretty villages* really *burn prettily* in a third. So misery becomes fiction, fiction pornography, pornography becomes real tears.

My Sarajevo acquaintance is an artist. She is making a video-game about the occupation of Sarajevo. She is convinced that it will help people understand what really happpend in Sarajevo, only through a compatible medium, she says, through a video-game.

My Sarajevo acquaintance is wrong. Tragedy becomes tragedy only when it is transposed into the genre. The fact that it provokes tears is not the event itself, but the rhythm and rules of the genre, the representation of reality and not reality itself, the funeral, in other words, and not the deceased.

'Soap opera . . .' I say to my acquaintance. 'Soap opera . . .'

The Confiscation of Memory

Shto by stalo vse ponjatno
Nado nachat' zhit' obratno.

A. Vvedenskij[1]

1.

I knew them because I was friendly with their son when I was a
student. We were 'going out' together, as we said then. Stanko
and Vera lived in a small two-roomed flat in the centre of Zagreb.
Stanko was a retired officer of the Yugoslav People's Army, Vera a
housewife. They had come to Zagreb from Bosnia. Their flat was
like a little museum of Yugoslav everyday life. On the walls hung
pictures of plump beauties lazing on the shores of romantic lakes
densely populated by moorhens and swans. On top of the
television was a Venetian gondola, on the fridge wooden herons
(the most popular Yugo-souvenir sold at that time on the whole
by Gypsies, 'from Triglav to Djevdjelija'). A picture of Tito hung
on the wall beside family photographs. The gleaming polish of
the heavy walnut furniture (the first post-war Yugoslav-made
bedroom fittings) was protected by little hand-embroidered
'throws'. Boxes decorated with shells and other seaside
mementoes with inscriptions ('A souvenir from Makarska', 'A
souvenir from Cres' . . .) made a kind of diary of their summer
holidays. Those were years when everyone 'went to the sea' – the

---

[1] These lines by the Russian avant-garde poet Aleksandar Vvedenskij contain the
humorous message that one should start living backwards in order for everything to
become comprehensible.

Adriatic, of course – every summer. On holidays organised by the trades' unions, of course.

On the shelves in peaceful coexistence resided various kinds of books: the ones my friend read (Schopenhauer, Kant, Hegel, Nietzsche, Kierkegaard . . .), Stanko's (books about Tito, monographs on Yugoslavia and the National Liberation War . . .) and Vera's (cheap paperback 'romances').

The flat was full not only of things but also of people, just like a station waiting-room. Through the flat came the neighbours' noisy children; they would come for a drink of water or a piece of bread spread with Vera's home-made jam. Every day Vera's friends would come, for 'a coffee' and 'a gossip'. Our friends would come as well, some of them would stop to play a game of chess and drink a glass of home-made Bosnian plum brandy with Stanko.

Vera kept preserves for the winter under the massive walnut double bed. There were tidy rows of jars of jam, gherkins, paprika, pickle and sacks of potatoes and onions. Once Vera called me into the bedroom, dragged a plastic box of soil out from under the bed and proudly showed me her freshly sprouted tomato seedlings. Every day Vera baked Bosnian pies and fed her neighbours, friends, the neighbours' children, everyone who called in. And many people called in, drawn by the life (and the beguiling cultural syncretism!) which bubbled cheerfully in the little flat like water in a kettle.

And then the children (Stanko and Vera had a daughter as well as a son) finished their studies and left home. Concerned for their parents, the children found another, larger, more comfortable flat and moved their parents in. When I went to see them, Vera burst into tears accusing the children of taking away her things, her souvenirs, her furniture, they had taken everything, she had only been able to save one thing. And Vera took me into the modern bedroom and dragged out from under the bed a picture of plump beauties lazing on the shores of a romantic lake densely populated by moorhens and swans.

'I keep it under the bed. The children won't let me hang it on the wall . . .' she said in the hurt tone of a child.

Vera still baked Bosnian pies, only no one came any more. Stanko invited people every day for a game of chess and a Bosnian brandy, but somehow it wasn't on people's way anywhere, or they didn't feel like playing chess. Yes, the flat was certainly larger and better, but with the change for the better life had definitively changed its taste.

In the name of a brighter future, Stanko and Vera's belongings, the guarantee of their emotional memory, had been 'confiscated'. The two old people found themselves, like fish out of water, deprived of their natural surroundings. People are not fish, so Stanko and Vera did not expire, but they had somehow abruptly aged, or at least that's how it seemed to me when I visited them . . .

2.

As I travelled, I knew that I would turn up among people who at some stage would start talking enthusiastically about things I would not understand. So it was that I once found myself in the company of some American acquaintances who were talking about children's books, their shared cultural inheritance.

'My favourite book was *Winnie the Pooh* . . .' I said, not quite truthfully. It wasn't until much later, when I was already an adult, that Pooh had become my favourite literary character.

My acquaintances looked at me in surprise. No one ever talked about Milne. Although I had been in America many times, I suddenly found myself on quite unfamiliar territory. For a moment I was a complete stranger, a being from another planet. And now, what a nuisance, this stranger would have to be told something that we never usually have to explain. Something like the fact that one and one makes two.

Some time ago I happened to be in the company of some Dutch friends. After a pleasant conversation about this and that, my Dutch friends and I were overjoyed to find that both they and I always watched the annual Eurovision Song Contest. The thought of the silly television spectacle aroused a childish gaiety in these grown-up people. And suddenly the atmosphere became warmer and more relaxed. For a moment we were a family, a European family.

As I travelled, I discovered that my American, Dutch, English friends and I easily talk about all kinds of things – about books and exhibitions, about films and culture, about politics and everyday life – but in the end there is always a bit of space that cannot be shared, a bit of life that cannot be translated, an experience which marked the shared life in a particular country, in a particular culture, in a particular system, at a particular historical moment. This unshareable and untranslatable layer in us is activated by a Pavlovian bell. And we salivate unfailingly, without really knowing why. That unknown space in us is something like a shared 'childhood', the warm territory of communality of a group of people, a space reserved for future nostalgia. Particularly if it should happen that this space is violently taken from us.

3.

There is an old joke about the Scots who, when they get together, shout out numbers and laugh at the numbers instead of telling the jokes. Why waste unnecessary words?

I believe that I can cross cultural borders easily, but nevertheless I observe that, while I may communicate with 'Westerners' with greater interest, I definitely communicate with 'Easterners' with greater ease. It somehow turns out that we know each other even when we don't, that we pick up nuances more easily, that we know we are lying even when we seem to be telling the truth. We don't use footnotes in our conversation, they are unnecessary, it's enough to mention 'The Golden Calf' and our mouths already stretch into a smile.

An encounter with an 'Easterner' is often an encounter with our own, already forgotten past. I have met Russians who enthusiastically mentioned the name of Radmila Karaklaijić[2] and Djordje Marjanović[3] or proudly displayed their Yugoslav-made shoes bought in the Moscow 'Jadran' shop. I have met Chinese people who when they heard where I was from delightedly pronounced 'Ka-pe-tan Le-shi'[4] and Bulgarians who enquired with incongruous rapture about 'Vegeta'[5].

All these names and things hardly meant anything to me, they belonged to an early socialist Yugoslav past which I hardly knew

---

[2] A Yugoslav pop star who was more popular in the, now former, Soviet Union than she was in, now former, Yugoslavia.

[3] Now a completely forgotten Yugoslav 'musical idiot', somewhat like the Czech Karel Gott.

[4] Kapetan Leši, the handsome and brave hero of Yugoslav partisan films, shot in the early nineteen sixties, completely forgotten today. In the meantime, he seems to have 'died' in China as well.

[5] 'Vegeta', seasoning for food, a popular Yugoslav export article, can still be found in Turkish shops in Berlin or Russian shops in New York's Brighton Beach. Together with 'Minas-coffee' (known affectionately as 'minasica'), 'Vegeta' has become a cult object of the Yugoslav diaspora.

was 'mine', but the recollection of them provoked the momentary prick of an indistinct emotion whose name or quality I was not able to determine at the time.

'If I haven't seen something for thirty or forty years it will give me that intense "punch" of nostalgia,'[6] says Robert Opie, a passionate collector of objects from everyday life and the founder of the Museum of Advertising and Packaging in Gloucester.

4.

Things with a past, particularly a shared one, are not as simple as they might first appear from the perspective of the collector. In this 'post-communist' age it seems that 'Easterners' are most sensitive to two things: communality and the past. Everyone will first maintain that his post-communism is different, implying at the same time his conviction that life in his post-communism is closer to that of the Western democracies than that of the other (post-communist) countries. The 'Easterner' is reluctant to admit his post-communist trauma in public, nor does he have the will to try to articulate it. He has had enough communist traumas (he holds the copyright to them too), but they have worn out, aged, or something, and don't seem to hurt any more. The cursed 'homo duplex', mentally trained to separate his private life from the collective, weary of the constant ideological pressure to live facing towards the future, exhausted by the excessive amount of 'history' that has happened to him, frightened by memories that keep popping up from somewhere, at this moment the 'Easterner' would most like to sink into the compliant and indifferent present, at least that's how it seems. It is only the younger and more honest of them, like the (former) East German playwright Thomas Oberlender, who will exclaim out loud: 'Why, I have two biographies and one life . . . !'

5.

Things with a past are not simple. Particularly in a time when we are witnesses and participants in a general trend of turning away from stable, 'hard' history in favour of changeable and 'soft'

---

[6] Unless you do these crazy things . . .': An interview with Robert Opie, in *The Culture of Collecting*, ed. John Elsner and Roger Cardinal, Harvard University Press, Cambridge, Mass., 1994, p. 29.

memory (ethnic, social, group, class, race, gender, personal and alien) and a new cultural phenomenon which, as Andreas Huyssen suggests, bears the ugly name of musealisation. 'Indeed, a museal sensibility seems to be occupying ever larger chunks of everyday culture and experience. If you think of the historicising restoration of old urban centres, whole museum villages and landscapes, the boom of flea markets, retro fashions, and nostalgia waves, the obsessive self-musealisation per video recorder, memoir writing and confessional literature, and if you add to that the electronic totalisation of the world on databanks, then the museum can indeed no longer be described as a single institution with stable and well-drawn boundaries. The museum in this broad amorphous sense has become a key paradigm of contemporary cultural acitvities.'[7]

6.

If we accept the 'museum' as a paradigm of the contemporary sense of temporality, then, at least as far as European-American culture is concerned, the places we occupy in the museum and our attitude to the museum do nevertheless differ.

For instance, although in the American intellectual market the key questions of our time at the end of the century are what is history and what memory, what is personal and what collective memory, and so on, it seems to the European outsider that the American attitude to the 'museum' is different from that of the European, particularly the East European. History, memory, nostalgia are concepts in which contemporary America has recognised a high cultural-therapeutic and, of course, commercial value. The stimulation of the recollection of different ethnic immigrant groups, encouraging the reconstruction of a lost identity (Afro-American, for example), opening immigrant museums (on Ellis Island, for example), establishing chairs at American universities, which, concerned with various cultural identities, are concerned with memory, the publishing industry, newspapers and television which readily commercialise the theme – all of this supports the idea of the new American obsession with 'musealisation'. The American market contains

---

[7] Andreas Huyssen, *Twilight Memories: Marking Time in a Culture of Amnesia*, Routledge, London/New York, 1995, p. 14.

everything, from documentary videocassettes of contemporary history to souvenirs of the recent past. Americans of all ages can purchase instant products to satisfy their 'historical' yearnings. And although in America everything rapidly 'becomes the past', it seems that nothing disappears. Television broadcasts series and films which were watched once by today's grandfathers and are now watched by their grandsons. The old *Star Trek* and *Star Trek, the New Generation*, the old *Superman* and the 'Supermen' of all the subsequent generations, are available simultaneously. In this way, the American lives a kind of eternal present, or at least that's how it seems to the superficial European outsider. The rich market of nostalgia seems to wipe out nostalgia, it appears that real nostalgia for something implies its real loss. But America does not know loss, or at least not in the sense that Europeans do. Thus, through the process of commercialisation, but also through the elasticity of an attitude to recollection which is constantly changing (making – remaking, shaping – reshaping), nostalgia is transformed into its painless surrogate, at the same time as its object.[8]

That, I repeat, is how it appears to the European outsider. Because what our European (or Euro-ego-centric) claims an absolute right to, without the slightest hesitation, is just that, History, and an understanding of History.

7.

Because for him, the European, History has got involved in his private life, altered his biography, it has caused him to perform 'triple axles', he was born in one country, lived in another and died in a third; it has caused him to change his identity like shirts, it has given him a feline elasticity. Sometimes it seems to him that, like a cat, he has nine lives . . .

Recently Europe produced the biggest souvenir in the world, the Berlin wall. The Berlin wall shattered into millions of little souvenir pieces: some turned into senseless objects and ended up

---

[8] The artistic representation of history often follows the idea of the commercial surrogate. Thus one American artist represents the Holocaust by using miniature children's toys (little SS officers, little camps and camp inmates), then he transfers the posing figurines to photographs, reproducing well-known documentary scenes. The children's toys in the photograph imitate the past horrific reality to perfection, only the most attentive eye will observe that it is a question of a surrogate.

in the rubbish-bin, and others into pieces of shrapnel which hit wounds which had long since healed, and opened up new ones. Today Europe rummages through drawers of memories, particularly those which contain the traumatic files of the First World War, the Second World War, fascism and communism. This feverish activity, connected with remembering, may have its origin in the fear of the possibility of forgetting. At this moment Europe is concerned with repeating the process of historical guilt: the old rubbish which European countries, in the process of creating and re-creating their own memory, have shoved under each other's doors, is trying to return to its owners. The processes are often sensitive and painful, particularly in the relationship of (former) West and (former) East Germany. The politics of remembering is connected also with artistic questions of its representation, the media, its consumability, commercialisation and morality. Europe is like the Teufelsberg with its contents bubbling out. (The Teufelsberg is the highest hill in Berlin, whose surface is covered in grass; under the grass lie millions of tons of Berlin ruins piled up after the Second World War.) Old souvenirs which had surfaced – flags, relics, red and yellow stars and black swastikas – are joined by new, still warm grenades, bullets and bombs freshly arrived from Bosnia.

8.

But let us return to a detail from the beginning of this story. Why did I tell my American acquaintances that my favourite book was *Winnie the Pooh*? Perhaps because for a moment I felt lonely, perhaps I wanted to be able to join them in the warmth of the collective steam of nostalgia by conjuring up a shared childhood, or perhaps, most likely, because I realised that an honest answer would have demanded too many explanatory footnotes and in the end have remained untranslatable.

My favourite children's book was *The Hedgehog's House*. This little, warm, innocent book became the property of generation after generation of children born in Yugoslavia. Its author was Branko Ćopić. I knew a circle of Zagreb students who studied Lacan, Foucault and Derrida assiduously, but proclaimed the 'silly' but 'dear old *Hedgehog's House*' their cult book, and amused themselves by reciting lines learned by heart. It was a free nostalgic gesture, a little test of memory of a generation. Branko Ćopić, otherwise a Bosnian Serb, committed suicide twenty years ago, having previously foretold in a dark postscript to one of his last books, all that would happen later. Today Branko Ćopić is a forgotten writer.[9] One day, when the ruins are cleared, he will find his place, according to his blood group, in the history of Serbian literature. Maybe Bosnian too, it depends on the generosity of spirit of the moment. In Croatia, Branko Ćopić no longer exists. For three reasons, it seems. The first is the war itself which is in its nature a human activity that encourages amnesia. The second is the fact that Ćopić was a Serb. And the third reason is the fact that Branko Ćopić belonged to the former, Yugoslav culture. If he existed, the hand of a nostalgic reader might well reach for him. And at a time of erasing one memory and constructing a new one (that is a time of enforced amnesia and enforced remembrance), every nostalgia, including the most harmless, is, rightly, considered dangerous.

9.

If the reader envisages the state as a house, it will be easier for him to imagine that for many inhabitants of former Yugoslavia, along with the war and the disappearance of their country, many other things have been confiscated as well: not only their homeland and their possessions but also their memory. In the general and obvious misery no one takes into account invisible losses. On the priority list of losses, both for the loser and for the observer, the first place is the loss of life itself, then the loss of those closest, then material goods. Only then come, if they ever do, intangible losses. To discuss them at a time of real death is inappropriate. The memory of *The Hedgehog's House* is an offensively luxurious emotion. However, this little book is not the only thing on the list of losses. And that list could be drawn up by some twenty million plus inhabitants of the vanished country (if they really could, if they really wanted to and if they knew who to do it for).

[9] A note by the Sarajevo journalist Branko Vuković describes a moving episode: a conversation with a young Sarajevo sniper of Muslim nationality. In delirium, the soldier, who had 'freaked out', said that, remarkably, the only thing that really 'turned him on' was the book *Eagles Fly Early*. This children's book, by Branko Ćopić, is a highly emotive topos of the cultural memory of several generations of Yugoslavs. The episode is, of course, virtually untranslatable, its emotional impact, weight and symbolism can be understood at this moment only by former Yugoslavs, and only by those of them who are more resistant to nationalist hatred, that is the less numerous.

Over the last five years, media consumers could hear from journalists, television reporters, politicians, historians, intellectuals and writers more or less the same story about the war in former Yugoslavia. In this interpretative package of the Yugoslav misfortune, there was a place for geographical maps and borders, national, religious, ethnic differences, languages and scripts, historical causes, the 'repressive' Yugoslav federal system, communism and post-communism, aggressors and victims, the repertoire of human evil, massacres, rapes and camps, the names of international negotiators and mediators, peacemakers and murderers, politicians and leaders. Numerous books have been published by historians and political analysts, journalists and writers, reporters and lovers of 'catastrophe tourism', stray inquisitives and politicians, photographers and hunters of strong emotions, experts on Eastern Europe and authorities on other people's misfortune. These numerous observers, participants and intermediaries, drawn by the spectacle of death, have accused one another of moral indifference and incompetence and scored for themselves intellectual, professional and moral points (however, there is no cash desk where these could be counted), fighting over other people's land.

In this heap of spoken and written words, few have mentioned the ordinary people. The anonymous citizens of the former country were and have remained the indifferent statistics of the killed, dispersed, vanished, refugees, survivors, identified by national group as Muslims, Croats, Serbs ... If for the local warlords people were simply indifferent cannon fodder, I wonder how it is that among the numerous interpreters of the post-Yugoslav misery so few pity the ordinary people. The misfortune of others is free and as a rule does not hurt. We may still pity, but it is hard for us to be in a position to comprehend the true dimensions of other people's loss. And those losses include such a difficult-to-grasp, many-faceted and complex thing as collective memory.

10.

Seen from outside, at this moment the Yugoslav peoples resemble demented gravediggers. They appear stubbornly to confirm the dark stereotypes others have of them. Included in that repertoire of stereotypes is the idea that, throughout their history, the Yugoslav peoples have done nothing other than bury and dig up human bones. At this moment, human corpses are being eaten by starving pigs or, at best, they end up in nameless, collective graves as a dark pledge to a 'brighter' future. And, truly, the Yugoslav peoples are, it seems, most blithe when they are in a position to destroy each other's past (gravestones, libraries, churches, monuments of cultural-historical value). At this moment they are confirming that they are masters of destruction: only true masters know how to remove one another's memory. Nor are they any more tender towards their own past: they will wipe it out or resurrect it, according to need, with the ease of a computer.[10] Through their activity of digging up and ritually mourning human bones and burying fresh ones without funeral rites, the Yugoslav peoples are spinning in a diabolical circle: it is impossible for them to come to terms with their own past, present and future.

On a different, and more elegant, level, this could also be the story of Proust who was forcibly deprived of the 'key' to his remembrance, a madeleine. At first glance a trivial thing, an ordinary madeleine. However, in the Balkans that 'key' is taken by force from its owners. The 'key' only comes to the surface many years later, when there is no longer anyone who would know how to open the door with it, and when the confiscators too are long gone, when it has become a meaningless thing.

11.

The citizens of former Yugoslavia suddenly found themselves in the situation of having two biographies and one life. The older ones even added three biographies to their life. The new, 'postcommunist', powers, taking over the knowledge of their communist-predecessors or simply applying their own, communist knowledge, know the great manipulative value of collective memory. For collective memory can be erased and rewritten,

[10] One of the freshest examples is the Croatian town of Knin. For several years Croatian state propaganda used Knin, 'the cradle of the Croatian kings', to construct national memory. Knin and its surroundings were populated by rebellious Croatian Serbs. In August 1995, when Knin was 'liberated' (that is, when the Croatian Serbs were driven out *en masse*), and when the Croatian flag was placed on the Knin fortress, the town lost not only its manipulative-propaganda value but also its 'memorial' value. Now, Knin is a town of ghosts, deserted and plundered. It was plundered by the Croats themselves. There are identical examples on the Serb side as well. One such 'hot' manipulative topos in the Serbian national memory is Kosovo, inhabited by the Kosovo Albanians.

deconstructed, constructed and reconstructed, confiscated and reconfiscated, proclaimed politically correct or incorrect (in the communist language: suitable or unsuitable). The political battle is a battle for the territory of collective memory.

With the collapse of multinational Yugoslavia began the process of confiscating the Yugoslav collective memory and its replacement by the construct of national memory. The war simply speeded up the process and radicalised the measures. Today, it seems, the work has been successfully completed: one memory has been erased in order to establish another.

In this process, some 'fortunates' have acquired the right to reclaim their 'property' confiscated some fifty years previously. This generous gesture depended on the general policy of self-design of each former Yugoslav state individually, on the policy of creating its own national image. Thus, for instance, in Croatia the right to reclaim their confiscated memory was extended to those who lost the Second World War, the ageing political émigrés, the Ustashas, collaborators with the Pavelić regime, the occasional guard in Croatian concentration camps, the occasional minister in Pavelić's government. The long-lived old men acquired a symbolic satisfaction: returning after so many years they were able here and there to see Ustasha symbols, here and there a street sign with the name of Mile Budak,[11] here and there the portrait of their leader Ante Pavelić. They were given the opportunity of rehabilitating their own past: they could not resist the opportunity of explaining to the Croatian public that the Croatian concentration camps during the Second World War were actually not particularly comfortable hotels. Some of them acquired a function in the new government, some published a book, some found a fragment of their past and the hope of its complete restoration in a group of young Croatian neo-Nazis. Why was it they, and not some others, who were given the right to the return of their property? Simply because they served the new authorities as welcome living fragments in constructing the national memory. The new authorities are rapidly working on the design of the new Croatian state. By all accounts they intend to shape Croatia into a state of interrupted historical continuity (that famous historical continuity was, presumably, interrupted

---

[11] Minister and Croatian writer, the dedicated signatory of the racial laws in Pavelić's Nazi statelet.

by the communists and the Serbs). Hence the connection with the four-year fascist Independent State of Croatia is presumably felt to be more natural than the lengthy connection with communist Yugoslavia.

All in all, today memory in the form of fragments and splinters of the past, the occasional symbol and the occasional souvenir, has been restored to the minority. For the sake of the minority, it has been denied to the majority, those for whom the construct called Yugoslavia had with time become their daily life.

12.

Today it turns out that many East European, former communist cultures had prepared their own death, by collecting the material of collective memory. Thus, for instance, from the first signs of its encroaching end, Russian alternative artists assiduously measured the pulse of the dying mammoth of communism. The works of Russian 'soc-artists': the Soviet political kitsch in the paintings of Komar and Melamid; the Soviet everyday reality, 'byt', in the paintings and installations of Ilya Kabakov; the language of Soviet pop songs, newspapers and the street in the poems of Dmitri Prigov; the linguistic collocations taken from popular Soviet almanacs, school primers and textbooks in the creations of Lev Rubinstein; the kitsch of Soviet communal living in the installations of Larisa Zvezdochetova; apt-art, and so on and so forth – with the disappearance of its context, this whole artistic 'archaeology' of Soviet daily life has changed its original function. The sharp tones of artistic subversion have today acquired the soft patina of nostalgia. In other words, the difference between American pop artists and their Americana and Russian soc-artists and their Sovietana is being established today, retrospectively. For while Warhol's Campbell soup may still be bought today in every American supermarket, the icons of Soviet daily life are disappearing. Whether they like it or not, the works of Russian soc- artists have consequently become the document of a vanished reality. Thanks to the assiduous, lengthy investigation of the mythology of Soviet daily life with which Soviet alternative artists were concerned, today the epoch which is no more has left a vast array of artistic material. That is why the present lively intellectual activity of the Russian intelligentsia connected with investigating collective memory is readily understood. The intelligentsia – philosophers, cultural historians, sociologists, anthropologists – are all today concerned with investigating the various layers of 'Soviet' cultural memory, not avoiding (and not ashamed) to investigate the mechanisms of collective and personal nostalgia.[12]

The picture is, of course, incomplete and not all layers of collective memory are touched on equally. Particularly not the more delicate of them: Stalinist camps, but also the many years of shared life in the multinational and multiethnic community that was the Soviet Union.

13.

What stimulates nostalgia, that prick of indistinct emotion, is just as complex as the topography of our memory. Just like the mechanism of dream, where the oneiric encounter with an insignificant and harmless object can provoke a quite disproportionate emotion, so are the mechanisms of nostalgia unpredictable and hard to read. Nostalgia is not subject to control, it is a subversive activity of our brain. Nostalgia works with fragments, scents, touch, sound, melody, colour, its territory is absence, it is the capricious corrective to adaptable memory. The strategies of its activity are deceit, capriciousness, subversion, suddenness, shock and surprise. Nostalgia knows no hierarchy of values, the 'material' it deals with is not divided into good and bad, acceptable and unacceptable, clever and stupid; on the contrary some 'silliness' is often its favourite choice.[13] The field of its activity is the unconscious, the chemistry of the brain, the workings of the heart, its mechanisms are often close to the phenomenon which neurologists call the 'phantom limb'.

[12] In her book *Common Places: Mythologies of Everyday Life in Russia* (Harvard University Press, Cambridge, 1994), Svetlana Boym ends her investigation of Soviet everyday life with the observation: 'And so it goes: one wishes to cure nostalgia through history, but ends up simply historicising one's own nostalgia.'

[13] At one time I had imagined a project of collecting 'mental souvenirs' of life in former Yugoslavia and asked my friends and acquaintances to participate. Regardless of social, cultural, generational, group differences I was interested in knowing whether it was possible to identify a common corpus of emotional topoi in our memory. The meagre 'material' I collected proves that such research is possible. Predrag Dojčinović, a poet and essayist who lives in Amsterdam exile, contributed his 'souvenir', a description of the wrapping of a 'Buco' cheese. This was a little square of processed cheese with a hideous portrait of a fat boy on the wrapping. This detail suggests not only the capriciousness of nostalgia but also its 'untranslatability' into other cultures, in other words the exclusivity of collective memory, its absolute copyright.

Precisely because of the elusive nature of nostalgia the authorities in the new states of former Yugoslavia have coined the term Yugo-nostalgia and given it an unambiguous meaning. The term Yugo-nostalgic is used as political and moral disqualification, the Yugo-nostalgic is a suspicious person, a 'public enemy', a 'traitor', a person who regrets the collapse of Yugoslavia, a Yugo-nostalgic is the enemy of democracy. The term 'Yugo-nostalgia' belongs to the new terminology of war.

14.

Whether nostalgia will one day succeed in articulating its object and determining its space is hard to predict. It is equally debatable whether such a thing, nostalgia, exists at this moment and if it does what its nature is. It is perfectly possible that the war has put an end to collective Yugo-memory, leaving behind only the desire for as speedy as possible oblivion.

Nameless ex-Yugoslav refugees scattered over all the countries and continents of the world have taken with them in their refugee bundles senseless souvenirs which nobody needs (a line of verse, an image, a scene, a tune, a tone, a word . . .). In the same bundle of memory jostle fragments of past reality, which can never be put back together, and scenes of war horrors. It is hard for their owners to communicate all these shattered fragments to anyone, and with time they wrap themselves into a knot of untranslatable, enduring, soundless distress. Those who stayed and preserved a roof over their heads will adapt more quickly, will learn the words of the new times and forget the old.

Confiscated memory behaves like a disabled body which from time to time suffers from the syndrome of the 'phantom limb'. They say that in Belgrade, in Serbia, people assuage their Yugo-nostalgia by listening to old hits of the Zagreb pop singers Arsen Dedić and Gabi Novak. They say that in Zagreb suburban taverns drunk people shout songs of Lepa Brena,[14] wondering later in their morning hangover 'what came over them'. They say that divided families and old friends meet in Skopje, in Macedonia (Skopje is the 'most natural' meeting place, there 'Yugoslav' products can

---

[14] Lepa Brena, an unusually popular singer of 'newly composed traditional' songs. The last 'adrenalin' unifying cultural topos of the nations and nationalities of Yugoslavia. Up until the last moment, she declared herself a Yugoslav. Today, Lepa Brena, a Muslim by nationality, in order to save the remnants of her market, declares herself a Serb.

be bought in the shops, and dusty, greasy photographs of Tito have not entirely disappeared from the walls). They say that when the Vojvodina-born pop singer Djordje Balašević held a concert in Ljubljana, many people from Zagreb travelled there, and also many from Belgrade. They say that in Zagreb, Belgrade, Ljubljana videocassettes of old 'Yugoslav' films are sold illegally. In Skopje, they say, a cassette of 'Yugo-hits' from the sixties is selling like hot cakes. Even the Croatian President, Franjo Tudjman, one of the fiercest proponents of the confiscation of Yugo-memory, in a speech at a moment of joyful excitement because of the 'great Croatian military victory' in Krajina (or the expulsion of the Serbs who lived there) accidentally used a Serbism, the Serbian version of the verb 'to organise'![15]

And, as we are discussing confiscators, let us mention also Slobodan Milošević, the first 'player' in the Yugoslav game of destruction. Stealing the name of Yugoslavia and applying it to Serbia and Montenegro, by simply manipulating the name, in other words, Milošević confiscated the symbolic territory of possible community, therefore also of Yugo-nostalgia. The ordinary, fearful citizen of former Yugoslavia, when trying to explain the simplest things, gets entangled in a net of humiliating footnotes. Yes, Yugoslavia, but the former Yugoslavia, not this Yugoslavia of Milošević's . . . Yes, nostalgia, perhaps you could call it that, but, you see, not for Milošević, but for that . . . former Yugoslavia . . . For the former communist Yugoslavia?! No, not for the state, not for communism . . . For what, then? It's hard to explain, you see . . . Do you mean for that singer, for Djordje Balašević, then?! Yes, for the singer . . . But that Balašević of yours is a Serb, isn't he?!

15.
Yugoslaviana – the mythology of everyday life which the citizens of former Yugoslavia built and shared for fifty years – is today sketching its outlines in the air. When chance brings them together – ex-Yugoslavs suddenly discover the charm of collec-

---

[15] The film director Želimir Žilnik conducted an unusually interesting test of collective memory in his documentary film *Marshal Tito Among the Serbs Again*. He took an actor with a remarkable physical resemblance to Tito, dressed him in a marshal's uniform and let him walk through the streets of Belgrade. Although all the passers-by knew that he was a surrogate, nevertheless, many of them, forgetting themselves, spoke with the surrogate as though he were Tito himself.

tive memory. Many are astonished at the realisation that 'all that' existed and disappeared 'just like that' without their even noticing. It occurs to some of them that the East German 'Trabant' is now a museum piece, while the Yugoslav 'Fićo'[16] has simply disappeared and it never occurred to anyone to put it in a museum. And what kind of museum anyway? Because where could you find anyone, in the new national states preoccupied with building their own national ego, prepared to take over 'foreign' discarded rubbish, fifty-year-long 'Yugoslav' cultural memory? Even if he were to do it, who would be able to read it properly today in the completely altered codes? Because memory consists of numerous untranslatable components which demand numerous explanatory footnotes, and, even with the footnotes, who would in fact understand something that entwined, grew together and evolved into a shared life of fifty years? For who would, really, accept the articulation of a vanished cultural everyday life (jokes, objects, television series, newspapers, pop music, language, humour, those warmest commonplaces of collective memory) and invest in it the effort required to 'musealise' it at least partially, when real museums and old libraries are being transformed by the demented Yugoslav gravediggers into dust and ash?

16.

> Where do you come from?
> From Yugoslavia.
> Is there any such country?
> No, but that's still where I come from.

This anonymous quotation comes from the beginning of a book entitled *Children of Atlantis*,[17] a collection of essays by young people, ex-Yugoslavs, refugees from the war. It is said that language produces reality. In the story of the disintegration of Yugoslavia and the war there are numerous cruel and terrifying examples that confirm this thesis. The word 'Atlantis', which refers to the myth of the disappearance of a country punished by the gods, erupted as a metaphor for Yugoslavia with the eruption

[16] The first car manufactured in Yugoslavia.
[17] *Children of Atlantis: Voices from the Former Yugoslavia*, ed. Zdenko Lešić, Central University Press, 1995.

of the war. The choice of Atlantis as a metaphor only confirms the general sense of its definitive disappearance.

We take our tale about collective memory back to the very beginning, to Cicero who, in his work 'De Oratore' tells the story of the poet Simonides of Ceos, the 'inventor' of memory.[18] According to the story a nobleman of Thessaly named Scopas invited the poet Simonides to a banquet at his palace in order for him to write a poem in honour of the host. Having received a message that someone was looking for him, Simonides got up in the middle of the banquet, left the palace and went outside. While he was outside the ceiling of the palace suddenly collapsed, killing the host and his guests. Their bodies were so crushed that the relatives of the victims could not identify them when they came to collect them for burial. However, Simonides, who survived, remembered where each one had been sitting at the table. The story says that thanks to Simonides, the inventor of memory, the relatives were after all able to bury their dead.

Although in this story the word 'memoria' means 'mnemotechnique', which is one of the five parts of Cicero's rhetoric, I shall take the liberty of telling it in my own way.

The story of Simonides tells us that the birth of memory preceded the accident, the collapse of the roof, death, disappearance. The story of Yugoslavia and its disintegration could be likened metaphorically to the scene of the banquet and the table with people sitting round it. Suddenly the shared roof over their heads collapses, killing the people at the table. Simonides, the survivor, asked by the relatives to identify the victims, does not manage to do his mnemotechnical job and relate what he remembers, because suddenly the remaining walls collapse, killing him and the relatives who had come to bury their dead. The new witnesses of the scene, struck by a double misfortune, are, admittedly, in a position to identify the victims, but only those they remember from the places where they happened to be when the remaining walls collapsed. And so each one remembers and mourns his own. The other victims do not exist. Not to mention the original ones.

The past must be articulated in order to become . . . memory. The citizens of Yugoslavia have been deprived of their common

---

[18] I quote Cicero's story from Frances A. Yates's book, *The Art of Memory*. I am grateful to Nenad Ivić, for drawing my attention to the cited example.

fifty-year-long past. That past will probably never have a chance to be articulated into a harmonious collective memory, but it will still be hard to erase as it came to life naturally, just as everyday life itself comes to life. In exchange for what has been denied them, the citizens are offered the construct of national memory, which many accepted with enthusiasm, thinking it was a firm foundation for a better future. However, the construct has not been adopted, because it has not had a chance to be, nor could it have been transformed into collective memory, because, in order for that to happen, generations would have to live it, as their everyday reality.

Looking from the outside it seems that the memory transaction has been successful. However, from the inside, nothing is ever really forgotten nor is it really remembered. Everything is there, present, as in Scopas's collapsed palace. And if we are to believe Umberto Eco who says that 'one forgets not by cancellation but by superimposition, not by producing absence but by multiplying presences',[19] then our story could easily slip in the opposite direction and instead of being about remembering it becomes a story about forgetting. In other words, a story about Atlantis where real lives and real people sink into a parable. And there, according to the genre, just one question is left: What was it that so angered the gods?

April 1996

[19] Umberto Eco, 'An Ars Oblivionalis? Forget it!' *PMLA*, 1988, p. 260.

Nice People Don't Mention
Such Things

On the table, in the glow of the wax candle, stood the tiny bronze Europa riding a galloping bull. Baločanski took the tiny figurine in his hand and began to examine it under the light holding it close to his eyes, so that he seemed to be sniffing at the little Europa like a dog.

Miroslav Krleža, *The Return of Philip Latinowicz*

1.

An acquaintance of mine in Zagreb once introduced me to the love of his life. She was a quiet, pale little woman who exuded calm.

'I'm going to marry her,' said my acquaintance. 'She's a wonderful sleeper, she can sleep for twenty hours a day,' he explained, tenderly.

Now they are happily married.

This little real-life episode may serve as a preface to the interpretation of a love story. Let us say, at once, that what we mean is the love between East and West Europe. And let us say, also, that in our story Eastern Europe is that sleepy, pale beauty, although for the time being there is little prospect of an imminent marriage.

2.

I wondered exactly when I realised that what was at stake was an attachment between two different halves. It must have been at the moment when I felt on my own skin that frontiers really do exist, that one enters countries and leaves them, and that for this simple spatial transaction one needs an identification document. Before, when I crossed frontiers freely with my Yugoslav passport I did not feel their reality.

Today I possess a Croatian passport and I know the offices of many consulates and embassies in European cities. For example, in order to obtain a small Dutch stamp in my passport, I have to show a letter of invitation, proof of the reason for my journey to the Netherlands, proof of health insurance, international or travel cover, proof that I have money and a return air ticket which confirms that I shall leave the country, in this case the Netherlands, by a set date.

At airports I stand in the queue for passport control. Signs over the booths behind which uniformed officials sit indicate my place. In some places it says *others*, in some there is merely an absence of the blue board with the ring of little yellow stars. My queue is long, it drags on slowly. The EU people in the parallel queue enter quickly. I notice that none of them looks in our direction. There is not a single glance expressing sympathy, curiosity or, if nothing else, contempt. They have no time, the queue is moving too quickly. But we, *others*, have plenty of time to observe them. We are different, our skin is often dark, our eyes dart suspiciously about or stare dully straight ahead, our movements are sluggish and subdued. No one chats or laughs in our queue, we are quiet, there is something surreptitious about us. The tension of our bodies testifies that we have only one thought in our heads: just to get across this frontier.

And when I cross it, I shall not say anything about this to my Dutch friends. Nice people don't mention such things. Besides, why should I? Once I have passed through passport control I can go and pray in a little Muslim or who knows which shrine at the airport itself, if I really feel like it. I'm welcome, cultural differences and identities are respected here.

However, my problem is of a different nature. My problem consists in the fact that I am not and do not wish to be different. My difference and my identity are doggedly determined by others. Those *at home* and these *outside*.

3.

I come from a Land of Blood Groups, from Croatia. There the dedicated blood-cell counters noted each of my blood cells. As a result I became . . . no one. Write: *no one*, I say to the officials in the booths each time they ask me my nationality, and they ask me often. Hurry up, they say, tell us what it is. Nationality: *no one*. Citizenship: *Croatian*, I repeat. We don't have that *no one* of yours in the computer, they say. The right to be *no one* is guaranteed me by the constitution of this country. Citizens are not obliged to declare their nationality if they don't want to, I say. In real life it's different, they say, everybody is obliged to be *someone*. That's just why we have wars, I say, because everyone agreed to belong to their own blood group. That's why we have wars, they say, because people like you wanted us all to be *no one*.

In the computers of Croatian officialdom, my name is entered in the category: *others*. I insisted on my position. They insisted on theirs: I no longer exist there. It's quite understandable, I myself insisted that I was no one. Now I live *outside*. Now, outside, I am what I no longer am *at home*: a *Croatian* writer. The representative of a country in which I barely exist, a country from which I ran away into exile, on the assumption that exile meant freedom from enforced identification.

Here, alongside my occupation, *writer*, they never fail to put that designation, *Croatian*. So along the way they learn the name of a new European statelet, stumbling over it, *Cro-Cro, Cro-a-tian*, that gives them some satisfaction. People respect ethno-identities, I understand that, they don't wish to offend, I must be extra sensitive about these things, that's just why there's a war in my country, after all. And so: me Tarzan, you Jane . . . The more politically aware will add: *former Yugoslav*. The more culturally conditioned will add: *East European*. The politically sensitive will add: *post-communist*. The gender-aware will add: *woman*. The best-read will add: *Central European*. (For heaven's sake, Croatia was always Central Europe, wasn't it? What do they mean, Balkans? What nonsense!) And it seems I have no way of taking off the labels they have so kindly stuck on to me. Because it is only with those labels that they can recognise me, place me, communicate with me, it is only with those labels, they believe, that they can read and understand me *properly*. I understand them, it is only through my otherness that they can realise their specialness.

And I, a *voluntary* exile with a Croatian passport in my hand, am obliged to show reciprocal kindness: they expect me to accept my identities as though they were real. It all reminds me of a role-playing game, and, although I am tired of games, I do after all agree to play. So, me Tarzan, you Jane . . .

4.

When I asked her to sketch her own, inner, map of Europe, one of my West European acquaintances said: 'This is where I am. Round me are Germany, Belgium, this is France, that's England, down there is Italy, and, yes, then there are Spain and Portugal as well, and here is a line. Beyond that line is nothing, a great blank . . .'

On her inner map, the great blank stretched eastwards from Berlin.

My acquaintance is not stupid or uneducated or insensitive. She was just being honest. And she told the truth: for many *Westerners* Eastern Europe is a mental empty space. It begins somewhere beyond the *iron curtain*, somewhere behind the *wall*, even now when there is neither a curtain nor a wall.

'And if something doesn't exist, I can't be anything other than indifferent to it,' said my acquaintance.

That innocent-indifferent ignorance gives rise to those numerous true anecdotes which serious people consider unworthy of repetition. For instance, the anecdote about a West European acquaintance of mine who, after visiting Russia, was touched to discover that Russians really loved small children . . .

5.

Of course, not all *Westerners* were indifferent. There were those who passed through the *wall* and the *curtain*, permitting themselves an affair with Eastern Europe. Today, in their post-traumatic state, they lick their wounds and endeavour to be indifferent.

I always wince uneasily when I see *Westerners* excited by the slightest sign of a possible return to communism. Television pictures of miserable people in worn clothes decorated with dusty communist medals waving flags on Red Square flash round the world with lightning speed. There they are, the *commies*, raising their heads again! The experienced and watchful followers of East European communist systems immediately reach for their pens and round on the poor supporters of a return to communism, vigorously writing their angry diatribes against the communist president chosen by some Poles or Bulgarians in their recent elections.

'*Ostalgia*' – nostalgia for the vanished East German everyday which is enacted by young (former) East Germans – is a newly coined term for an emotional trend, whose followers need not necessarily be East Europeans.

The Westerners' excitement at television shots of communist zombies on Red Square surfaces via a complex route. Suddenly they are seeing on the screen the image of their East European sweetheart the way she might be once again. And what was she like?

Eastern Europe was a different world from the West. If nothing else, then for years she confirmed the *Westerner*'s conviction that he lived in a better world. Eastern Europe was the dark reverse side, the alter ego, a world which Western Europe could have been like, but, fortunately, was not. And that is why the *Westerner* loved her. He loved her modest beauty, her poverty, her melancholy and her suffering, her . . . *otherness*. He also loved his own fear, the quickening of his pulse when he travelled there, he was excited by that entry into the empire of shadows and reassured by the reliable exit-light: passport, embassy, credit card. He loved his own image of himself shopping cheaply, oh so cheaply. There, in the East of Europe, he inhaled a kind of personal freedom, yes, over there he felt closer to what he really was. Over there time was not measured according to agendas and schedules, it's true that there were shortages of all kinds, but there was an abundance of time. The *Westerner* came to Eastern Europe, she could not go to him, and that was freedom too, freedom from reciprocity. Eastern Europe was always there, waiting for him, like a harem captive. He loved her with the love of the master. He was the researcher and coloniser, he placed his little flags joyfully in the territories he mentally conquered.

It was freedom from reciprocity.[1] Eastern Europe was his secret, a mistress content with little. At home he had a faithful

---

[1] 'In short, the Western Europeans came to have a strong and growing interest in keeping Europe divided. [. . .] The more secure that division, the easier it was to imagine a closer and more prosperous union of nations on the west of the line – while at the same time holding out the illusory prospect of that union's hypothetical expansion to the east "one day".' (Tony Judt, *A Grand Illusion? An Essay on Europe*, New York, 1996)

wife, order and work. Like every mistress, Eastern Europe only strengthened his marriage.

6.

'The times we live in are disgusting!' a West European acquaintance of mine complained to me recently. 'You can't distinguish Russians from French people any more, and when you go abroad there's nothing to bring back any more! You can buy everything everywhere!'

7.

Things have changed. Grey, silent Eastern Europe has begun to speak, to cross frontiers, and, hey, she doesn't seem to need the *Westerner* any more. He feels disappointed, no, not only because of the loss of an intimate territory . . . His former mistress is increasingly like his own wife! Russians send their children to the best English and Swiss colleges, buy diamonds in Amsterdam and chateaux in France . . . They speak English without an accent – who would have thought it, before they could not pronounce an ordinary *full stop* without that Slav bleating, and look at them now – they all stand straighter, they slip effortlessly across frontiers, they're everywhere, you can't walk down the street without bumping into them, they're all over the place, they're buying up whole quarters of Paris, Berlin, London, they've become greedy, it's all the mafia, of course, they've inhaled their first mouthful of freedom and now they think that no one can get in their way . . .

And our *Westerner* feels a kind of discomfort (*What if Eastern Europe moves here, to me?!*), loss (*Where are the frontiers? Is the whole world going to become the same?*), slight contempt (*Oh, couldn't they think of anything better to do than resemble us?*), self-pity (*When I took them jeans, they liked me!*) . . . And as he watches the shots of ageing *commies* on Red Square, the *Westerner* wonders whether it would not have been better if that wall had stayed where it was.

8.

And what about the *Easterners*, did they love the *Westerners*, and if so, how did they love them?

Easterners did after all know more about Western Europe. Or their knowledge had a different quality. In their inner map of

Europe there were no indifferent empty spaces. In many homes there was a map of Europe on the wall; in the kitchen, as in a museum, people kept empty containers from Danish biscuits, English tea and French cheese. These little museum exhibits and the map of Europe were sad substitutes for the countries they were firmly convinced they themselves would never see. Western Europe was a dark object of desire, for it was a world in which people really lived . . . more humanly.

Easterners loved foreigners. Foreigners were walking geography, a small-favour service (they could take something, bring something), their addresses were carefully preserved in address books. (*What if I should by some miracle really make it out?*) Foreigners were living confirmation that the world about which he, the *Easterner*, had dreamed, really existed. The only thing was that these foreigners weren't people. Their lives were too good for them to be considered people, that was it. Because what made the *Easterners* (in their own eyes) superior was the unshareable experience of humiliation. Humiliation was the only thing *Easterners* could place their copyright on, it was their inner legitimation, the unique *Made in Eastern Europe* product . . . The misfortune of humiliation is a broad manipulative field, the *Easterner* gladly created an institution of his misfortune. Here he was an expert, besides, his superiority in the domain of emotion had always been acknowledged . . . What about the *Westerners*? God knows what it was that beat in their Western breasts in place of a heart . . .

But the *Easterner* did understand all his own East Europeans – all those poor Romanians, Bulgarians, Poles – but he did not like them. They were all in the same shit, the same contemptible human trash. And no one could make him consider them his *brothers*. What kind of brotherhood was that supposed to be, brotherhood in misfortune!?

All in all, the *Easterner* did not doubt that he was a European, but his language gave him away. He never said 'We Europeans' but always 'Europe and us'. The *Easterner* lived in the mousetrap of that traumatic paradox, without being aware of either the mousetrap or the trauma or the paradox.

9.

These commonplaces jotted down in haste from an imaginary list of frustrations (and fascinations) between East and West Europe are as inaccurate as they are accurate. Originating in the production of figments, belonging to the realm of cultural stereotypes, these commonplaces serve to crystallise some traumatic points which, whether they are true or false, do, it seems, really hurt.

The twentieth century is characterised by psychoanalysis: by its discovery at the beginning of the century and its trivialisation at the end. Contemporary television confessionals in which ordinary viewers come before an audience of millions and simulate their traumas – personal, collective, social, historical – reduce trauma to the level of popular, cheap emotions accessible to all.

That is why one should believe an acquaintance of mine, a Russian, who, after an attack of unduly violent anger apologised: 'You see, my nerves have been historically damaged . . .'

10.

Since ancient times, Europe has built its identity on the contrast with the *East*, with *Asia*. Hippocrates and Aristotle did not blame the differences on people, but on the climate. According to Aristotle, it was because of the cold climate that Europeans were courageous, but not particularly able or wise. The connections between them are weak, they are incapable of managing others, nor do they like others to manage them. Equally, it is because of the climate that the inhabitants of Asia are gifted, but they lack courage and will. That is why they tend to be servants or else they gladly rule over people.

A similar set of characterological oppositions has been current for many centuries. It is on this contrastive base – initially innocently conditioned by climatic differences – that with time new elements in the construction of the European identity were gradually built up (enlightenment, culture, science, civil society, civilisation, as opposed to primitive cultures, Christianity, as opposed to other religious systems, freedom, equality, brotherhood, rationalism, and so on and so forth).

The mental construct called *Europe* has been the concern of European thinkers, artists, rulers (secular and religious), warriors (let us remind ourselves that even Hitler fought against *Asia*, while German soldiers died *for Germany, for Europe!*). Europe has always built its identity and its sense of self in opposition to an 'other': to *Asia*, to the *East* (to *barbarians*, to the *inferior*, to the *primitive*, to *communism* to *émigrés, Gastarbeiters, Islam* . . .). Europe has rarely integrated, rather it has tended to banish. So the inhabitant of Europe has adopted not only knowledge of geography but also the basic notions: *us*, Europeans, and *them*, people from beyond the border.[2]

Others and frontiers, these are the two conceptual points around which Europe has built its identity. For almost half a century Europe was divided by a security wall. The Western half experienced the wall as a shield, the Eastern half as an insult. Inert, servile *Asia*, in this case Eastern Europe, slumbered behind the wall, in a befuddled, totalitarian trance. Today Western Europe is afraid of the consequences. They are not only of a practical nature (fear of huge migrations from the East to the West). A certain unease follows the disappearance of the opponent, the mirror in which Western Europe contemplated itself for so long, nurturing its narcissism.[3]

Meanwhile, the war which occurred in Europe, in Yugoslavia, only confirmed the aforementioned set of frustrations and once again proved their vitality.

II.

The first thing a foreigner notices when he endeavours to discover from a citizen of former Yugoslavia why the war came about is an inability to articulate a reply and the wide use of the language of emotion. With time, following the media, the citizens did manage to memorise a few general formulae. However, these merely simulate rational discourse, for the language of trauma very quickly breaks through what has been learned. For instance, Serbs will swear that they meant no one any harm, but that no one in Yugoslavia had ever *liked* them. They will interpret the genocide they perpetrated against the Muslims, if they accept that they did perpetrate it, as revenge for unrequited love.

[2] 'One is tempted to say that the post-war creation (or, rather, re-creation) of Europe proved to be perhaps the most seminal, and thus far the most lasting consequence of the communist totalitarian episode. After many false starts before, this time the new European self-identity re-emerged, in an almost textbook fashion, as a *derivative of the boundary.*' (Zygmunt Bauman, *Life in Fragments. Essays in Postmodern Morality*, Oxford, 1995, p. 244)

[3] 'The otherwise self-sufficient, self-satisfied, even selfish "Europe" centred in Brussels became a beacon for the rest of the continent and source of respect and credibility for itself because of the promise that *this* Europe was not Zollverein, no mere neo-mercantile partnership of the rich and famous, no temporary practical and empirical solution to daily economic dilemmas. *This* Europe was the Europe of all Europeans – even if there were practical political impediments to their immediate membership of it.' (Tony Judt, *op. cit.*, p. 42)

One reason for the generally accepted language of trauma is its broad political and journalistic legalisation. That is the language spoken by political leaders, elected representatives, that is the language in which debates are carried out in the newly founded parliaments, and it is the language of the media, the language of ordinary people.

'That journalist of yours really doesn't like us,' said an embittered Bosnian Muslim refugee to me recently. He is now teaching at an American university. That 'yours' meant *Croatian*.

'What do you mean?'

'She writes about us as though we were some kind of "Shiptars"!'[4]

If we accept the logic of an amorous trauma, then we can say that the former Yugoslav peoples lived a double, parallel trauma: one directed inwards, the other to the outside world; one towards another nation in the former shared country (often several of them!), the other towards . . . Europe.

The beginning of the European *he loves me, he loves me not* episode is marked by the moment when the peoples of former Yugoslavia placed *Europeanisation* in the place of honour in their transitional ideological package. (*We're going into Europe!*) At that moment Europe was trembling at the possibility of *balkanisation*, and itself clinging ever more tightly to its own *Europeanisation*, which is also, they say, called *Brusselsisation*.

12.

What does the word 'Europe' mean for the former Yugo-peoples? At the beginning of the transitional process *Europe* was a metaphor for a direction and aim (transition), for a system of values, for democracy, a better life and an equal place under the protective umbrella of the quality label: *Europe*.

For the Croatian media, political leaders and ordinary people Europe was a territory, from which the Balkans, Serbia, were erased. (The Serbs do not belong in Europe.) That is why the Croatian political scene keeps doggedly sending love signals to its Europe: we are anti-communists, Catholics, we are a democratic country, we are defending Europe from Serbo-Bolshevism, communism, Byzantinism, barbarism, balkanisation, we are a civilisational, European, Christian shield which will prevent that terrible *East* from reaching Vienna. (Metaphorically and

4 'Shiptar', derived from the Albanian word for Albanian, is used as a derogatory term.

literally what's more, for the Croatian authorities drove out the majority of their own citizens of Serbian nationality!) At the same time Croatia was building an identity she herself projected, adapting her image to imagined, self-evident European standards.

And when Croatia finally became an internationally recognised European state, the euphoria was followed by disappointment. For she had been recognised not because she had in any case always been in Europe, not because that was where she belonged in every sense, not because she was *equal*, but simply because at a given moment she was a victim. Realising that formal international recognition still does not mean an invitation to dinner (maybe just permission to peer from outside through the window of the illuminated restaurant where the gentlemen are dining), collective feelings altered. Europe turned from a long desired beauty into a faithless *whore*.[5]

Bosnian Muslims, the greatest victims of this war, have similar emotions – a mixture of hope of assistance and deep disillusion. However, the Serbian media and public opinion are also soaked in the same emotions. There too the pendulum of collective emotion towards Europe swings from the idea of Belgrade the *Europolis* to an insurance company which bears the name *Evropa* and apparently offers its services with the advertising slogan: *This is the only Europe that thinks of you!*

All this creates a complex traumatic field.[6] Dreaming their

[5] Let us add that the metaphor of a country or a continent as a *whore*, a *fallen woman*, or else a *sick old woman*, which often circulates in the former Yugoslav media with reference to Europe, is not the exclusive copyright of the wretched Balkan peoples. An American journalist crossing the (former) Yugoslav frontier experienced the local landscape in the following poetic way: 'The earth here had the harsh, exhausted face of a prostitute, cursing bitterly between coughs.' (Robert Caplan, *The Balkan Ghosts. A Journey Through History*, New York, 1994, p. 27)

[6] 'For Europe is not only a place where we have always been, but also an aim towards which we are moving. Its presence in us is experienced just as powerfully as its absence. It is the territory of the most sublime values of justice, liberty and equality, but at the same time the place where these values are perverted. It is as much the object of our adoration and desire as the object of disillusion and abomination. As its chosen people who save it now from its fiercest enemies, now from itself, we are more European than Europe itself, but also more anti-European. For not only do we sacrifice ourselves for it, we are also its victim. As the altar of our sacrifice, it is the gleaming monument of our glory, but also a festering sewer down which our hopes ebb away like illusions. So how is it possible that all these unbearable contradictions should exist in our Croatian identity in harmonious symbiosis, as in a legal system of madness? So that Europe is nothing other than a figment of our imagination?' Boris Buden, *Barikade*, Zagreb, 1996, p. 139.

dreams, the newly emerging European statelets are left to wait in the vestibule of Europe. Each of them thinks itself more worthy and that, because it is *more European* than the others, it will be first in line. It is highly debatable when and whether *Europe* will ever allow them in. For the time being they are accorded the attention one accords to the inferior and to children. And the statelets put on a show of infantilism, immaturity, play the role of the victim. At the same time that is what they really are: infantile, immature, victims.

The statelets which have hatched out of the ruins of communism still do not exist on the mental map of Europe. On the other hand Europe (whatever it means) is an inseparable part of their newly acquired identity. The statelets see this relationship solely as a story of unrequited love. If we ask the question why these statelets think they ought to be loved, and, since we are talking of love, who it is they themselves are prepared to love, our questions are unlikely to be answered.

13.

Does this Europe (this projection created by the traumatised imagination of the small nations of former Yugoslavia) also have *feelings* or are they reserved only for the wretched?

Europe read about the Balkan situation through its own established, long-standing stereotypes about *that part of the world* (not of Europe, note!). It approved the disintegration of Yugoslavia, for that state was in any case *an artificial creation*, in which the small nations did not have the opportunity to realise their national self-awareness and statehood like other, *normal* European countries. The disintegration of Yugoslavia was equated in European minds with the collapse of communism (*The Soviet Union, for instance, such communist federations are not viable!*) and therefore had a positive connotation. Disintegration went along with democratisation. Proudly waving its own unification, Europe supported disintegration in a foreign territory. Emphasising the principles of multiculturality in its own territory, it abetted ethnic cleansing elsewhere. Swearing by European norms of honour, it negotiated with democratically elected war criminals. Fiercely defending the rights of minorities, it omitted to notice the disappearance of the most numerous Yugoslav minority, the population of anational, 'nationally undetermined' people, or the disappearance of minorities altogether. When the war really flared, it was suddenly horrified at the bloodthirstiness of *tribal* account-settling and withdrew into a corner. And it immediately drew a border-line (*It's incomprehensible! Those must be ancient ethno-customs! These people are not like us!*). To start with many Europeans rushed into the polygon of the war (let us recall, among others, Lord Owen who sliced Bosnia into ethnically pure cantons with a surgeon's satisfaction) and then withdrew. Now they are writing their memoirs.

In that dark corner of Europe, some European liberal thinkers found a provincial, museum Europe which, imagine, still read books and had real paintings on its walls (e.g. Finkielkraut), or a romantic, peasant Europe uncorrupted by the evils of urban civilisation, in which one could still eat plums unpolluted by pesticides (e.g. Handke). Their writings may also be read as texts which affirm a new non-transparent racism, concealed by the mask of European concern (*It's true that in the Balkans people slit each other's throats, but they do really love small children!*).

Europe did, of course, also help, it received refugees, offered them generous assistance in the form of food, money, medicine and other things. But it was not all loss, something was also earned: a positive moral and political self-image, a still firmer reason for homogenisation along Brussels lines, and who knows what else.

But still, does this West have feelings? Certainly, feelings is just what it has in abundance. European (and American) journalists, intellectuals, artists, analysts, thinkers, experts on countries in transition acquired with the war in Yugoslavia an opportunity once again to show off their colonial love, the love felt for a victim. They did not enter into a dialogue with the victim (*What dialogue! The victim is by definition dumb!*), they confiscated its tongue (*The victim's role is to suffer, and not itself to articulate its misfortune*), they became its interpreters (*The language of the victim is in any case unusable in the codes of the Western market*), representatives of its misfortune for which they would, of course, take their percentage . . . It is true that in all of this they were disturbed by the insatiable egocentricity of the victim. It did not once occur to the victim that others were impatiently waiting in line: Rwanda, the Chechens . . .

It is precisely feelings and sympathy that the West brings as its gifts. Dozens of West European (and American) writers, artists, film directors, photographers are today camping in the field of the Bosnian misfortune. They listen attentively to what the victims say and make notes so that they can later call the world to account, prick its indifferent heart, ennoble themselves through another's misfortune, give Western emotional standards a little shake. And who dares accuse the sated West of indifference? On the contrary, it is precisely feelings that have invaded the Western market.

14.

The iconographic image of Europe crowned, dressed in a robe with the design of a geographical map, on which the sixteenth-century designer did not forget either *Lithvania* (on the contrary, it's larger than *Moscovia*), or *Vangaria*, or *Sclavonia*, nor *Bvlgaria*, nor *Polonia*, nor *Macedonia*, has been transformed today into an indifferent blue board with a ring of little yellow stars. The ring of little yellow stars is a modern substitute for the former Imperial crown, or more exactly, it is a crown deprived of the lovely head of its famous bearer. The new emblem of a United Europe, its modern iconographical representation, suggests only a number (stars – members) unlike the earlier ones which seethed with meaning like tarot cards. Today everyone is free to read his own meaning of Europe into it.

And many do. The great European ideas are today most naturally adopted as parody. Ideas of internationalism are most consistently acted out by representatives of the global mafia as they build the powerful network of their secret routes from China to South America. Newly baked European nationalists are today the fiercest proponents of European ideas of a democratic society. Post-communist profiteers and thieves passionately promote the European idea of work and the proliferation of capital. Post-communist dictators, mafiosi and dogs of war are today the greatest proponents of peace and peaceful coexistence between peoples. United Europe does not seem to recognise or does not wish to recognise the differences. Or it refuses to do so. For it already is Europe, clearly and conclusively defined.

However, it is not only ideas which mutate, people also mutate. That fact conceals some hope, if that's what it is. While an increasingly clear division between the *compatible* and the *incompatible*, those *within* and those *outside* strengthens intolerance on both sides, so the frighteningly numerous migrations caused by the collapse of the communist systems and the war are bringing into being new people, cultural mutants, 'wossies'.

15.

Let us end our disjointed story in the genre which we promised at the beginning. The result of a love affair is usually descendants. So, let us say something about them. The descendants of the love affair from the beginning of our story are today the new inhabitants of Europe. They too are divided: some express loyalty to the nation, others loyalty to money. However, we are interested in the third group: the *stateless, nomads, bastards, wossies* . . . Those who unite in themselves the traumatic *Wessie* and *Ossie* genes. They do not respect their forebears.[7] They belong to a new tribe of people *of no fixed abode*. They feel most natural in an aeroplane. They are hard to recognise because they are good at mimicry. Their skill is the skill of *humiliation*,[8] their achievement is mental, personal freedom. If nothing else, they have won the freedom not to blame anyone for their own loss. Mutants have sharpened sight and hearing. They are sceptical, deprived of rights, they possess nothing, they are *sub-tenants*.[9] They are *Trümmerleute*, people who mentally clear up the ruins, because they have emerged from ruins, people who can therefore build a new idea about life, a new morality. In their former lives they had a chance to test available ideas about good: they had a home, and a homeland, and a nation, and a community, and successful careers. Today nothing can be taken from them, because they have nothing. Little can be given to them, because they once had everything. That fact gives them a kind of advantage. They do not consider Europe a privilege. Their privilege is the loss of illusions. Europe is for them just a

---

[7] 'We insist on our dislocation, rootlessness, our illegitimacy. We have not been given an identity [. . .]. Our forebears are not what determines us, we choose our forebears [. . .]. We build our own identity, capturing the past from the conformism of history, building our archaeology of the civil society.' (*Arkzin*, 8.11.1996, p. 2)

[8] 'It is saddening because if there is anything good about exile, it is that it teaches one humility. One can even take it a step further and suggest that exile is the ultimate lesson in that virtue.' (Joseph Brodsky, *On Grief and Reason*, New York, 1996, p. 25)

[9] 'We are poor relations, and the poor relation sees better than the property owner. France is divided into property owners and sub-tenants. I belong to the race of sub-tenants,' said the Polish poet Adam Zagajewski, who now lives in France, in an interview.

temporary place of residence, the choice of country is most often random. Let us not forget, they belong to the countless *race of sub-tenants*.

And finally, what gives me the right to judge such things, where is the proof, where are the facts? Let us remember, this is after all only a story. I myself am a *Trümmerfrau, a sub-tenant, a bastard, a nomad, a Wossie*. I have no other proof.

And perhaps the idea of Europe, the figment of its East as opposed to its West and vice versa, the dilemmas about better and worse worlds, will be solved by those who are yet to come. That is why the end of this story belongs to them.

When the war in former Yugoslavia began, many people thought of going abroad, and discussed where they might go and where it was possible to go, to America, Europe, Australia or New Zealand. Remembering the best of the accessible worlds, which was not (nor could it be) determined by frontiers, or countries, or ideologies, a child suggested: 'Mum, let's emigrate to McDonald's . . .'

November 1996

8

Souvenirs from Paradise

'With a bestial, butcher's instinct Pedro Vicario raised his knife and aimed another blow at almost the same place. It was amazing that the knife remained clean again,' Pedro Vicario informed the investigator.

Gabriel Garcia Marquez, *Cronica de una muerte anunciada*

1.

Early one morning the number 6 tram collected its passengers at the New Zagreb Zaprude stop and set off on its route into the centre of town. The tram was approaching the next stop when excited voices coming from the other end of the car forced the passenger who was standing beside the driver's cabin to look round. A well-dressed youth was furiously hitting a quite help-less old man. 'Give it to him! That's the way! Throw him off, the filth!', other passengers encouraged the youth. When the tram doors opened at the next stop, the youth gave the old man a violent kick. He fell off the tram, flat on to the pavement. The youth calmly returned to his seat and opened a newspaper. The tram set off. The passenger who was standing by the driver's cabin turned to the driver:

'Didn't you see what happened back there?'

'It's not my job to see, just to drive.'

'But you're still responsible for what goes on in the tram . . .'

'It's my job to drive . . . Let the police handle it . . .'

'That guy there has just beaten up an old man . . .'

'He was probably drunk . . .'

'That's no reason to beat someone up, is it?'

'He must have been annoying everyone . . .'

'But that guy almost killed him!'

Obviously irritated, the driver stopped the tram.

'Get off!'

'I beg your pardon?'

'And next time bug someone else, not me!'

The episode in the Zagreb tram in August 1997 is an unusually exact metaphor of post-Yugoslav everyday life. The theatre of terror in Croatia is open daily, public and free. The actors change, but everyone, like it or not, is drawn into the newly established rules: as participant, as accomplice, as supporter or as observer.

Let's go back to the tram episode and say that half the passengers were on the young rough's side, while the others were indifferent. One passenger tried to protest. Let's add that the reader need not agree with the use (or misuse) of this episode, but no one should doubt its reality. For the passenger in the Zagreb tram that August morning was me.

2.

The Yugoslav war is a dispiriting tale about human solidarity. Very few people sympathised with the Slovenes, when the war began, just as the Slovenes themselves unanimously closed the doors of their new state immediately after that war. The Croats showed no solidarity to anyone, just as few showed any to the Croats. The Serbs had no sympathy for anyone at all, and no one showed any understanding for the Serbs. Few people had ever shown solidarity to the Albanians, just as the Albanians were deaf to other people's troubles. And so on and so forth.

The story of solidarity does not stop at the frontiers of the newly created angry little states. Those who hoped that a feeling of solidarity would develop within the nationally homogenised communities were mistaken. Everyday life, harsh and brutal, discloses a disheartening absence of the most elementary human compassion. Just like the Zagreb tram episode, people are quick to express solidarity with the strong, whoever they are.

The question arises of how different the people who unanimously supported the ruffian in the tram are from those Serbs who mowed down innocent Muslims in Srebrenica or those Croats who killed innocent Serbs in Pakračka Poljana ... Yes, war dehumanised people, but people were astonishingly ready to accept their own dehumanisation.

3.

Recently in a Zagreb factory two women workers were accused of putting flowers in the windows of their office on the day Vukovar fell. Typical office surroundings, pots of flowers in the window, were the cause of the serious allegation of betrayal of the homeland. Some hundred patriotic staff members signed their names in support of the Managing Director's patriotic decision that the women should be immediately dismissed. One member of staff allegedly tried to say something in his colleagues' defence (They've been putting flowers in the window for years, you know ...). He was apparently dismissed as well.

'If love of one's homeland is fascism, then I publicly admit that I am a fascist,' a local neo-fascist publicly announced to a local paper.

4.

Post-war everyday life in Croatia is terrifying and difficult. For the time being no one has dared look into the accounts, but the losses are enormous and obvious. Nevertheless, hypnotised by their own nightmarish reality, the citizens continue to vote yet again for their local robbers and mafiosi, for their local dictators, spendthrifts and liars, for their local tyrants, murderers and criminals, for the people who have ruined them, the people who have made them their hostages and accomplices. But the deadly knife, just like the one in the quotation from Marquez, remains clean, no matter how often it is used.

5.

'It is not just that we live every day among this normal monstrousness and not only that we have got used to monsters, that we've grown close to them, but we are ourselves turning into monsters: living under the violence of totalitarian nationalism means day by day to be more and more prepared to accept that violence,' announced the writer Radomir Konstantinović for a Belgrade newspaper in August 1997.

'I'm not a monster. I'm a writer,' announced the war criminal Radovan Karadžić, at almost the same time to a journalist from *Süddeutsche Zeitung*.

'I'm not a prostitute! I'm a pleasure activist!' announced an American prostitute on some American television programme.

'That's not me . . . That's not my life . . . That's just temporary . . .' some poor factory worker announced confusedly in some local documentary film.

6.

While, slowly but surely, invoices from the tribunal in the Hague reach the debtors, demanding payment, the image which the authorities and the citizens of the new states have of themselves bears less and less resemblance to the factual image of that reality.

'How could I be an aggressor against my own country?!' wonders Radovan Karadžić to the *Süddeutsche Zeitung* journalist.

If no one knows who they are any more, if everyone refuses to be what they are, if no one is what he is, in other words, then what happened did not actually happen at all. And there we have the most effective way for Marquez's knife to stay permanently clean.

7.

Did the Yugoslavs ever know who they were? Yes, there were Slovenes who were Yugoslavs at the same time, Croats who were Yugoslavs along the way . . . There were those who had no national affiliation, who were just Yugoslavs, those whose silent disappearance in the general nationalist racket no one managed to notice. The citizens of Yugoslavia persistently refused to identify themselves with Eastern Europe (we're not Russians or Bulgarians, for God's sake!). Some agreed to cultural brotherhood with Central Europe (Croats and Slovenes mostly, convinced that the Serbs did not belong there). As a rule Yugoslavs refused to acknowledge their connection with communism (we're a socialist country, that has nothing to do with Russian communism). They saw themselves as neither East nor West, neither communism nor capitalism. For a time they were non-aligned, but Africa was too black and too far away for them to be open to the non- aligned brotherhood imposed on them. They refused to be called Balkan (that's all right for the Macedonians, they're closest!)[1] They were angry if some uninformed foreigner shoved them into the eastern bloc, behind the iron curtain, and they always pulled out the same trump card: Tito's historic 'no' to Stalin. Some refused, but not too loudly, to be connected with Yugoslavia (that wretched passport!), preferring to introduce themselves as Croats or Serbs. When they needed to and when they didn't, they pulled out their own history as an argument, even though they never really knew it. Many were anti-fascists and communists, many simply presented themselves as such. And when the new Croatian state authorities began to work systematically on touching-up the Croatian Ustasha past (pretending not to do so all the time), some Croatian citizens proudly became neo-fascists. Many former Yugoslavs became nationalists, chauvinists, racists,

---

[1] Maria Todorova writes with unusual accuracy about this confused self-image in her brilliant study *Imagining the Balkans*, Oxford University Press, 1997.

neo-Ustashas and neo-Chetniks, meta-fascists and justabit-fascists. Many victims became executioners, but some executioners also ended up as victims. Few remained communists, everyone became anti-communist.

Today it is clear that the constructs of national and state identity, which were proffered as an authentic substitute for the 'inauthentic', 'schizophrenic' Yugoslav one, are not in fact as firm and harmonious as the national designers at first thought. The constructs crumble and collapse, while the local designers dissect and reassemble the pieces in increasing panic, driving the already deranged citizens into madness.

8.

Antonomasia is a rhetorical figure. Those few people who know tropes and figures will certainly have noticed the striking frequency of this figure in the Croatian (and not only Croatian) media. 'Vukovar – the Croatian Hiroshima' is an example of antonomasia. The figure was used by good poets as a means of countering cultural and historical amnesia, while bad ones used it simply for tasteless exaggeration. The frequent use of this figure in the Croatian media can be read also as a symptom of the malfunction of Croatian state-forming mechanisms.

In August 1997 Croatian television broadcast a documentary film entitled *Tudjman, Croatian George Washington*.[2] What makes this film, of all the many television programmes, sculptures and publications that glorify the Croatian President particularly interesting? Because this well-paid state project is proof of the haywire self-image of a presidential personality. Why is the figure of a state president important at all? In frustrated, inauthentic communities which are obliged to imitate existence, for they hardly exist, the president is usually the people's choice, a representative figure, 'the soul of his people'. So the President's authorised film biography not only records collective frustrations precisely but, by making them public, legitimises them.

Blatantly touching up his own biography, Tudjman frees the audience of guilt for their own conversion. What lies did Tudj-

---

[2] This was supposedly an American documentary film. The directors of the film were named as Joe Tripician and Jakov Sedlar, and the screenplay was written by Hrvoje Hitrec, Andrew Brokaw and Chris Anderson. The text was read by the American actor Martin Sheen. The film was first shown on Zagreb television on 4 August 1997.

man tell? A great many.[3] That he is a university graduate. As an officer of the Yugoslav People's Army (JNA), he studied at the Higher Military Academy in Belgrade. He lied that the authorities did not permit him to publish his doctorate because his thesis conflicted with the partisans' account. It is true that the Arts Faculty in Zagreb refused to recognise this amateur historian's doctorate, so Tudjman was granted a doctorate in suspicious circumstances at the provincial university of Zadar. He lied that his parents were killed by communists because of their critical resistance to the new communist authorities. There is evidence that Tudjman's mentally ill father first killed his wife and then himself. He lied in portraying Tito as a merciless dictator. Tudjman was a colonel under Tito and his devoted subordinate for many years. He lied terribly in off-loading all the blame for the war in Bosnia on to the Bosnian President Alija Izetbegovič. He lied when he presented himself as a peace-maker ('I could never even watch a chicken being killed!'). He lied when he said he had invited the Croatian Serbs to stay in Croatia. The Croatian Serbs were systematically driven out of Croatia, and in the last brutal round called 'Storm' they were evicted *en masse* and many of them killed.

Tudjman lied about a great many things and concealed a great deal as well. However, the more important fact is that, in a semi-totalitarian community such as Croatia, Tudjman's spectacular autobiographical touch-up legitimizes lies, but at the same time the truth about disfunctional inauthentic collective identity. And the citizens can relax. For how many times have they themselves had to lie, to pretend (as though life was some kind of circus, for God's sake!) in order to stay where they are undamaged, or at least as little damaged as possible?

But still: why *Tudjman, Croatian George Washington*? A more natural antonomastic version would be 'Tudjman, the new Ante-Pavelič'. Although on many occasions this amateur-editor stuck his seven-year state-forming film on to the long-standing tradition of Croatian statehood (but Croatia was an independent state only as the Nazi NDH), for the sake of the world, Tudjman

[3] According to data from the article by Darko Hudelist 'A fated farce on Croatian State Television' (*Globus*, August 1997), with the quite unnecessary note that the author is more willing to believe a journalist who is well informed about the President's biography than the President himself who is not well informed about his own autobiography.

rejected that editorial connection. Another, perhaps more natural connection would be 'Tudjman, at last the wholly Croatian
Tito'. Although in his native village of Veliko Trgovišče, the
house where Tudjman was born is in the process of being
reconstructed in order to become a museum like Tito's birth-
place in Kumrovac (Kumrovac is just a few kilometres away from
Veliko Trgovišče), nevertheless, after so much public vilification
of communism and Yugoslavism, Tudjman cannot re-enter a
connection he has abandoned.

Hence the most appropriate comparison seemed to be the
remotest one – with George Washington. It could please the
Americans, make indirect amends for the regular anti-American
sentiment of the Croatian media, and, as a Croatian George, he
could ask for American financial support. In addition (for nothing
is impossible), it opens up the remote possibility that in some
future revision of American history, George Washington should
be remembered as . . . an American Tudjman.

And finally, if the historical inauguration of the Tudjman-
Washington connection succeeds, then the funds spent by the
state will be returned indirectly to the history being written by
the state. But if by any chance the film biography should be
proclaimed a shameful scandal, its true author will be able to
withdraw: he did not write the screenplay, he did not direct the
film, it was an American production.

9.

Croatia's prime tourist slogan, *Croatia – a small land for a big
rest*, printed on many tourist publications, evidently did not
satisfy Tudjman's state-building visions. Once the author of
Small Nations and Big Ideas had proclaimed himself the Croatian George Washington, by the same semantic logic Croatia
ought to be a little America. However, that would mean that the
small country had a small George. This confusion over the issue
of size was finally resolved in July 1997. Under her maiden name,
the wife of the Croatian minister of tourism took part in a
competition for the best Croatian tourist slogan and, surprise-
surprise, she won. The slogan goes *Croatia – paradise on earth*.
Now the semantic puzzle was finally completed. Tudjman
retained both his mythic role as forefather (Adam) and his
historical role as founder of the state (George Washington). The
dimensions thus became unimportant, because no one has yet

established whether paradise is in fact large or small. But everyone knows that it is unique. And that means that the Serbs, whom some ambitious representative of theirs declared *a heavenly people*, are kept at a reasonable distance. Because what would a *heavenly people* do in *paradise on earth*. It remains only to recall the most important thing: paradise is the home of the innocent.

10.

Is that really how things stand? The film *Tudjman, Croatian George Washington* ends with Tudjman's revision of the Bible and announcement that God did not create the world in his own image but in the 'image and scale of man'. This final message is only apparently intended for an international television audience. Its deeply subconscious addressee (although neither the sender of the message nor the addressee can know it) is in fact – the Hague tribunal! So, paradise is inhabited only by people after all.

Because just a few days after the film was first shown a local lawyer and former Minister of Police, a person whose name is certainly on the lists of those responsible for war crimes, declared in an interview that 'God did not populate the world with angels but with people'.[4] This sentence was also subconsciously addressed to the judges in the Hague.

And just a week later a member of the notorious Croatian military unit 'Autumn Rain' confessed in an interview for the same newspaper that he had liquidated eighty-six people, Croatian Serbs, with his own hands, and said: 'I am a great believer. God forgives everything up to a certain point.'[5] In this case we can say that he was quite consciously directing his message towards the Hague.

And immediately after that, a Croatian volunteer was decorated with the Tudjman medal, this was a person who had given orders for numerous crimes against Serbian civilians in Croatia, a war criminal tenaciously protected by the Croatian justice system for several years now. He became very angry in a television interview and snarled towards the Hague: 'Well anyone can be accused. Even Jesus was nailed to a cross, wasn't he?'

---

[4] *Feral Tribune*, 25 August 1997, pp. 28–30
[5] *Feral Tribune*, 1 September 1997, pp. 15–19.

11.

In August 1997, Belgrade was visited by the star of the Venezuelan television soap opera *Cassandra* (Croatian television broadcasts an equally mammoth, equally soapy *Marisol*). The arrival of the collective favourite Cassandra provoked real hysteria among her local admirers. Serbia has been living with Cassandra for months now. There is a story going around that some Bulgarian woman appears every week in one of the Belgrade markets where she earns a decent artistic wage by telling people gathered round her the contents of the next few episodes (Bulgaria started showing 'Cassandra' somewhat earlier). More than a thousand hopefuls participated in a federal contest for the girl who looked most like Cassandra. For the second round, for a short list of two hundred, sixty thousand readers of *Politika Express* responded. They say that some of the girls underwent plastic surgery for the occasion.

It was the inhabitants of the Serbian village of Kučevoi who went furthest. When the heroine Cassandra ended up in prison in one of the TV episodes, the furious people of Kučevoi sent a petition (with around two hundred signatures!) to the president of Venezuela demanding the immediate release of the innocent Cassandra. They went further still by writing to the Vatican to ask that Cassandra be proclaimed a saint, and then to the Hague tribunal, asking that it be made possible for Cassandra to be given a fair trial in Serbia.

The people of Kučevoi, who had remained deaf and dumb in face of the fascist policies of their state, the war, poverty, corruption and crime, the death of their own sons, the death of other people's sons, these ostrich-people, in other words, suddenly demonstrated unheard-of human solidarity, political maturity and a reasonable understanding of democratic procedures in the pursuit of their aims.

If a group of American citizens were to decide to promote Superman or Mickey Mouse as their future presidential candidate, it would be a real treat for the analysts of the postmodern age. The inhabitants of the village of Kučevoi voluntarily turned off the programme of their own reality and elected to live in a television world as though it were their own most intimate reality. Thus the inhabitants of Kučevoi are performing Baudrillard's thesis about the loss of the real which is today 'our reality' about the 'hallucinations' which are the only way left us of feeling that we are alive.

On the other hand, the real, enormous number of young people who have left their homeland because of the war and scattered over the world (and whose disappearance incidentally no one has noticed) live a quite real life in – a virtual homeland. Recently, on the Internet, who knows from where, came the message:

'Is there anyone out there from Kučevoi?'

12.

'We aren't Serbs, we're Cassandra's people,' the inhabitants of the village of Kučevoi could have proclaimed.

'I'm not a monster. I'm a writer,' declared Radovan Karadžić.

'I'm not Tudjman. I'm the Croatian George Washington.' This could have been the title of the documentary film.

So it is confirmed yet again that literature, art, history, religion, television, things of 'the soul and spirit' are the most rewarding field for manipulation. In some circumstances this can be declared a dangerous minefield, and in others an ecological-recreational park for moral purification.

13.

Tudjman's spectacular television hagiography includes two photographs: one taken in 1962, the other a year later. They are photographs of Miroslav Krleža with Franjo Tudjman. The photographs happened by chance to capture an instant when the great writer was with the virtually anonymous politician. Tudjman is using these photographs today to shore up his positive image: they confirm the President's inclination towards literature, towards art . . . He could of course have made use of the gaggle of local writers who wag their tails cheerfully whenever they see him, but he didn't, because after all he does know that Krleža is the greatest. So these chance photographs are today the most precious souvenirs of Tudjman's biography.

But in fact, are the photographs really accidental?

14.

Miroslav Krleža's novel, *Banket u Blitvi* (*Banquet in Blitva*), or *comoedia blithuanica*, describes the small, muddy, backward, European statelet of Blitva, which 'after thirty European nations had slaughtered each other for four years' emerged from the 'bloody flood' as an independent state ('like a tin rattle', says Krleža). The action of the novel takes place around the two main characters, Colonel Kristijan Barutanski, the dictator of Blitva who came to power by 'wringing several thousand Blitvan chickens' necks', and Niels Nielsen 'a neurotic, conceited European intellectual'. By contrast with the cynical and pragmatic Colonel Barutanski for whom Blitva is a 'bloody borshch', the 'romantic' Niels Nielsen asks himself and his fellow citizens: Blitvans, Huns, Blatvians and Kobilijans, the simple question – are they all really 'mad dogs' and how much longer and why will they go on 'tearing at their own flesh'? The key moment in the novel is Nielsen's open letter to Colonel Barutanski, a classic analysis of the personality of a dictator.[6]

In his first outline of the novel in 1935, Krleža saw Blitva as 'a variation on the by then already acute political theme of the birth and growth of a fascist psychosis in various regions and countries of Europe on the eve of the Second World War'. The first two parts of the novel were published in 1938 and 1939, and already in 1941 banned and burned. After the war *Banquet in Blitva* was reissued (1953), and the critics of the time interpreted it as an allusion to the circumstances of the Yugoslav monarchy prevailing between 1918 and 1941. 'The characters of this novel are those of the contemporary international political drama, which is being played out before our eyes on numerous European stages,' wrote

---

[6] 'Blitva is now governed by your laws,' writes Niels Nielsen to Kristijan Barutanski. 'Through all the centuries of its dark history, Blitva was never free, not for one moment, and now, under your personal rule, Blitva stands for bloody lawlessness in a succession of violent crimes. Blitva, less free today than she ever was in the hardest days of foreign slavery, is being lacerated by you personally with your spurs, as you assure us that you are today the only guarantee of our civil liberty.' Describing the colonel who 'wears an operetta helmet adorned with a swan's feather' and his cabinet which resembles 'a circus cage' in which 'the ministers grimace like monkeys on their golden chairs', Nielsen continues his accusation: '[. . .] Your whole sinister band does nothing other than trade under the Blitvan state flag, as though Blitvan sovereignty were your commercial share company, and you were the only, patented shareholders of that firm. [. . . .] You gleamed "like a brilliant meteor over Blitva's centuries of darkness" (to use the image coined by your semi-official *Blitva Gazette*), in its sentimental description of your state coup [. . .] when you forced your way partly with machine guns and partly with ordinary infantry rifles and cannon through more than three thousand Blitvan citizens and settled on the golden throne in Beauregard, following your historical calling to "liberate and cure Blitva, which you created, from its most critical sickness, its so-called Parliamentarism" . . .'

Krleža in a note on the occasion of the appearance of the third part of the novel, which he completed 1962–63.

At that same time, in 1962 and 1963, Krleža appeared in two photographs with a virtually anonymous colonel whose name was Franjo Tudjman. He had no inkling then that he was being photographed with the future prototype (or just a variation) of his hero, Colonel Kristijan Barutanski!

15.

In the end does everything end in literature, or is it the other way round?

'About suffering they were never wrong. The Old Masters: how well they understood its human position', begins a poem by W. H. Auden entitled 'Musée des Beaux Arts'. The poet describes precisely a painting by Pieter Breughel the Older, *The Fall of Icarus*. The painting is in the Brussels Museum of Fine Arts.

In June 1997, during my second journey to the periphery of Europe, Zagreb, I found myself very briefly in the centre of Europe, Brussels. If anyone is ever in a European city for the first time, briefly and by chance, then it is wisest to follow the direction taken by the first Japanese person he comes across. Because as a rule the Japanese person will join his own kind, like an ant. And ants always know where to find the sugar lump, the tourist heart of the city.

Brussels is the administrative heart of Europe, blue, surrounded by little gold stars, at least that is what is suggested by the heart-shaped Euro-souvenir. Warm rain pours over Brussels. The Japanese walk with recently purchased umbrellas. The umbrellas are blue, edged with little gold stars. I pad obediently after them, creeping through the moist artery of the heart of Europe.

Like Indians in reservations, the inhabitants of Brussels sell souvenirs which sum up the European past: guns, swords, medieval knights' robes, reproductions of famous European battles, plaster busts of famous military commanders. Among the numerically dominant busts of Napoleon there is one of Beethoven, a paperweight. The people of Brussels sell souvenirs of their present, their European unification: glasses, key-rings, pencils, postcards, umbrellas . . . All the rest is lace and chocolate. And the plump Manneken-Pis whose proud jet refreshes the numerically dominant Japanese.

To the chance traveller, Brussels can seem for a moment like the perfect stage for the end of the (European) twentieth century. Weightless Japanese glide over the stage with their Gucci and Ferragamo shopping bags. In the corners of the stage, street-musicians play: mouth-organs, balalaikas, Jews' harps . . . Russians, Romanians, Croats, Serbs, who knows where they all come from. The European East moves in the summer to the European West waiting for someone to throw a coin into their hats. All the rest is lace, chocolate, and – souvenirs. To the chance traveller, it may all seem sweet and small. Indeed, it may even seem that the warm rain has made Europe shrink like a cotton rag that has been badly washed.

I did not go to the Museum of Fine Arts. I did not see Breughel's painting, although, it seems to me, it was because of it, because of the painting that I ended up here 'by chance'. Instead, I bought a sumptuous postcard with a reproduction of *The Fall of Icarus* and a translation of Auden's poem into several languages . . . 'They were never wrong, the Old Masters' . . . Could the old masters have imagined that their lament (one in paint, the other in words) over the indifference of the world, their personal footnote of protest at the world as it is and as it has always been ('. . . how everything turns away quite leisurely from the disaster . . .'), would end up on a cheap souvenir?

Could Miroslav Krleža, the great European writer, have foreseen the ironical twist by which he, who long ago described the tiny, muddy Blitva and its dictator, Colonel Kristijan Barutanski, would end up as a trophy, a souvenir in his literary character's television hagiography? Could he have imagined that present-day intellectuals loyal to the colonel would use him as a rag to polish their own citizens' conscience, maintaining with absolute authority that 'if he were alive today, Krleža would be Tudjman's adviser'?

The old masters knew that the price of falling is calculated into every attempt at flight, just as Krleža, the old master, did after all know that 'every isolated, individual effort in the struggle against crime and deceit ends up as a romantic adventure'.

So what is left us? Just a footnote? Yes, a footnote. Because there is still hope that the present living replica of the literary hero, the dictator Kristijan Barutanski, will one day become a footnote (and perhaps not even that) in Krleža's novel written long ago.

We are left, then, with 'a box of lead letters' as Krleža suggests with a bitter smile from his pre-computer age, 'that isn't much [. . .], but it's all that man has so far thought up in defence of human dignity.'

August-September 1997

Glossary

(A few brief notes for those readers who still find the author's position unclear.)

Homeland:
My homeland was called Yugoslavia. But its borders did not coincide with the borders we learned in school. My homeland was somewhat larger, stretching from Triglav in Slovenia to the Black Sea. Because that's where we went every summer to visit my grandparents.

Among the Slovenes, Croats, Bosnians, Serbs, Montenegrins, Albanians, Macedonians, I felt Yugoslav, and that's how I described myself in my identity documents: a citizen of Yugoslavia, mixed, anational, unspecified, nationally indifferent . . . There were people like that living in Yugoslavia, Yugoslavs, and it didn't bother anyone at the time. Or at least that's how it seemed.

Identity:
A few years ago my homeland was confiscated, and, along with it my passport. In exchange I was given a new homeland, far smaller and less comfortable. They handed me a passport, a 'symbol' of my new identity. Thousands of people paid for those new 'identity symbols' with their lives, thousands were driven out of their homes, scattered, humiliated, deprived of their rights, imprisoned and impoverished. I possess very expensive identity documents. The fact often fills me with horror. And shame.

My passport has not made me a Croat. On the contrary, I am far less that today than I was before.

I am no one. And everyone. In Croatia I shall be a Serb, in Serbia

a Croat, in Bulgaria a Turk, in Turkey a Greek, in Greece a
Macedonian, in Macedonia a Bulgarian . . . Being an ethnic
'bastard' or 'schizophrenic' is my natural choice, I even consider
it a sign of mental and moral health. And I know that I am not
alone. Violent, stubborn insistence on national identities has
provoked a response: today many young citizens of former
Yugoslavia, particularly those scattered throughout the world,
stubbornly refuse any ethnic labels.

Patriotism:
In my language there is a word for 'love of one's homeland':
domoljublje. I don't feel that love. All the more since 'homeland'
is on the whole synonymous with 'state'. All the more so since
people take them, homelands, from me and give them to me if it
occurs to them, and still ask me to love them unconditionally.
Any forced love, including that of one's homeland, strikes me as
perverse.

Nationalism:
Nationalism is the ideology of the stupid. There is no more stupid
and tedious ideology than nationalism. Nationalism as a religious and therapeutic refuge is the option of those who have
nothing else. Blood is only somewhat thicker water.

Fascism:
Nationalism is often only a nicer name for fascism. The 'Yugoslav' war was a fascist struggle for new national and state borders.
The winners are powermongers, mafiosi, criminals, war profiteers, national tycoons, and the losers the now ethnically
cleansed peoples.

Communism:
The most stygmatised set of ideas and ideological practice, which
serves today as an enormous bank for laundering a bad conscience, both personal and collective. The phrase 'it's all the fault
of communism' relieves millions of people who lived in it and
participated in it of all responsibility. Combined with nationalism, it becomes even more effective. I hate all Russians, said a
Romanian. Why? Because they were all communists.

The therapeutic function of communism lies above all in its officially declared death: life can really now start again from scratch. Dead communism is an effective therapy: it offers people an irresistibly agreeable sense that they were both victims and the righteous who helped to shift the heavy iron curtain a millimetre or two.

The process of passing from a worse to a better life resembles an improvised waiting-room and has a pleasant name: transition. Transition is for many an exceptionally exciting time of (criminal) freedom.

National history:
History really is written by the victors. As the victors are always men, there are no women, children or losers in history. The victors swiftly occupy the academies, publishing houses, universities, ministries of culture and education, and similar useful institutions which will transform their victory into one, coherent, national history. National history is the hyper-revised biography of the nation. The authors of the new histories relate to history as to gossip, that is they know that it takes far longer to deny or re-fashion gossip than it does to create it. And they know that few people are interested in later revisions. So gossip, myths and confabulations often become great national truths.

Language:
The language I write was called until recently Serbo-Croat (or Serbian and Croatian), and it was the language spoken by Croats, Serbs, Bosnians and Montenegrins. Today people are trying to force me to recognise Croatian as my mother-tongue, and Serbian and Bosnian as – foreign languages!

I like the irony of the recently coined abbreviation for the divided language: BSC. That is the term used by officials of the Hague Tribunal in their internal communications for the language spoken by the recently-arrived war criminals. BSC: Bosnian-Serbian-Croatian.

Language is an instrument of communication. I do not 'buy' the thesis about language as the 'national essence'. All the more so since several hundred thousand people sacrificed their lives for such an 'essence'. When they need them, the national language and national literature are abundantly manipulated by the state-makers. I refuse to serve affairs of state.

A nation's writer:
My Croatian passport does not make me a Croatian writer. It is easiest and most profitable to be a national writer, particularly if the nation is small. I have chosen a less profitable way: I do not wish to belong to anyone, not to a people, nor a nation, nor a national literature. If I have to belong to someone, then it's to my readers. Wherever they may be . . .

A writer's nation:
I refuse to be a writer of 'my nation', especially of a nation which destroys books. Over the last few years, tons of books, dozens of libraries, many schools have been destroyed. Dozens of writers have been thrown out of the school curriculum and literary life. The literary map has changed just as the map of the former country has: writers are now divided according to ethnically cleansed cantons.

Izabel Skokandić, the unqualified director of a small library on the island of Kŏrcula, recently threw dozens of books into rubbish skips. There is not much to choose between the director of the library and the better-known poet-general Karadžić-Mladić (who destroyed the national library in Sarajevo).

At the beginning of the 1998, Izabel Skokandić executed several members of 'my family': Oscar Wilde, Ivo Andrić, Branko Ćopić, Mark Twain, Jack London, Victor Hugo, Ivana Brlić-Mažuranić . . .

Exile:
The experience of exile, just like the experience of my homeland, is one of my earliest experiences. As a child, obsessed with a secret passion, I used to get up in the night and in the dark turn the buttons on our first 'Nikola Tesla' radio. Those solitary nocturnal navigations through the sounds of different languages are among the most exciting experiences of my life.

Today, living in exile, I do not 'buy' the thesis that every exile is traumatic. On the contrary, I consider my decision to possess only a suitcase one of the better ones of my life. Repressive homelands are far more traumatic.

Besides, I remember the film *The Wizard of Oz*. Interpreting that film as a story about home and flight (i.e. about exile), Salman Rushdie says: 'So, Oz finally *became* home; the imagined world became the actual world, as it does for us all, because the truth is that once we have left our childhood places and started to make up our lives, armed only with what we have and are, we understand that the real secret of the ruby slippers is not that 'there's no place like home', but rather that there is no longer such a place *as* home: except, of course, for the home we make, or the homes that are made for us, in Oz: which is anywhere, and everywhere, except the place from which we began.'[1]

Witches:

A milieu which destroys books has no mercy towards their authors either. Several years ago, my (national) cultural milieu declared me a 'witch' and burned me on a media pyre with undisguised glee.

At the same time, the university professor of literature with whom I had worked for some twenty years on the culture of 'challenging' (the professor's term), suddenly rejected 'challenging' as a method of intellectual and artistic thought. He opted for the culture of the no-conflict collective. Instead of writing about the smell of the recent conflagration, he wrote flattering articles about the 'dignity of Croatian literature'. As a 'witch', I was thrown out of local literary life.

Today, from the perspective of my nomadic-exile, I can only be grateful to my former cultural milieu. I invested my own money in the purchase of my broom. I fly alone.

March 1998

[1] Salman Rushdie, *The Wizard of Oz*, British Film Institute, London, 1992, p. 57.

Note

Most of these essays were written between 1991 and 1994. Many of them have been published in various European periodicals, newspapers and collections (*Le Temps Moderne, Lettre Internationale, Die Zeit, Index on Censorship, Vrij Nederland, NRC Handelsblad, The Times Literary Supplement, The New Left Review, Neue Zürcher Zeitung* and others). The first edition of the book appeared in the Dutch language at the beginning of 1995, and somewhat later in German.

The Croatian edition of the book appeared at the end of 1996.

The English edition differs from the first, Dutch, one: a few essays and postscripts have been added. The author is grateful for the efforts of the translator Celia Hawkesworth who had to incorporate all the changes and additions.